LANGUAGES OF SENTIMENT

ADVANCES IN CONSCIOUSNESS RESEARCH

ADVANCES IN CONSCIOUSNESS RESEARCH provides a forum for scholars from different scientific disciplines and fields of knowledge who study consciousness in its multifaceted aspects. Thus the Series will include (but not be limited to) the various areas of cognitive science, including cognitive psychology, linguistics, brain science and philosophy. The orientation of the Series is toward developing new interdisciplinary and integrative approaches for the investigation, description and theory of consciousness, as well as the practical consequences of this research for the individual and society.

Volume 18

Gary B. Palmer and Debra J. Occhi (eds)

Languages of Sentiment
Cultural constructions of emotional substrates

LANGUAGES OF SENTIMENT

CULTURAL CONSTRUCTIONS OF EMOTIONAL SUBSTRATES

Edited by

GARY B. PALMER
University of Nevada at Las Vegas

DEBRA J. OCCHI
University of California at Davis

JOHN BENJAMINS PUBLISHING COMPANY
AMSTERDAM/PHILADELPHIA

TM The paper used in this publication meets the minimum requirements of American National Standard for Information Sciences — Permanence of Paper for Printed Library Materials, ANSI Z39.48–1984.

Library of Congress Cataloging-in-Publication Data

Languages of sentiment : cultural constructions of emotional substrates / edited by Gary B. Palmer, Debra J. Occhi.

p. cm. -- (Advances in consciousness research, ISSN 1381-589X ; v. 18)

Papers presented at a conference held 1996 and sponsored by the Society for Linguistic Anthropology.

Includes bibliographical references and index.

Contents: Linguistic anthropology and emotional experience / Gary B. Palmer and Debra J. Occhi -- Language, primordialism, and sentiment / Harold Schiffman -- Lamenting death, or, The death of lament? / James M. Wilce Jr. -- Dignity in tragedy : how Javanese women speak of emotion / Laine Berman -- Public and private voices : Japanese style shifting and the display of affective intensity / Cynthia Dickel Dunn -- From hiren to happi-endo : romantic expression in the Japanese love story / Janet S. (Shibamoto) Smith -- Sounds of the heart and mind : mimetics of emotional states in Japanese / Debra J. Occhi -- Bursting with grief, erupting with shame : a conceptual and grammatical analysis of emotion-tropes in Tagalog / Gary B. Palmer, Heather Bennett, and Les Stacey -- The convergence of sociocultural theory and cognitive linguistics : lexical semantics and the L2 acquisition of love, fear, and happiness / Howard Grabois -- Language and emotion concepts / Zoltán Kövecses and Gary B. Palmer.

1. Language and culture Congresses. 2. Emotions Congresses. I. Palmer, Gary B., 1942- . II. Occhi, Debra J. III. Society for Linguistic Anthropology (U.S.) IV. Series.

P35.L338 1999

306.44--dc21 99-33999

ISBN 90 272 5138 X (Eur.) / 1 55619 434 X (US) (Pb; alk. paper) CIP

John Benjamins Publishing Co. • P.O.Box 75577 • 1070 AN Amsterdam • The Netherlands

John Benjamins North America • P.O.Box 27519 • Philadelphia PA 19118-0519 • USA

Table of Contents

Introduction: Linguistic Anthropology and Emotional Experience 1
Gary B. Palmer and Debra J. Occhi

Pragmatic and Social Constructionist Approaches

Language, Primordialism and Sentiment 25
Harold Schiffman

Transforming Laments: Performativity and Rationalization as Linguistic Ideologies 39
James M. Wilce, Jr.

Dignity in Tragedy: How Javanese Women Speak of Emotion 65
Laine Berman

Public and Private Voices: Japanese Style Shifting and the Display of Affective Intensity 107
Cynthia Dickel Dunn

Cognitive Approaches

From *Hiren* to *Happî-endo*: Romantic Expression in the Japanese Love Story 131
Janet S. (Shibamoto) Smith

Sounds of the Heart and Mind: Mimetics of Emotional States in Japanese 151
Debra J. Occhi

Bursting with Grief, Erupting with Shame: A Conceptual and Grammatical Analysis of Emotion-Tropes in Tagalog 171
Gary B. Palmer, Heather Bennett and Les Stacey

The Convergence of Sociocultural Theory and Cognitive Linguistics: Lexical Semantics and the L2 Acquisition of Love, Fear and Happiness 201
Howard Grabois

Theory

Language And Emotion Concepts: What Experientialists and Social Constructionists Have in Common 237
Zoltán Kövecses and Gary B. Palmer

Name Index 263

Subject Index 265

Introduction

Linguistic Anthropology and Emotional Experience

Gary B. Palmer
University of Nevada at Las Vegas

Debra J. Occhi
University of California at Davis

We ordinarily take our naïve desire to know the emotions of others as natural. In American popular culture, conscious emotional experience is a focus of interest that shows up in the themes of TV talk shows, melodramas, and even broadcasts of so-called hard news. "Can you put into words what you are feeling right now?" Such are the urgent questions with which nosy news reporters badger victims of tragedies, harrass bereaved relatives, and fawn on winners of sporting events. Watching the victims and stars on the network news and in everyday life, we try to discover how they "feel" about things not only by paying attention to physical cues, but also by listening to their talk and how they use it to "express" or "convey" emotions. American anthropologists and linguists, being products of their culture, have similar interests, often shared by colleagues from other nations. Susanne Niemeier (1997: viii) noted that "the domain of emotions has recently reappeared on the scene of scientific discussion ... becoming again one of the fashionable topics in separate or joint endeavors in psychology, philosophy, ethnology, sociology, and linguistics."

Perhaps it is our simple primal interest in people combined with a culturally ingrained curiosity about emotions and feelings that accounts for the current lively scholarly interest in emotional experience and the language of emotions in other cultures. We are now seeing these personal and vernacular interests in emotional experience channeled into scholarly and scientific pursuits that are cross-cultural and cross-linguistic. But sometimes we are brought up short when we encounter languages spoken by people that do not share our enthusiasm for verbalizing descriptions and expressions of emotional experience, as has been observed in Japanese (Shibamoto Smith, this volume), Javanese (Berman, this volume) and in the Filipino languages Tagalog and Ilongot (Palmer and Brown 1998; Rosaldo 1990). In such languages, emotional talk is typically interpreted in pragmatic terms rather than as a register of conscious experience. These are the cognitive and pragmatic poles of language, but there are surely other languages that occupy intermediate positions and complex mixes of usage. The problem of how emotions are conceptualized, described, expressed, and realized in purposive actions in each language and culture, however local or global in scope, coherent or fragmented, establishes the outline of an intriguing research project. The papers in this volume contribute to that project by examining languages of sentiment in a variety of societies.

This volume of papers originated from a 1996 session on "Languages of Sentiment" sponsored by the Society for Linguistic Anthropology of the American Anthropological Association. The purpose of the session was to explore the communication of sentiments in a variety of languages, where sentiments are defined as emotions that are culturally defined and organized; sentiments are socially constructed emotions. Because our own orientation is toward cognitive linguistics, our thoughts in organizing the session were to discover through language to what extent people in different societies experience the same and different emotions because of their cultural backgrounds. Languages would afford the windows on their emotional worlds. This Humboldtian and Boasian notion that language reveals ethnic psychology is an old, but still valid one in anthropology and linguistics,[1] but it has recently ceded place of prominence to approaches that focus on the pragmatic dimensions of discourse as performance (Duranti 1997).

But the announcement of the SLA session allowed for a range of theoretical approaches to the problem of language and emotion. In addition to our cognitive linguistic relativism, we anticipated submissions from interpretive anthropologists, pragmatists, postmodernists, and those seeking universals of emotional expression. We got a bit of everything, though not always in packages that could be clearly labeled as one approach or the other. Nevertheless, we find two dominant orientations in the papers: the cognitive and the pragmatic. We have therefore made these the basis for the division of this volume into sections. These deal generally with the problem of what emotion-language reveals about emotional thought and the problem of how emotional language serves social and interpersonal goals.

In anthropology, the cultural study of emotions usually begins with Radcliffe-Brown's 1922 study of social sentiments in the ceremonial life of the Andaman Islanders. Because Radcliffe-Brown emphasized the primacy of the needs of society, he theorized that sentiments (organized systems of emotional tendencies centered about some object) serve to regulate the conduct of individuals in conformity with social needs. In his theory, sentiments are affected by social values, which in turn are reflected in legends and ceremonials. In an Andaman legend, the killing of a cicada brought darkness on the world. This legend was held to express the bane of social dysphoria by inducing the fear of darkness. Radcliffe-Brown believed, paternalistically, that the Andaman Islander was "not himself capable of thinking about his own sentiments" (Radcliffe-Brown 1922: 324). It was up to the ethnographer to work out their implications.

Configurationists of the 1930s saw emotions as belonging to personality patterns that were shaped by their ambient cultures, so that under given circumstances, all members of a culture were likely to display the same emotions. The rhetoric of these authors presented only the stereotype or exemplar for consideration. Ruth Benedict (1959 [1934]: 141) wrote of the "jealousy, and suspicion … that are characteristic of Dobu," an island society near New Guinea. Here, she said, "suspicion … runs to paranoid lengths" (151), and "the Dobuan, therefore, is dour, prudish, and passionate, consumed with jealousy, suspicion, and resentment" (168). Of the Kwakiutl of Vancouver Island, she wrote: "The characteristic Kwakiutl response to frustration was sulking and acts of desperation" (218). She asserted that the gamut of emotions recognized in Kwakiutl society "from triumph to shame, was magnified to its utmost proportions" (220). Such dramatic statements seemed overblown and drew criticism for stereotyping and ideological bias. Personality studies in the following decades attempted to allow for individual variation and to find particular causes of emotional response in family structure, socialization techniques, and even nutrition (Barnouw 1973). Nevertheless, it is probably fair to say that most anthropologists have always implicitly assumed that each culture offers a unique or characteristic range of experiences, which shape its participants' emotional responses.

Perhaps the greatest contribution of recent work on the topic has been to question the very concept of emotion. Are emotions feeling states or ideas? Are they located in the mind or the body, or do they cut across both domains, occupying physical sites in each? Or perhaps this formulation is too crude and emotions should be regarded as evidence for the unity of mind and body. There seem to be two approaches to the problem. One is to be vague, allowing empirical research to proceed with minimal constraints. For example, Besnier (1990: 421) advocated the use of the term *affect*, defined broadly and malleably as "the subjective states that observers ascribe to a person on the basis of the person's conduct." The other approach is to refine the model in the hope that we will actually get it right. Scholars pursuing cognitive and cognitive linguistic approaches have argued that emotions should not be regarded as mere feeling states based in physiology, because they are governed by dimensions of cognition or rationality (White 1992; Kövecses 1987, 1988, 1990; Lazarus 1995; D'Andrade 1995; Wierzbicka 1986), thus giving a more complex model with at least two primary aspects whose elements have to be described and set into proper relationship with one another.

Catherine Lutz (1988; Abu-Lughod and Lutz 1990) has also deplored the separation of cognition from emotion, but she cut into the problem from another angle, criticizing previous studies for essentializing emotions as psychobiological universals and reifying a culture-bound distinction between emotion and cognition that does not apply in non-Western societies. She proposed instead that emotion is pragmatic social action. Since what one tries to accomplish through emotional talk depends upon what one knows, it is not surprising to find her combining emotional pragmatism with an interest in cognitive scenarios, as seen in her assertion that "To understand the meaning of an emotion word is to be able to envisage (and perhaps to find oneself able to participate in) a complicated scene with actors, actions, interpersonal relationships in a particular state of repair, moral points of view, facial expressions, personal and social goals, and sequences of events" (Lutz 1988: 10). This is also the stance taken by Palmer (1996).

A postmodernist approach to emotion questions the possibility of objective, neutral, or impartial descriptions. Rosaldo (1993: 21) would seek the meaning of emotions in "case studies that are embedded in local contexts, shaped by local interests, and colored by local perceptions." He criticized structural studies of rituals that fail to describe the force of emotions, which can only be gotten at by taking the perspective of the experiencer, and that can only be done when the ethnographer has had comparable experiences. He claimed it was only after experiencing rage at the death of a brother and his own wife, anthropologist Michelle Rosaldo, that he was able to understand the motivating force of rage to bereaved Ilongot headhunters. It follows that languages of sentiment can only be apprehended by ethnographers who have attained similar experiences. And, if all meanings are local as Rosaldo claimed, the same must be true of sentiments. But, how restrictive is *local*? Rosaldo seems to generalize about Ilongot rage, so perhaps the scope of local can be as extensive as ethnic group, community, or small-scale society.

What are the language communities of interest to the authors in this volume? The scope of interaction described in these papers ranges from the global effects of capitalism (Wilce), to Tamil nationalistic linguistic ideology (Schiffman) to conversations in Japanese (Dunn). Seven of the contributors focus on Asian languages and cultures, including one paper each on Indonesian (Berman), Tagalog (Bennett, Palmer, and Stacey), Bangla (Wilce), and Tamil

(Schiffman), and three on Japanese (Dunn, Occhi, Shibamoto-Smith). In fact, this volume could justifiably claim to be a book on *Asian* languages of sentiment with supplementary orientational and theoretical essays. Berman, Dunn, and Wilce describe and analyze actual discourse events, while Bennett, Palmer and Stacey, Occhi, Shibamoto-Smith, and Grabois analyze linguistic data gathered from a variety of sources, including discourse, interviews, experimental settings, and popular media.

What is the range of sentiments covered in this volume? Some are deep-seated and lasting: Schiffman explores language primordialism, which includes "the sentiments that are evoked when language is perceived to be threatened," other sentiments related to public performance of verbal genres, and "the kinds of sentiments that move people to attempt to purify their language of 'foreign' elements and restore it to a state of former or imagined grace." Berman describes how Javanese women reframe the pain of humiliation in a discourse of dignity and express sentiments they term *sedih* (sad) and *enek* (sickening). She also discusses the disgrace, helplessness, and fear resulting from rape. Wilce records Bangla lamentation and mourning attendant on death. Shibamoto-Smith analyzes conceptions of love found in Japanese romance novels. Grabois delineates the lexical organization of love, fear and happiness. Together, then, these authors deal with primordialism, humiliation, sadness, disgust, love, fear, and happiness. Of these sentiments, primordialism seems to exist on a conceptual plane different from the rest. It is more abstract, observer-centered (etic), and internally differentiated. Other sentiments discussed by the authors of this volume seem more diffuse or mundane, the kinds of sentiments that people experience daily or frequently. Dunn's paper examines how Japanese discourse styles express emotionality, especially speaker anxiety, pleasurable feelings, strongly-felt affective bonds which promote group solidarity, and the notion of *honne* 'real personal feeling.'

Two of the papers range more widely over language that expresses a variety of emotions: Occhi touches on all the Japanese emotions that are lexicalized with mimetic terms, the most commonly occurring being a pounding heart, anger that comes with a quick, queasy surge, irritation, thrill or anticipation, happiness or excitement, anxiety or apprehension, and extreme anger. Similarly, Tagalog figures of speech analyzed by Bennett, Palmer and Stacey include expressions for pride, shame, bravery, grief, sadness, anger, fear, shame, happiness, love, alertness, lust, and shock. From these papers we get a sense of how a variety of sentiments may be lexicalized and grammaticized with the same linguistic devices: mimesis, metaphor, and metonymy. The language-specific lexical-grammatical configurations of emotion-language show that native speakers may perceive a domain of emotions or sentiments as distinct from other experiential domains.

The Papers

Pragmatic and Social Constructionist Approaches

The papers in this section tend to be both pragmatic and social constructionist, sometimes explicitly so, sometimes only by implication. In setting up this group of papers in opposition to the cognitive group, we are not asserting that cognitive approaches are free of social constructionist assumptions. The paper by Grabois, for example, is both cognitive and explicitly social constructionist, drawing not only on Lakoff and Langacker, but also on Vygotsky and Luria. However, it does seem to us that the papers taking cognitive approaches use methods unsuited to demonstrating pragmatic and social constructionist explanations for emotions. Rather, they tend to take it for granted that emotions are culturally defined, and they make it their task to discover culturally specific emotion language. They describe emotion lexicons in greater detail and they analyze the grammar, as in the paper by Occhi, and semantic organization of these lexicons, as in the papers by Shibamoto-Smith, Bennett, Palmer and Stacey, and Grabois. By contrast, the papers in this section are more concerned with demonstrating that emotion language is an interactional resource applied to social purposes.

"Who loves Tamil the most?" One of the remarkable facts about humanity is that people recognize languages to be distinctive practices, much as they recognize differences in styles of dress and architecture or even the different assortments of feathers on species of birds. They then invest their own languages and those of others with emotional values. Language becomes the object of sentiment rather than its instrument or projection. Harold Schiffman tells us that, "there is in some cultures (some would say *all* cultures) an observable phenomenon that seems to be a kind of meta-characteristic of the group: they see their language … as *essential* or as *the very essence of* their selfhood or ethnicity…without which the group would, in their own estimation, cease to have meaning, or even cease to exist." He refers to the general phenomenon as it applies to language, religion, blood-lines (caste, race, descent, etc.), and territory as *primordialism*. As applied to language, it becomes a part of *linguistic culture*, a term which he offers as an alternative to *linguistic ideology*. He shows how Tamil linguistic primordialism renders the term Tami 'mother' and 'mother's milk' synonymous with 'mother tongue.' Tami inspires devotion to linguistic purism, which is challenged by the question "who loves Tamil the most?" Taken together with several papers on Russian in Athanasiado and Tabakowska (1998), Schiffman's paper may be a harbinger of rising academic interest in language and nationalism.

In James Wilce's study of Bangla lament we see a sort of world systems theory of linguistic change towards a more referential view of language, away from a context that values performative aspects of linguistic praxis. The participant in modern, capitalist society does not publicly lament; she says "I am feeling sad" (Urban 1996: 176, cited in Wilce). Wilce adduces his own field data to support this argument for the Weberian privatization of emotion, but he also surveys changes to genres of lament in Greek, Taureg, Iranian, Indian, Pakistani, Tlingit, and Kaluli societies. The traditional expressions of grief most often fade and disappear, but they may also undergo revivals and reinvestments of old forms with new meanings. To Wilce's findings we would add the following observation: If lamentation is a way of intensifying selected aspects the grieving experience, it follows that members of cultures with traditions of lament would experience a different consciousness of grief. It also follows that the specific nature of the conscious experience of grief in lamentation societies is culturally determined, because it is colored by those aspects that are selected for dramatization. Wilce recognizes this and attempts to maintain a Whorfian relativity within the perspective that attributes the demise of traditional verbal expressions of sentiment to the global spread of capitalism.

Laine Berman also relates local emotional talk to a wider social context, but where Wilce saw local events as reflecting global process, Berman ties them to symbols of power embedded in traditions inherited by the Javanese nation state. That is, power is supported by harmony, which is maintained by the values of detachment (*iklas*), forbearance (*sabar*), and acquiescence (*trimå*). Thus, power is maintained by suppressing emotional talk. Javanese appear to devalue the language of sentiment, so emotional talk must be indirect and subtle. Berman takes a social constructionist stance in examining how this Javanese rhetoric of emotional control enforces hegemony, particularly sexual discrimination against women. But her stance is also pragmatic, because emotion is "analyzable through its meaning, force, location and performance in the public realm of discourse" and evaluative, because "Emotion is the ordering, selecting, and interpreting work we accomplish as we manage the fragments of our lives." Through examination of personal and private discourses of and about violence towards women, she challenges the dominant view that emotional control is best exemplified by men, and that women enjoy a kind of freedom of speech and behavior based on their lower social status. In her data, the women are constrained in speech and other responses, and are actually held responsible for the uncontrolled and improper behavior of men, particularly in cases of rape. As in other cases of oppression, women actually perpetuate their discrimination through adhering to proper feminine values, such as propriety, which Berman deftly extracts from a variety of discursive events.

Berman and Wilce show how Javanese and Bangla discourses proceed under oppressive circumstances when they are motivated by the strong emotions of humiliation and grief. Dunn examines grammatically defined speech styles in Japanese to discover how speakers signal affective stances of intimacy and remoteness. Her paper is based on speeches given by group leaders at the same club meeting at a Japanese women's university. Their styles and behavior distinguish private intimacy (*ura* 'back side') from public formality (*omote* 'front side'), which respectively create in-group *uchi* versus out-group *soto* stances. Dunn's characterization of styles includes an analysis of verb-endings, sentence-final particles, and postposing. Her data include two attempts, by two of the officers, to rouse the membership towards better participation in future events. The speech of the first speaker includes strong elements of intimacy and is framed as a personal appeal, contrasting strongly in terms of indexing strategies to the second, who deliberately distances herself from the audience. The intimacy of first speaker's presentation also contrasts to an earlier, more formal presentation of her own. Dunn argues that the choice of style communicates speakers' emotional states, such as anger, more effectively than an outright scolding would have done.

Cognitive Approaches

In linguistic anthropology, cognitive approaches to language could once be described succinctly as lexical semantics, which involved mainly the study of taxonomies and componential analyses of particular semantic domains, such as life-forms and kinship. Today, cognitive linguistic approaches are more likely to examine polysemy in small sets of spatial particles, blended clause constructions, models underlying metaphor and metonymy, and the cultural scenarios governing noun classifiers (Lakoff 1987; Langacker 1991; Fauconnier 1997; Palmer 1996). But where do emotions fit into this work? Can emotions also be seen as cognitive constructions, or are they simply feelings whose primary referents are physiological? One author, Zoltán Kövecses (1986, 1988, 1990, 1991a, b, 1994, 1998, In press), has argued convincingly that cognitive models structure talk about emotions in English and other languages. In this work he has shown that emotions are structured by metaphorical models, metonymical models, propositions, and narrative scenarios. He has found a number of specific models that apply cross-linguistically, and in some cases universally. So it would appear that emotions are cognitive constructions, at least in part. And if that is the case, it follows that emotions must participate in reasoning processes, unless these are locally defined as some sort of abstract thinking divorced from emotion by training. Thus, sentiments become not merely the motivators of our discourse, but also the channels through which it moves. To a great extent, sentiments constitute the permissible plays in the games set up by our cultures.

This point is demonstrated in Janet Shibamoto Smith's study of Japanese romance novels, which she reads "in an attempt to understand contemporary formulations of a cultural model of the Japanese emotion *ai* 'love'. The Japanese novels share a market with Harlequin novels translated from English, which, even in translation, retain metaphors, metonymies, and plots similar to those listed in Kövecses's description of the cognitive model of love in American English, which includes the idea that "the intensity of the attraction goes beyond the limit point." Shibamoto Smith asks whether this holds true for Japanese true love. She finds instead that Japanese true love must be contained within the family or other appropriate social vehicle. Rather than true love guaranteeing the stability of the relationship as in the English model, it is the social container that guarantees the love in Japanese. What constitutes a successful pair bond depends on the scenarios native to the original language of the narrative. Indigenous Japanese models rely on a different set of values and use different means of describing love experiences and behavior, and these differences are distinguishable at the level of bodily awareness as well as in speech. The narratives of Japanese true love lack the metaphors of heat and descriptions of throbbing, boiling, and melting that one finds in the English Harlequin romances. Although English love narratives are successfully translatable into Japanese, it remains to be seen how they affect their readers. Do the translated love styles remain foreign, or do they become incorporated into Japanese thinking, behavior, and language?

Debra Occhi analyzes the Japanese terms called *gitaigo*. These are sound-symbolic lexemes of emotional expression, such as *doki-doki*, which can signify a pounding heart in anticipation of meeting an object of romantic interest, when used in the appropriate grammatical construction. Such expressions are at the most iconic pole of the iconicity-conventionality scale of emotions posited by Kryk-Kastovsky (1997). Occhi's work shows that a single *gitaigo* can have one sense based on physiological experience and another sense that is a metonymical extension referring to a social scenario that arouses feelings similar to those of the basic notion. Thus, her work points the way to the merging of experientialist with social constructionist approaches advocated by Kövecses and Palmer (this volume). Her research explores the epistemology of emotional states as they are attributed to self and other across different word classes in Japanese. She compares constructions containing *gitaigo* to those containing adjectives, whose grammatical behavior is much better understood. The paper includes a variety of statements by native speakers, particularly linguists, about the nature of *gitaigo*.

These reveal an ideology that assigns *gitaigo* to intuitive naturalized states and attributes to them a strong evocative potential.

Extending Kövecses's cross-linguistic comparisons of emotion metaphors to Tagalog, authors Gary Palmer, Heather Bennett, and Lester Stacey provide evidence for universals, as well as for language specificity in emotion imagery. Tagalog makes extensive use of the seemingly universal metaphors THE BODY IS A CONTAINER FOR EMOTION and EMOTION IS FORCE OR INTERNAL PRESSURE, but in Tagalog one can be *bursting* with grief, a concept which seems unfamiliar to a speaker of English, who is more likely to be *stricken* with grief. While Tagalog grief bursts out from within, sadness is imposed from without, tightening the chest, weighing upon it, and injuring the heart. In Tagalog, as well as English, the metaphor of thick skin signifies that one is impervious to what might arouse emotions in others. It is interesting to compare metaphors of emotion that use the source domain of taste. The Tagalog metonym *maasim ang mukha* 'sour face (ill feeling, hatred)' may be compared to the Japanese use of *amae* 'sweet, of taste/behavior', which Shibamoto Smith compares to *ai* 'love' in romantic fiction. Analysis of the grammar of emotional tropes reveals that emotional processes typically happen in body parts, with body-part terms functioning as actors or undergoers of static processes, but, grammatically speaking, emotional processes are not caused to happen by external agents. While previous work on Filipino languages suggests that the contexts in which one actually describes emotional experience are very limited (Palmer and Brown 1998; Rosaldo 1990), it is clear that Tagalog has a rich lexicon of emotional imagery. Future research should attempt to discover the contexts in which this lexicon is put into play.

More than any other in this volume, the paper by Howard Grabois integrates social construction with cognitive theory. His theoretical focus on the social construction of consciousness derives from the sociocultural theory of Vygotsky and Luria. In this respect, his paper on how second language learners assign meaning to the lexicon of emotion complements the recent work of Péter Bodor (1997) on the problem of how children develop competency in the use of emotion language. But Grabois also utilizes the cognitive linguistic theory of Lakoff, Langacker and others. For example, he compares Lakoff's (1987) description of Dyirbal noun classifiers in terms of category chaining to Vygotsky's chain complexes. Following Vygotsky (1987), he makes an useful distinction between *sense*, which is "a complex, mobile, protean phenomenon," "firmly rooted in specific discourses," and *meaning*, which is stable and decontextualized, what Langacker would no doubt refer to as entrenched and schematic meaning. Adopting Langacker's view of semantic networks to Vygotsky's view of language as socially distributed knowledge, Grabois says, "we can begin to see meaning as that part of the network which is most stable among the individuals who comprise a speech community, and sense as that part of the network which is most individual." Though speech is social in its origins, "once appropriated by the individual, it goes 'underground' and becomes inner speech." Grabois then asks "whether or not it is possible to establish inner speech in a non-native language."

In Grabois' study, the target language is Spanish. He explores semantic networks that ramify out from the terms for *love*, *fear*, *happiness*, and *death* by giving word-association tests to both native speakers and non-native speakers whose first language is English. He shows that non-native speakers may, given sufficient time and interest, be able to acquire native-like lexical organization of semantic networks for these emotion terms, thus demonstrating that it is possible to establish inner speech in a non-native language. His study also reveals important cross-linguistic differences in the associations of emotion terms. He found, for example, that the term *heart* and others related to it by metonymy play a more central role in the semantic network of *love* than does the corresponding Spanish term *corazon*. He concludes that social networks are of great importance in the acquisition of native-like semantic networks. For native speakers of Spanish, *happiness* evokes more connotations of nature (*playa, mar, naturaleza*) while native speakers of English respond with terms for domestic imagery (*children, puppy*). Most interesting is his discovery that native speakers of English are most likely to respond to fear with terms for its effects "i.e. anxiety, nervous, stress, sweat, scream, shaking," while native speakers of Spanish are more likely to respond with its "objective conditions." If we add this observation to differences already noted between English and Asian languages, it begins to look as though speakers of English, American and Canadian at least, have an unusual proclivity to verbalize the domain of emotional experience.

Experientialist versus Social Constructionist Accounts

The book closes with a survey article by Zoltán Kövecses and Gary Palmer, who posit a complementary relationship between two of the most prevalent approaches taken in contemporary research on language and sentiment: social construction theory and the search for universals of physiologically based emotional experience. They review major concepts in emotion studies, including basicness, metaphor and metonymy, theories of meaning ("label," "core meaning," "dimensional," "implicational," and "prototype"), and the relation of scientific to folk theories of emotion. Kövecses and Palmer observe that while emotions are emergent from physical experience, they are nevertheless more frequently evoked by social events rather than physical ones. Both reliable physical responses and appropriate social scenarios are needed for adaptive social interactions. The unstated implication is that this adaptive behavioral synthesis is governed by emotions. One could also argue that cultural adaptations are governed by sentiments. They assert that "emotion concepts must frequently blend universal experiences of physiological functions with culturally specific models and interpretations, and emotion language must reflect this blend." Finally, they conclude that "an emotion concept typically integrates content pertaining to all spheres of experience: social, cognitive, and physical. It also invokes imagery pertaining to language and discourse. This complex content is organized as a more or less stable configuration." This conceptualization applies as well to sentiments, that is, culturally defined emotions. By applying this integrated perspective to natural language, it should be possible for researchers to obtain more exhaustive descriptions and realistic analyses of languages of sentiment.

Languages of Sentiment and the Consciousness of Emotions

In this section we consider four problems: (1) whether different cultures have a heightened or lowered awareness of certain emotions, (2) the relative burden of the lexicon in the verbal expression of emotions and the communication of emotional imagery, and (3) whether the cognitive-linguistic approach is better suited to the study of consciousness of emotions than the pragmatic or social-constructionist approach to language, and (4) how the emotional language and consciousness of individuals relates to collective emotional consciousness.

Linguistic Relativity in the Awareness of Emotions

When we ask whether different cultures have heightened or lowered awareness of certain emotions, we are usually thinking of basic emotions: anger, joy, fear, sadness, or disgust, or emotions with high salience in English, such as love and hate. Languages do appear to differ greatly in their focus on different emotions, but the data are difficult to compare and interpretation of the significance of differences is fraught with difficulties. Data presented by Palmer, Bennett, and Stacey suggest that anger has high salience in Tagalog, but that hate is low in salience. They present 16 expressions for anger, yet only one expression glossed as 'hate'. Anger also has high salience in Tahitian. Robert Levy (1984: 218–219) refers to it as "hypercognized", with "a large number of culturally provided schemata for interpreting and dealing with it" (Levy 1984: 218–219). On the other hand, Tahitian lacks words for severe grief and lamentation. Levy found "no unambigous terms which represent the concepts of sadness, longing, or loneliness." By comparison, Tagalog has *dalamhati* 'affliction, grief, extreme sorrow' and *lungkot* 'sorrow, sadness, grief', of which at least the latter is a salient emotion. In Indonesian anger is lower in salience than it is in English (Heider 1991). It is interesting that these differences, which are apparently significant though difficult to verify, in the salience and lexicalization of anger and grief occur among three languages belonging to the Austronesian family: Indonesian, Tagalog, and Tahitian. Yet such differences may be situational and hard to verify, especially if emotional expression is suppressed to avoid disharmony, as among the Utka Eskimo described by Jean Briggs (1970), or oppression, as among Javanese women described by Berman in this volume. Briggs (1970) reported that the Utka denied the existence of their ill-tempered feelings and in fact she was able to record only four emotion terms pertaining to hostility. Except in exceptional circumstances, expressions of annoyance and ange were uttered only in the third person. In Java, Berman found that even the discussion of emotional events was not necessarily sufficient to evoke emotion-language: "contextualizing emotion talk to actual situations of abuse can not always assist us in pinpointing emotion as a discursive event, especially where emotion is represented through silence or reframing."

In Tagalog, Palmer, Bennett, and Stacey encountered over 20 expressions for fear and shock, suggesting high salience for this emotional domain. In English, Grabois found *fear*, and the responses it provokes ("i.e. anxiety, nervous, stress, sweat, scream, shaking") to be a focus with greater scope and complexity than the Spanish *miedo*. Unlike *fear*, *miedo* is strongly associated with the concept of aloneness (*soledad*).

Palmer, Bennett, and Stacey list only seven Tagalog expressions for love, yet it would be dangerous to conclude that the emotion has low salience in that language, because expressions involving *mahal* 'love' occur frequently in popular romance videos and plays. The unusual grammar of expressions for love involving the heart as a proposed participant suggest that we are witnessing the borrowing and phrasal calquing of emotional linguistic constructions from American romantic literature and media. In this context, it is particularly interesting that Grabois observed that *heart* plays a more central role in the expressions for love used by native speakers of English than *corazon* does for native speakers of Spanish, which is the other likely source for borrowings of emotion-lexemes into Tagalog. Shibamoto-Smith makes a similar observation of possible emotional-linguistic change in progress that can be seen in the Japanese consumption of Harlequin romance novels translated from English. The men in the translated romances use more language expressing sexual desire than the men in romances authored by Japanese. These Tagalog and Japanese examples illustrate how cultures may cultivate novel emotional experiences and language rather than constraining individuals to follow entrenched sentiments. Since people all over the globe are tuning in to Western media, and since much of what they consume pertains to sentiments, it has become difficult to find societies for which we can say with certainty that their languages of sentiment are entirely local.

The Burden of the Lexicon

In communicating emotional imagery, what is the burden of the lexicon versus other modalities of language and culture in expressing emotions and communicating emotional imagery? Merlin Donald (1991) has pointed out that emotional expression evolved early in human prehistory, much earlier than language, as part of an overall mimetic pattern of social communication. This raises the question of what happened as language evolved. To what extent did language become just another vehicle for the mimetic expression of emotion? The lexicon of mimetic emotion terms in Japanese discussed by Occhi, suggests that language did assume some of the mimetic function, but the fact that the Japanese pattern of lexical emotion-mimesis is culture-specific shows that the terms are cultural and social constructs rather than strictly organic products of language evolution.

The consciousness of emotions expressed by mimetics seems to depend on the circumstances. The fact that Japanese mimetic terms occur in well-defined grammatical constructions (nominal syntax) with well-defined patterns of prosody (LHHH) argues that the emotional imagery which they evoke is entrenched and conventional, and therefore low in salience in many speaking situations. On the other hand, when questioned about their usage of the terms, speakers are able to describe physical sensations and contexts of usage in terms of typical social scenarios ("if you're thinking about coming net fishing in Chigasaki you are *waku waku*, and if your sweetheart is going to be waiting there you are *doki doki* as well"). Thus, the level of consciousness of the emotional imagery of mimetic terms in Japanese may depend upon whether speakers are being reflective regarding their usage.

As shown by the Japanese mimetics, emotions also find expression in the prosody of language, including variation in speaking tempo, volume, pitch, and in the length of vocal segments. The capacity for prosody in general appears to be inherited from primate communication, but in humans it has co-evolved with linguistic capacities, so that prosodic signalling of emotions must be more complex in humans than in non-human primates even apart from the *emotion-*

lexicon. This in turn suggests that humans are capable of a greater range of emotional experiences, which they contemplate and verbalize using a surprising variety of vocal skills and reflexes. In the course of human evolution, it was probably the case that those who could cultivate a relatively more differentiated spectrum of emotional expression and express it verbally were more effective in their social coordination and organization and therefore more effective in propagating their genes.

The emotion-lexicon itself seems to play only a small part in emotional expression, probably secondary to gesture, posture, facial expression, visible physiological responses such as blushing, and prosody. Palmer and Brown (1998) found that speakers of Tagalog do not readily describe their emotions or use the emotion-lexicon to express them. When asked about their feelings while watching video romances and melodramas showing scenes involving disrespect or abuse of women, consultants were most likely to describe scenarios of abuse followed by reactive scenarios of revenge, or even suicide. Nevertheless, Tagalog does comprise a sizable lexicon of emotion terms, many of which can be inflected for mood (realis or irrealis) and aspect (completive or incompletive) and given derivational affixes signaling whether participants are actors, undergoers, or locations. In a study of the Tagalog lexicon of cognition and emotion, Palmer (n.d.) assembled 42 terms for emotions (*pakiramdam*) and desires (*hangad*) with definitions and classifications in Tagalog. Nine of the 42 are borrowings from English and Spanish. Of course, the boundaries between the domains of emotion, desire, thought, and even social behavior are a bit fuzzy. The term *kapiling* provides just one example of a term that conflates emotional experience with social cognition:

> *ang kapiling ay isang uri ng pagsasama na hindi lamang pisikal kundi ang pagsasama ng puso at damdamin*
> '*kapiling* is a way of being together that is not physical but a togetherness of the heart and emotions';

In addition to the 42 emotion-lexemes, Palmer, Bennett, and Stacey (this volume) list 78 emotion-tropes. Together, the two lists yield an emotion-repertoire of at least 120 terms. If we take into account inflections, derivations, and prosodic transformations of the lexicon, it is clear that hundreds, if not thousands of discriminations can be made within the lexical domain, this in a language where the description of emotions and use of emotion-declaratives seems secondary to discussion of events and scenarios that produce emotional experience. Conventional polysemies add yet another dimension to the semantic matrix of the emotion-lexicon.

Furthermore, emotion-terms often predicate complex cognitive models, such as the Japanese and English models of romantic love that Shibamoto-Smith compares in her paper. The [Japanese] *happî-endo* model speaks of mutual dependency expressed in leaning…and clinging…, properly contained (contra the Kövecsesian model of American love as something that escapes or overflows its container) within the respective relevant *uchi*-units of the romancing pair." Shibamoto-Smith's paper illustrates how languages of sentiment engage the well-known value systems of American individualism and Japanese orientation to reference group. Wilce refers to a Bangla model of emotion. He observes that "Amina's … assertion that Latifa's passionate speech makes her 'head even crazier' resonates with a model of mental health linked with humoral heating and cooling. People place their hands on another's head to sense physical signs of overheating believed to accompany excess passions that can make them insane."

It is unlikely that any speakers are conscious of an entire cognitive model at any particular time. Discourse situations and events heighten the salience of various aspects of models making them partially accessible to conscious introspection. Cognizance of salient elements is typically distributed across multiple speakers and usage events (Borofsky 1994). The question remains as to whether all functioning elements of cognitive-linguistic models must ultimately be accessible to the distributed awareness or multiple consciousnesses of the community of speakers.

While a voluminous semantic discrimination matrix exists as a theoretical possibility, there are well-traveled pathways which represent emotional experiences that are recognized and reproduced by each culture and given conventional definition in the lexicon. Semantic maps, engraved by discourse history, are unique in important respects to each culture and language. As a case in point, Grabois uses experimental methods to establish that the term *death* is more likely to evoke affective responses (*dolor* 'pain', *tristeza* 'sadness', *soledad* 'aloneness', *pena* 'suffering', and *angustia* 'anguish') in native speakers of Spanish than in native speakers of English, who are more likely to respond with words that describe ceremonies (*funeral*, *coffin*, *cemetery*, *grave*, *casket*).

Another area that would reward further study is the role of grammatical constructions in languages of sentiment. The nominal syntax of Japanese emotion-mimetics has already been mentioned. Palmer, Bennett, and Stacey observed that the most common grammatical structure of Tagalog emotion-tropes is [PREDICATE *ang* ARGUMENT], which is found in 46 out of 78 expressions. The predicate-initial construction in Tagalog has been characterized as signifying the "participation of emotion, of suspense, to emphasize a conception" Lopez (1940: 11). It contrasts with a [SUBJECT *ay* PREDICATE] construction, of which there are only four instances.

The study of the syntax of emotion-language may also contribute to our general understanding of language and consciousness. Stamenov (1997: 330) has argued that "syntax seems to represent as its 'direct referent' basic aspects of the structure of consciousness." It follows that distinctive emotion-grammar refers to a corresponding structure of emotion-consciousness. Palmer, Bennett, and Stacey (this volume) show that Tagalog emotion-metaphors and metonyms manifest dual grammatical structures (understood in the cognitive linguistic sense of a symbolic linkage of phonology with semantic or conceptual structure), but in addition, they link the foregoing to the dual conceptual structures of metaphorical and metonymical thinking, providing evidence in favor of the heterogeneous dual-focus system of consciousness proposed by Stamenov (1997).

The Cognitive-Linguistic Versus the Pragmatic or Social-Constructionist Approach

On first consideration, it might appear that cognitive approaches give us more purchase on the consciousness of emotion than do pragmatic and social-constructionist approaches. A cognitive approach enables one to rapidly and systematically record the emotion-lexicon and discover cognitive models and maps that theoretically underly the usage of terms and the organization of lexical domains. This requires teasing out the interpenetrations of emotion, cognition, physical experience, and social scenarios in the meanings of terms. Such meanings are often obtained as definitions available to the conscious introspection of native-speaker consultants. The cognitive approach also requires that one describe the polysemy for each term (its range of conventional meanings). One can also consider the cognitive grammer of emotion-expressions.

Having done this cognitive homework, one is prepared to take a pragmatic or social-constructionist approach to discover how terms are actually deployed in discourse. Which of several possible meanings of a term is brought to bear? Why is the use of an emotion-term or genre suppressed? Is it because the emotional scenarios evoked in the minds of listeners conflict with their preconceptions and preferences? Of Javanese, Berman asks "do women *avoid* the expression of emotion (as Heider suggests), are they more emotional and hence less *alus* then men, or do the Javanese have a more subtle system for expressing emotion than has yet been identified by scholarly research?" She locates emotional expression of abused women in shifting narrative registers which function as a kind of deixis that indexes emotional evaluations of events. She shows, too, how oppressed women factory workers show emotion by quoting speech of their oppressors and repeating quoted speech. The emotion-lexicon plays little part in these narratives. Where emotion words, such as *sedih* (sad) and *enek* (sickening) are used, they describe the misuse of power, but not the actions of individuals or personal feelings of victims. This restricted use of the emotion-lexicon is governed by the strategy of coordinated resistance.

Schiffman looks at how language itself becomes the object of deliberately emotional rhetoric. He describes an extraordinary history in which at least nine Tamils have voluntarily given their lives for their language over the past four decades. Not only does this suggest that Tamils can get highly emotional about their language, but it must also say something about the act of speaking Tamil. Since the language is so highly valued, displaying it by speaking in political contexts must be an emotional experience. It is as though every word uttered adds a token to an extended construction, a primordial expression of sentiment arousing imagery of motherhood and ethnicity, which constitute the primary meanings of speaking. Yet politicians can also make their love of Tamil explicit by resorting to the emotion-lexicon. The deployment of language, whether conscious or unconscious, can, in and of itself, be an emotional experience.

Donald (1991: 236) has compared discourse to a daily plebiscite that ratifies our linguistic symbols. This is exactly the point where the pragmatic and social-constructionist perspectives come to bear on the language of sentiments. To verbally express an emotion is often, perhaps always, a political act. This is clear in the papers by Berman, Dunn, Schiffman, and Wilce. Berman shows that Javanese women must avoid using the emotion-lexicon because of the political consequences. Dunn shows how a speaker of Japanese deploys a complex array of grammatical emotion-markers to build audience rapport. Schiffman links emotion to linguistic culture. Wilce describes how the genre of lamentation with its expressive texted weeping is erased by those who favor the cool language of global modernization. As lamentation dies, so does a tradition of emotional experience. It is not a question of convention versus novelty, but a replacement of one set of conventions by another. It also follows that to discriminate a new emotion and give it words is to commit a novel political act. The more emotions recognized, consciously or not, the more complex the politics.

But the methodological prescription for a dose of cognition followed by a dose of discourse is too simplistic. Meanings are sometimes discovered only in discourse itself and remain hidden from more static techniques of elicitation. Because every situation is in some respect novel, discourses in socio-political events produce inchoative emotional significances unyielding to prior elicitation. Discourses produce new emotion words as well. Discrepancies must always arise between what people know about their emotion-language and what they discover about it and ratify, or fail to ratify, in actual discourse. By starting from discourse, one can listen to the emergence of emotion-language and the emergent conscious experience that is predicated by new expressions. One can be certain that definitions are grounded in social action and captured undistorted by later reflections biased by ideologies of emotional expression. We conclude that the pragmatic approach to discourse is essential to the linguistic study of conscious emotional experience. Studies of emotional consciousness can benefit from regular feedback between cognitive and pragmatic observations of emotion-language.

Language and the Collective Consciousness of Emotions

Kövecses and Palmer (this volume) take the discussion of emotion and consciousness as an opportunity to raise the old question of how individual experience relates to collective experience (See, for example, Borofsky 1994). They suggest that the emotion-constructs of individuals in part elaborate the collective emotional consciousness in the aggregate while also partly preserving shared emotion-prototypes, even though no single person may possess an entire emotion-prototype. This linguistic analysis provides us with a new approach to Radcliffe-Brown's theory of social sentiments.

Thinking about the problem in this way has surprising consequences for our view of the evolution of language, consciousness, and emotions. Much recent speculation has focussed on knowledge as a crucial element in the mutual feedback process that bootstrapped early humans into fully functioning language users (Donald 1991; Bickerton 1995). Kövecses and Palmer suggest that it is the more intellectualized emotions, such as hope, pride, respect, and shame, that may be both more consciousness-dependent and more language-dependent. They argue that "the emerging ability to conceptualize socially structured emotions beyond the basic ones may have provided a springboard for the co-evolution of consciousness and language in relations of mutual feedback." This is because emotional language shapes potentially adaptive human relations and institutions.

Together the papers in this volume cover a wide variety of sentiments and they provide useful case studies, some described discursively, others analyzed in grammatical detail. They exemplify two major analytical approaches and they illustrate several methodologies, including participant observation, use of data from questionnaires and interviews, analysis of popular media, and the use of native-language reference materials. They provide ethnographic descriptions of pragmatic uses of languages of sentiment in the contemporary world. They add to our knowledge of cultural differences in emotional emphasis and how these are manifested in emotion-lexicons. They show us how cognitive-linguistic and pragmatic approaches can complement one another in studies of emotion-language and the consciousness of emotions. There is much to ponder in these papers, but even so, they barely scratch the surface of what remains to be done. Besnier's (1990) listing of the linguistic devices by which languages may express affect offers a good survey of the possibilities for further study. Nevertheless, we are hopeful that readers will find that the papers in this volume advance the study of languages of sentiment.

August 26, 1998
Las Vegas and Sendai

Notes

1. The many interesting papers presented at the LAUD Symposium on Humboldt and Whorf, held in Duisburg, Germany, April 1–5, 1998, demonstrate the viability of linguistic relativism that is cognitively oriented. The proceedings are to be published in two volumes with the following working titles: "Explorations in linguistic relativity" (Vol. 1), Martin Pütz and Marjolijn Verspoor, Eds., and "Evidence for linguistic relativity" (Vol. 2) Susanne Niemeier and René Dirven, Eds.

References

Angeliki Athanasiadou and Elzbieta Tabakowska (eds) 1998. *Speaking of Emotions: Conceptualization and Expression*. Berlin/New York: Mouton de Gruyter.

Barnouw, Victor. 1973. *Culture and Personality*. Revised Edition. Homewood, IL: The Dorsey Press.

Benedict, Ruth. 1959 [1934]. *Patterns of Culture*. Boston: Houton Mifflin Company.

Besnier, Niko. 1990. Language and Affect. *Annual Review of Anthropology* 19: 419–51.

Bickerton, Derek. 1995. *Language and Human Behavior*. Seattle: The University of Washington Press.

Bodor, Péter. 1997. "On the usage of emotional language". In Niemeier, Susanne and René Dirven (eds), 195–208.

Borofsky, Robert. 1994. "On the knowledge and knowing of cultural activities". In Robert Borofsky (ed) *Assessing Cultural Anthropology*. New York: McGraw-Hill, Inc., 331–347.

Briggs, Jean. 1970. *Never in Anger*. Cambridge: Harvard University Press.

D'Andrade, Roy. 1995. *The Development of Cognitive Anthropology*. Cambridge: Cambridge University Press.

Donald, Merlin. 1991. *Origins of the Modern Mind: Three Stages in the Evolution of Culture and Cognition*. Cambridge, Mass: Harvard University Press.

Duranti, Alessandro. 1997. *Linguistic Anthropology*. Cambridge: Cambridge University Press.

Fauconnier, Gilles. 1997. *Mappings in Thought and Language*. Cambridge: Cambridge University Press.

Heider, Karl. 1991. *Landscapes of Emotion: Mapping Three Cultures of Emotion in Indonesia*. Cambridge: Cambridge University Press.

Kövecses, Z. 1986. *Metaphors of Anger, Pride, and Love: A Lexical Approach to the Structure of Concepts*. Amsterdam: John Benjamins.

———. 1988. *The Language of Love. The Semantics of Passion in Conversational English*. Lewisburg, PA: Bucknell University Press.

———. 1990. *Emotion Concepts*. New York: Springer-Verlag.

———. 1991a. "A linguist's quest for love". *J. Social and Personal Relationships* 8: 77–97.

———. 1991b. "Happiness: A definitional effort". *Metaphor and Symbolic Activity* 6: 29–46.

———. 1994. "Ordinary language, common sense, and expert theories in the domain of emotion". In J. Siegfried (ed) *The Status of Common Sense in Psychology*. Norwood, New Jersey: Ablex, 77–97.

———. 1998. "Are there any emotion-specific metaphors?" In Angeliki Athanasiadou and Elzbieta Tabakowska (eds), 127–152.

———. In press. *Metaphor and Emotion. Language, Culture, and Body in Human Feeling*. New York: Cambridge University Press.

Kryk-Kastovsky, Barbara. 1997. "Surprise, surprise: the iconicity-conventionality scale of emotions". In Niemeier, Susann and René Dirven (eds), 155–169.

Lakoff, George. 1987. *Women, Fire, and Dangerous Things: What Categories Reveal about the Mind*. Chicago: University of Chicago Press.

Langacker, Ronald. 1991. *Concept, Image, and Symbol*. Berlin/New York: Mouton de Gruyter.

Levy, Robert. 1984. "Emotion, knowing, and culture". In Richard A. Shweder and Robert A. LeVine (eds), *Culture Theory: Essays on Mind, Self, and Emotion*. Cambridge: Cambridge University Press, 214–237.

Niemeier, Susanne. 1997. Introduction. In Niemeier, Susann and René Dirven (eds), vii-xviii.

Niemeier, Susann and René Dirven (eds). 1997. *The Language of Emotions: Conceptualization, Expression, and Theoretical Foundation*. Amsterdam/Philadelphia: John Benjamins Publishing Company.

Palmer, Gary B. 1996. *Toward a Theory of Cultural Linguistics*. Austin: University of Texas Press.

Palmer, Gary B. n.d. "Tagalog expressions pertaining to mental experience: cognition and emotion in a Western Austronesian language". Unpublished ms.

Palmer, Gary B. and Rick Brown. 1998. "The Ideology of Honor, Respect, and Emotion in Tagalog". In Angeliki Athanasiadou and Elzbieta Tabakowska (eds), 331–355.

Radcliffe-Brown, A. R. 1922. *The Andaman Islanders*. New York: The Free Press.

Rosaldo, Michelle. 1990. "The things we do with words: Ilongot speech acts and speech act theory in philosophy". In Donal Carbaugh (ed), *Cultural Communication and Intercultural Contact*. Hillsdale, NJ: Lawrence Erlbaum Associates, Publishers, 373–408.

Rosaldo, Renato. 1993. *Culture and Truth: The Remaking of Social Analysis*. Boston: Beacon Press.

Stamenov, Maxim I. 1997. “Grammar, meaning, and consciousness: what sentence structure can tell us about the structure of consciousness”. In Maxim I. Stamenov (ed) *Language Structure, Discourse and the Access to Consciousness*. Amsterdam/Philadelphia: John Benjamins Publishing Company, 277–342.

Urban, Greg. 1996. *Metaphysical Community: The Interplay of the Senses and the Intellect*. Austin: University of Texas Press.

Vygotsky, L. 1987. *The Collected Works of L.S. Vygotsky; Volume 1, Problems of General Psychology*. Robert W. Rieber and Aaron S. Carton (eds). New York and London: Plenum Press.

Pragmatic and Social Constructionist Approaches

Language, Primordialism and Sentiment

Harold Schiffman
University of Pennsylvania

> The words of childhood — these early companions in the dawn of our existence, with which our whole soul was interwoven, when can we ever mistake them? When can we ever forget them? Maternal language was our first world, it conveyed the first sensations that we felt, the first activity and cheerfulness that we enjoyed. The associated ideas of place and time, of love and hatred, of joy and activity, and all that the ardent and rising soul of youth comprehends in them, all this is thus perpetuated, and language becomes a stock.[1]

The term primordialism has been used in a number of ways by social scientists and others dealing with the phenomenon of "primary sentiments" or notions present (at least to some observers) in some societies, that are perceived by culture-bearers and analysts alike as being *essential* to their self-definition. Without these primordial ("first-order" or original or fundamental elements), a list of which usually mentions language, religion, blood-lines (caste, race, descent, etc.), territory, and perhaps some others, the group in question could not imagine themselves to exist.

The concept of primordialism, whether or not language is involved in its perception, is not without its detractors, and we shall have to deal with the assault on the notion, particularly as an *analytical* construct, below. What we are interested more in here is the notion of primordialism as *self-defined*.[2]

Thus, whether or not we accept primordialism as analytically necessary, useful, or helpful, there is in some cultures an observable phenomenon that seems to be a kind of meta-characteristic of the group: they see their language (or their religion, or their genetic relatedness) as *essential* or as *the very essence of* their selfhood or ethnicity (whatever this means, however defined),[3] without which the group would, in their own estimation, cease to have meaning, or even cease to exist. To preserve this meaning, or this existence, the group (or its members) then resort to actions that are deemed "primitive, dangerous, politically fissiparous" by analysts and opponents, but in the eyes of the group's members, are necessary and natural. The fear that lurks in the minds of most analysts, and some political leaders, is the "havoc wreaked … by those … states that did passionately seek to become primordial rather than civil political communities …" (Geertz 260), the best (or worst) example in our time being Nazi Germany.[4]

Therefore, we do not need to accept or reject primordialism as an analytic device in order to be able to study its characteristics or manifestations in a given group or language community,[5] just as we do not need to accept common and popular notions about race in order to study the phenomenon of racism. In the case of race, of course, anthropologists have long since abandoned the idea that there are a fixed number of races, or of a set basic defining, essential racial characteristics, but racism as a kind of *belief system* continues to be manifested in the world's cultures, whether or not there is any kind of "scientific" basis to the notion. Similarly, linguists do not need to validate the idea that a given language, say Japanese, has essential characteristics that are qualitatively different from other languages; we can study the belief systems and attitudes that seem to be observable in Japanese linguistic culture (cf. Miller 1982) as a phenomenon totally independent of the structure and form of the Japanese language. But for the Japanese, the structure and form of their language is intertwined with their belief systems about their language, which seem to the Japanese (as Miller reports it at least) to be uniquely essential to their "culture" and without which Japanese culture would cease to exist.

For the purposes of this paper, of course, the aspect of primordialism that we are interested in is the *emotional* or *sentimental* aspect — the sentiments that are evoked when language is perceived to be threatened, or the sentiments displayed in certain circumstances such as public oratory, the public (or even private) reading of poetry, the public (or private) incantation of sacred texts, the performance of song, or the kinds of sentiments that move people to attempt to purify their language of "foreign" elements and restore it to a state of former or imagined grace.

It is common nowadays to refer to such ideas or belief systems as *ideologies* and to condemn them as being always related to systems of hegemony, perpetuation of inequality, imperialism, colonialism, patriarchalism, or whatever. I resist the temptation to use the term "ideology", since I find it fraught with many methodological inexactitudes, the least of which is the lack of rigor in its application. I prefer instead to think of these belief systems, ideas, etc. about language to be part of which I call *linguistic culture*[6]. Already twenty-five years ago Geertz pointed out that

> [i]t is one of the minor ironies of modern intellectual history that the term "ideology" has itself become thoroughly ideologized. A concept that once meant but a collection of political proposals, perhaps somewhat intellectualistic and impractical but at any rate idealistic [...] has now become, to quote *Webster's* "the integrated assertions, theories, and aims constituting a politico-social program, often with an implication of factitious propagandizing".... Even in works that, in the name of science, profess to be using a neutral sense of the term, the effect of its employment tends nonetheless to be distinctly polemical...

Geertz goes on to point out that some would list "the main characteristics of ideology as bias, oversimplification, emotive language, and adaption to public prejudice." (Geertz 1973: 193).[7] We lack, in other words, a way to deal with these phenomena that does not get into either a denial of their existence, or a need to utterly condemn them, lest anyone in our audience think that we give them some sort of credence, or that they are in any way credible.

In this paper I will attempt to avoid condemnatory prose in favor of what some would call a misguided and hopelessly futile "objectivity" in the study of linguistic primordialism. And because the notion of "ideology" is itself hopelessly contaminated, both from the left and the right, I shall abjure it in favor of simply attempting to examine belief systems concerning language as an observable phenonenon of some linguistic cultures, and try to delineate any common features and origins that I can discern, especially regarding their emotive and sentimental imagery.

Primordialism and "Primary Factors"

The search for primordialism leads one into many thickets, and one I hope to avoid is the concern of an earlier generation of anthropologists, such as Needham 1978, for what he called "primary factors", i.e. what aspects there exist about culture, or even of human beings, that might be termed universal or primary. If it could be determined what structures, or organizational systems, or ideas even that *all* cultures displayed or possessed, one could perhaps justify the primordialism, the attachment, the bond that certain primordial features had for various peoples. But in today's approach to the same questions, it is typical to deny the primordial, to see everything as a social construct, and therefore the embarrassing persistence, in some cultures, of attachments that social anthropologists now want to see as anything *but* primordial, leads to puzzling conclusions. Some would even deny the primacy of emotion, or at least of affect, which makes us wonder why anyone would harbor strong feelings toward language, or kinship, or religion, or territory, when surely these emotions and feelings are all *just* social constructs, perhaps just the artifact of the analysis?

To summarize thus far: we need to distinguish between factors (phenomena, proclivities, constraints, determinants) that the anthropologist seeks to isolate as primary (primordial) among the cultures of the world, and the things (phenomena, proclivities, attachments, etc.) that peoples themselves call prim/ary/-ordial (such as religion, language, race, gender, blood lines, whatever) especially as these are felt (by peoples) to be essential to their *ethnicity*, their sense of peoplehood, their basic group identity, which tends to be transmitted generationally.

For Geertz, primordial attachments derive from the "assumed givens" of social existence — region, kin, sharing of religion, language, social practice. But the *sentimental* nature of these attachments is embarrassing for the social scientist — the attachment is "romantic" and thus inappropriate to the objectives of social science. From a discussion of the subjective romantic, one can quickly degenerate into crude statements about cultural determinism, leading to stereotypical assessments of national character, superior vs. inferior, and so on.

I would add that these factors are also impossible to *quantify* and quantificatory social science has shied away from them, almost as if they would contaminate the purity of their scientific analysis. As Stack (1986: 2) puts it the term "lacks rigor, explanatory power, and predictive value of structural analyses of behavior." Thus, the primordial explanation explains everything and nothing, and ignores other factors. But as Geertz continues,

> The general strength of such primordial bonds, and the types of them that are important, differ from person to person, from society to society, and from time to time. But for virtually every person, in every society, at almost all times, some attachments seem to flow more from a sense of natural — some would say spiritual — affinity than from social interaction.

Here we are *truly* in trouble: *spiritual* affinity? "These congruities of blood speech, custom [etc.] are seen to have ineffable and … overpowering coerciveness." (Geertz 1973: 259)

Thus, the bonds of personal affection, consanguinity, practical necessity, common interest, or incurred obligation are important, but more important is the unaccountable absolute import attributed to the very tie itself. The ties are felt to be like some kind of magnetism, or some kind of magic; they are irresistible, ineffable, intangible; they exist at some higher plane, perhaps on a spiritual plane; they are non-rational, or even irrational. And they can be counted on to stir up deeper sentiments than any "common interest" kind of practical bond.

Unleashed, they may lead to civil war (Sri Lanka), or genocide (Nazi Germany, Ruanda, Cambodia).

Who are the Primordialists?

Since primordialism is a vague and non-rational "attachment" rooted in sentiment and other poorly defined and difficult to quantify notions, it is also perhaps difficult, or even dangerous, to identify or label groups that would seem to exemplify primordialism par excellence. This despite the need for examples from language loyal groups that have already been identified, such as those given by Geertz. Some groups, however, do stand out, and seem even proud to be noted for their intense attachment to their language. The Tamils are one of these, and by some measures, perhaps among the strongest; the Japanese are another, and the French are not far behind. I have dealt with various expressions of what might be called primordialism *par excellence* in my 1996 book; in addition to the Tamils, Japanese and French, I cite passages written about Arabic and Navajo.[8]

What then might be the metric by which we measure primordialism? If it exists, how is it manifested? Are there varying degrees of primordialism? If it is gradient, what is the grading scale? As Johnson and Lakoff point out, however, things that are not quantifiable, such as sentiments (*love* is their prime example) are almost always described in metaphorical terms: love is a physical force (akin to electromagnetism or gravity), a patient (especially a mad one), or it is magic, or war. Even the supposedly measurable one (physical force) however, is not, in the case of love, described in terms of MHz or G's, and the others are described only in terms of further metaphoric devices (Johnson and Lakoff 1980: 49).

Given the well-known reluctance, nay inability of the social sciences to quantify primordialism, or even to touch it with a ten-foot pole, do the linguistic primordialists themselves have ways to assess it? Since the social scientists consider it impossible, should it not also be an impossible task for the the culture bearers themselves? The answer is no; the primordial bond is ineffable, it is not to be quantified, but this is in fact its special allure. It can, in fact be *qualified*, i.e. qualities can be ascribed to it, and various expressions of it can be assessed. What *can* be measured is the level of *devotion* to the object of their admiration, and primordial linguistic cultures come readily equipped with ways to measure it.

Though many cultures refer to the native language as the "mother tongue", (an appelation that may have originated in France during the French Revolution) the Tamils also have the notion of *tamiṛ taay* ('Tamil as mother') who is pure, virginal, immutable, quasi-divine; she gives us life, nourishes us with her milk; we must protect her with our lives if need be:

> … *Tamilttāy* … the apotheosis of the language as goddess, queen, mother, and maiden. Indeed in the discourses of Tamil's devotees, there is ready slippage between *tamil*; *Tamilttāy*; *taypāl*, 'mother's milk'; *tāy*, 'mother' and *tāymoli*, 'mother tongue,' all of which over time come to be synonymous with each other. (Ramaswamy 1997: 17).

But we (the outside observers) do not measure her primordial qualities; they are to be measured by the devotion of her devotees, because the strength of her qualities is seen in the strength of devotion she inspires. Even this can only properly be measured by a culture bearer, an insider to the linguistic culture. Only an insider can tell if the devotee is pure in his/her devotion, and pure in his/her service to the language. If his/her heart is pure, *Tamilttāy* will speak to him/her, and s/he will speak a *pure* Tamil as well.

Linguistic Purism

Linguistic purism is therefore one expression (one that can perhaps be measured) of primordial devotion in the Tamil world. I have dealt with this in a recent work:

> In many linguistic cultures there exist movements that have as their goal linguistic *purism*. This has been defined in a number of different ways, but often involves religious or quasi-religious fundamentalism and a return to (or a search for) linguistic *authenticity*; it often takes the form of removing from the language elements (usually lexical) that appear to be foreign, or corrupt, or lacking in true authenticity in the linguistic culture in question.[9]

Annamalai's definition is widely used:

> Purism is the opening of the native sources and closure non-native sources for the enrichment of the language. Though the native sources are open in general, the dialectal and literary sources are often treated differently. The opening and closure can be seen as applied to materials and to models. Models are the derivational, compounding and syntactic patterns. … The factors which lead to purism may be, theoretically, internal or external to the language … More important than any structural consideration is the attitude of speakers toward native and non-native elements …. The attitude … is determined by socio-cultural, political and historical factors which are external to language. There are certain conditions some or all of which must be present for the puristic regulations to emerge in any language … [such as when the] social order is undergoing change with power relations redefined. (Annamalai 1979: 3–5)

Purism as language policy

As we can see, devotion to linguistic purism is a kind of language policy — there is an attempt to control where vocabulary comes from, what sources (external or internal) it will draw from, what syntactic and derivational process it will utilize. Central to all of this is a *belief system*, consisting of some or all of the following:

- A belief that there exists somewhere, perhaps in the past, or in a particular textual tradition, a state of "purity" that the language can aspire to, or return to; A belief that there are people with special knowledge, capable of making decisions about what is pure and what is not;
- A belief that purity is a good thing, capable of renewing or strengthening the moral fiber of the language, its linguistic culture, or its speakers; purity/ purism, therefore is *salvific*;
- There may also be a belief that purity is associated with a religious state, i.e. by keeping the language pure we keep religion pure, which helps keep the world from disintegrating.
- Purism may be associated with religious fundamentalism and fundamentalist movements, with political movements, nationalism, national integration, millennialism, and many other kinds of social, political and cultural phenomena.

Puristic movements in linguistic cultures come and go, they wax and wane. As Annamalai points out, they are often associated with changes in the social order or when power-relations are being redefined. They are often very unscientific, relying on dubious ideas about what is native and what is not, and as a result many aspects of the movement get "fudged" because of ignorance of the history of various words, or because it becomes too complicated to remain consistent.

Loan Translation

For example, many puristic movements allow "loan translation" of borrowed elements, which means that if a word can be coined that effectively translates the pieces of the borrowed word, the concept can be kept. Thus German, which went through a period of purism (but has now emerged from it) consciously coined terms like *Fernsprecher* for "telephone" and *Fernsehen* for "television" but in recent years has abandoned attempts to *calque* foreign words and now simply borrows, mostly from English. In Tamil, … borrowed words from Sanskrit, Hindi, English and other languages were (and are) consciously exponged in an attempt to return to the purity of Old Tamil; when television broadcasting came to South India, Tamil, too had to find a Tamil word, and resorted to a loan translation *tolaikaaṭci* (*tolai* means 'distant' and *kaaṭci* means 'show') in lieu of using the English word or the All-India Sanskritic *dūrdarṣan*, which is itself a loan translation from "tele-vision". But even Old Tamil contains some loan words (from Sanskrit) but when it was pointed out that the word *aracu* "government" was originally from Sanskrit *rāj*, the solution was to declare quite simply that Sanskrit had borrowed the word from Tamil, rather than the opposite. Purism may rely on philology and "scientific" linguistics for arguments it finds useful, but if the arguments reveal inconsistency and error, they can be twisted to suit the goals of the puristic movement (Schiffman 1996: 61–63).

Tamil linguistic culture has some metrics by which it can measure puristic usage, though even these are fraught with some difficulty. But Indian linguistic culture comes ready-made with various devices, since ancient "standards" are available against which usage can be compared. For most Indian languages, Sanskrit and degrees of Sanskritization are ready at hand; for Tamil, older stages of Tamil are also available, and the exclusivity of these models (no other language emulates them) adds another notch to the fervor of Tamil primordialism. One can emulate the grammar, vocabulary, the syntax of earlier models, and the ability to expatiate at length on any topic is highly valued. (Here objective measures are ready at hand; a stop watch can serve nicely to measure the length of utterances.)

But even within Tamil culture (and Indic culture at large) length of utterance or archaicity of grammar is somewhat mundane; other measures, more ineffable, less objective, are more highly valued.[10] The question really is, who loves Tamil the *most*, and how shall we know this?

The use of Metaphor

By one objective measure, such as willingness to sacrifice one's life for the language, the Tamils surely rank near the top: by documented estimates, at least 9 Tamils have voluntarily given their lives for their language during various demonstrations and actions during the last four decades (Ramaswami 1997: 1), and unofficially, the loss of life by Tamils fighting for an independent Tamil Eelam in Sri Lanka ranks very high. In fact the invocation "remember the martyrs!" is often used whenever enthusiasm for Tamil causes is seen to be flagging, and can penetrate even discussions of how to encode Tamil characters in Unicode, a debate one might consider essentially devoid of potential emotional content.

But the quality of primordialism that seems to be admired most is the most ineffable sort, and that is the creative use of Tamil itself, especially in the use of metaphor. At the 6th World Tamil Conference in Kuala Lumpur in 1987, I observed a display of this creativity that I had never before been fortunate enough to witness.[11]

The (as of this writing) current Chief Minister of Tamilnadu, Mr. Karunanidhi, then out of power, attended the conference and gave a keynote address. This featured speech was perhaps only possible because the then Chief Minister, Mr. M. G. Ramachandran (better known as MGR) was literally on his death-bed back in Madras, and because he was unable to attend, attendance by any other members of his party was also forbidden. Mr Karunanidhi profited from this situation by using the keynote address to obliquely attack MGR on the issue of who loved Tamil the most (a metaphor for the question of who ought to be the next Chief Minister). Since it would have been unseemly to attack MGR directly, he chose to construct an elaborate metaphor, in which he described a chaste, virginal bride (i.e. the Tamil language) who had been "left standing at the altar". In rich detail he described her beauty, the glory of her raiment, the auspiciousness of the moment (chosen by astrologists), the splendor of the guests in attendance at the wedding. But *where was the bridegroom?*, he asked. Again and again he described the trials and tribulations of this chaste virgin, again and again he asked *where was the bridegroom?*, and we, the audience, could only compare the situation of this jilted bride to the situation we found ourselves in — waiting in the grand hall for the chief guest (MGR), who never appeared. What was keeping him? Did he lack ardor? Did he not love (his) Tamil (bride), or did he not love her *enough*? Was he not strong enough, ardent enough, deserving enough of her? Could he not lift the veil and behold her chastity, her beauty, reserved for him? But we could also see the bride's plight as the plight of Tamil linguistic culture, jilted by her saviour on the political scene, while the once-revered leader (MGR) languished on his deathbed, his government paralyzed.

The metaphor went on and on, a seamless web of submetaphors and other poetic devices, full of the alliteration that Tamils love, but never once was the perfidious bridegroom mentioned; the question *maappiḻḻai engee?* (where's the bridegroom?) hung in the air, and as it was repeated again and again, the audience began to chime in. Never once was MGR's name mentioned, and never once was it stated that Tamil was the jilted bride. But it was clear that another bridegroom must be found. Who would come forward? On and on the metaphor was built. The speech, the use of favored literary devices, the linguistic skill showed the expertise of the speaker to elaborate advantage. *He* was the obvious candidate, he was the obvious choice to fill the gap. Only he possessed the linguistic skills, only he could rescue the bereft bride, weeping for her suitor. Mr.

Karunanidhi didn't have to say "I love Tamil more;" he *demonstrated* it in his mastery of the rhetorical style. The question seemed to answer itself.

This speech, though in itself a virtuosic performance of a particularly Tamil sort, in some ways seems to me to epitomize Tamil primordialism. There are a number of features, and I would like to enumerate them.

- Tamil is anthropomorphized as a woman, especially a pure, virginal, beautiful woman; sometimes the woman is called *Tamil̠ taay* 'mother Tamil' and in imagery, she is the mother of us all (or of all Tamils.) She has given us life, the life-breath (*uyir*) without which no Tamil can speak (Ramaswamy 1997).
- The love of the Tamil devotee is above caste, creed and religion; any Tamil, whether Hindu, Muslim or Christian, can love Tamil, and Mother Tamil loves all her devotees equally.
- Love of Tamil is best expressed in devotional poetry or prose (such as the oratorical metaphor of Mr. Karunanidhi) spontaneously generated in praise of her. The creativity of the poetic construct is *in, of,* and *for* Tamil; it is Tamil's finest moment to be praised in the most creative (ineffable, spiritual) use of the language.
- Other expressions of devotion, such as the more mundane memorization and recitation of classical texts, or the long-drawn out generation of alliterative prose oratory (known as the DMK style) almost devoid of meaning, is admirable, but cannot hold a candle to the oeuvre produced by the likes of Mr. Karunanidhi.

Conclusion

Primordialism, or at least linguistic primordialism, despite its problematicity for anthropologists and other analysts as an analytical concept, seems to be still alive in the world today, and shows no signs of dying out, or being replaced by more "modern" constructs. Linguistic primordialism is as important to people in as highly-industrialized a country as Japan as it is to speakers of smaller, less technologically-developed linguistic cultures. Just as it seemed to be at one point an essentially *premodern* phenomenon, it now seems also (or still) to be a *post-modern* one. The dissolution of the large economic empires and multinational states created in this century, often as a result of the aftermath of world wars, or as the product of new economic systems, has seen the rebirth of primordialism of various sorts, including the linguistic, and far from being a nineteenth-century phenomenon, now seems destined to continue unabated into the twenty-first.

Notes

1. Die Worte der Kindheit — diese unsre frühen Gespielen in der Morgenröthe des Lebens! mit denen sich unsre ganze Seele zusammen bildete —, wenn werden wir sie verkennen? wenn werden wir sie vergeßen? Unsre Muttersprache war ja zugleich die erste Welt, die wir sahen, die ersten Empfindungen, die wir fühlten, die erste Würksamkeit und Freude, die wir genoßen! Die Nebenideen von Ort und Zeit, von Liebe und Haß, von Freude und Thätigkeit, und was die feurige, heraufwallende Jugendseele sich dabei dachte, wird alles mit verewigt — nur wird die Sprache schon Stamm! (Herder 1770: 89)
2. Fishman (1997: xviii) refers to this as the "inside" view of the language and ethnicity connection. by culture-bearers, or in the case of a language, by the speakers of the languages themselves.
3. See Smolicz's notion (Smolicz 1979) of "core values" here.
4. It may be necessary in some cases,of course, to see some primordial attachments, at least those that are overtly declared as the basic ones, e.g. National Socialism's *Blut und Boden* ('blood and soil/territory') as metaphors for something else — the Nazis defined "German soil" as in fact that soil where German was spoken, but did not declare the German mother-tongue to be itself primordial, since there were some German speakers who were excluded because of *Blut* (the Jews); this also made certain other considerations of *Boden* problematical, e.g. German-speaking Switzerland and the pockets of territory occupied by ethnic Germans in eastern Europe, such as the German-speaking communities along the Volga.
5. As Fishman puts it, studying positive ethnolinguistic consciousness is like doing gender research but decrying sexual harrassment, or doing religious inquiry but condemning religious bigotry (Fishman 1997: 6).
6. By linguistic culture I mean the sum totality of ideas, values, beliefs, attitudes, prejudices, myths, religious strictures, and all the other cultural "baggage" that speakers bring to their dealings with language from their culture. Linguistic culture also is concerned with the transmission and codification of language and has bearing also on the culture's notions of the value of literacy and the sanctity of texts. It also includes, of course, the language itself. (Schiffman 1996)
7. Geertz repeats the old saw that "I have a belief system, you have prejudices, and he has an ideology."
8. Here are quotes that assert strong evaluations of the special characteristics of the languages in question, especially their first-order characteristics, in particular, how the languages originated, or how they came to assert their dominance over others:

   On Arabic:

   > Muslims consider the Koran to be holy scripture only in the original Arabic of its revelation. The Koran, while it may be translated, is only ritually valid in Arabic. This is connected with the notion of Arabic as a "sacred language". Language itself is sacred, because of its miraculous power to communicate and to externalize thought. In this sense, language is essentially the same as the Divine power of

> creation. In order to create, God speaks a Word in the Spirit; similarly, man externalizes what is within his mind by formulating words with the breath, by giving breath "form" in sound. The power of words to transmit to another consciousness the knowledge of the speaker lies in the fact that true words *are* themselves what they mean, or were at their origin; they are the object itself in sound. (Glassé 1989: 46).
> Thanks to the relationship of words to their roots, as if to a supraformal archetype, a deeper and more universal sense often superimposes itself upon a particular meaning in a phrase in classical Arabic. Simple statements, which are the rule in the Koran, open, under the right conditions of receptivity, into astonishing and vast horizons; the world is reduced to ripples in consciousness. These and other qualities make Arabic an imcomparable medium for dialogue between man and God in prayer (Glassé 1989: 47).

On Japanese:

> For modern Japan, the Japanese language is a way of life, and the enormous amount of speculation, writing, and talking about it that goes on at every level of Japanese life constitutes an entirely distinctive and marvelously self-contained way of looking at life. In modern Japan, the Japanese language is never allowed to be taken for granted, not by anyone, not for a single moment. … The language not only serves the society as a vehicle for daily communication, but it also manages, … to be a cult and myth as well. … To the Japanese today, the Japanese language is not simply the way they talk and write. For them, it has assumed the dimensions of a national myth of vast proportions (Miller 1982: 4–5).

On Navajo:

> To the Navajo, man can think only with symbols, so some symbols must have existed before thought. The first few sentences of the first paragraph of the emergence myth read: "The one that is called "water everywhere". The one that is called "black earth". The one that is called "first language." … These phrases are significant in that they indicate that in the beginning were the word and the thing, the symbol and the object. … Symbol is word, and word is the means by which substance is organized and transformed. Both substance and symbol are primordial, for in the beginning were the word and the element, the symbol and the symbolized. (Witherspoon 1977: 46)

For the Navajo the world was actually created or organized by means of language. The form of the world was first conceived in thought, and then this form was projected onto primordial unordered substance through the compulsive power of speech and song. (*ibid.* 1977: 47).

9. Excellent studies of purism can be found in Wexler 1974, Annamalai 1979, and Jernudd 1989.

10. In fact, in Indic linguistic culture, the pundits themselves consider servile punditry of a knee-jerk kind to be lowest on the ranking scale. Those who memorize the Vedas, e.g., have less prestige than those who commit other texts to memory, since Vedic is so dense that there can be little comprehension of it, and gross memorization is all that is necessary.

11. In fact, I had usually avoided devotional speech-making if I could, because I found it mystifying and difficult to comprehend. At one such rally, several weeks after arriving in India the first time, I asked my "host" at the rally to translate, since I couldn't follow the rhetoric, and couldn't understand the speech. "Neither can I," he replied, "but isn't it *beautiful*!"

References

Annamalai, E. 1979. *Movement for Linguistic Purism: the Case of Tamil*. Central Institute of Indian Languages: Mysore.

Annamalai, E. n.d. "Notes and Discussions; The Standard Spoken Tamil — some Observations." Unpublished ms.

Fishman, Joshua A. 1997. *In Praise of the Beloved Language: A Comparative View of Positive Ethnolinguistic Consciousness*. Contributions to the Sociology of Language 76. Berlin; New York: Mouton de Gruyter, 1997.

Geertz, Clifford. 1973 *The Interpretation of Cultures: Selected Essays*. New York: Basic Books.

Glassé, Cyril. 1989. *A Concise Encyclopedia of Islam*. London: Stacey International.

Grassi, Ernesto. 1994. *The Primordial Metaphor* tr. by Laura Pietropaolo and Manuela Scarci. Binghamton: Italian Academy of Advanced Studies in America.

Herder, Johann Gotfried. 1770. *Abhandlung über den Ursprung der Sprache* ed. by Wolfgang Proß. Munich: Carl Hanser Verlag.

Jernudd, Björn. 1989. *The Texture of Language Purism: an Introduction*. Vol. 54 of Contributions to the Sociology of Language. Mouton de Gruyter: Berlin.

Jernudd, Björn and M. H. Ibrahim. 1986. "Introduction". In *Aspects of Arabic Sociolinguistics. International Journal of the Sociology of Language* 61.5–6.

Johnson, Mark and George Lakoff. 1980. *Metaphors We live by*. Chicago: University of Chicago Press.

Kövecses, Zoltán. 1990. *Emotion Concepts*. New York: Springer Verlag.

Markel, Norman. 1998. *Semiotic Psychology: Speech as an Index of Emotions and Attitudes*. Berkeley Insights in Linguistics and Semiotics 26. New York: Peter Lang Publishing.

Miller, Roy Andrew. 1982. *Japan's Modern Myth: the Language and Beyond*. New York: Weatherhill.

Needham, Rodney. 1978. *Primordial Characters*. Charlottesville: University Press of Virginia.

Ramaswamy, Sumathi. 1997. *Passions of the Tongue: Language Devotion in Tamil India, 1891–1970*. Berkeley and Los Angeles: University of California Press.

Schiffman, Harold F. 1996. *Linguistic Culture and Language Policy*. New York and London: Routledge.

Shils, E. 1957. "Primordial, Personal, Sacred and Civil Ties". *British Journal of Sociology* 8(2).130–145.

Stack, John F., Jr., ed. 1986. *The Primordial Challenge: Ethnicity in the Contemporary World*. New York: Greenwood Press.

Smolicz, J. J. 1979. *Culture and Education in a Plural Society*. Canberra: Curriculum Development Center.

Wexler, Paul. 1974. *Purism and Language: A Study in Modern Ukrainian and Belorussian Nationalism (1840–1967)*. Bloomington: Indiana University.

Witherspoon, Gary. 1977. *Language and Art in the Navajo Universe*. Ann Arbor: University of Michigan Press.

Transforming Laments

Performativity and Rationalization as Linguistic Ideologies

James M. Wilce, Jr.
Northern Arizona University

Rationalization and Lament[1]

> That great historic process in the development of religions, the elimination of magic from the world [its disenchantment, entzauberung] … which … repudiated all magical means to salvation as superstition and sin, came here to its logical conclusion. The genuine Puritan even rejected all signs of religious ceremony at the grave and buried his nearest and dearest without song or ritual … (Weber 1958: 105).

> However it has been achieved, traditional women's lament has been almost eliminated from the modern western world. Only in isolated pockets… can we find, usually in the memory of the older women, some last remnants of the songs for the dead that were once improvised at every funeral. (Holst-Warhaft 1992: 6).

Bangladeshi ideologies of language, music, and affect reveal an interesting contradiction. Bangladeshis, Islamist and otherwise, are quick to state that lament tunes "come from the heart" irrepressibly. Yet in their next breath, Islamists condemn these heart expressions as willful, narcissistic self-indexing. In the ensuing conflict, Bangladeshi lament — tuneful, texted weeping — seems destined to share the fate of European lament traditions.

Such a loss betokens the transformation of consciousness inherent when a community begins to "imagine" itself as a "rational public" (Anderson 1991; Calhoun 1992) with modern nationalist identity and goals. Whereas older forms of community self-consciousness arose out of matters pressing to groups like families or autonomous and wandering religious orders, modernist production of culture in terms, inter alia, of emotion and performance genres arises in mass media (Babb and Wadley 1995). Foucault's notion of "a discipline" captures the ties between traditions of discourse as "disciplines" (academic or otherwise) and transformations of people and their consciousness as they "become disciplined," internalizing the new disciplines characteristic of an era. That sort of sea-change in consciousness, documented by Foucauldian scholars like Bose (1995) even in India, accompanies the rise of nationalism. It is by no means limited, however, to spheres normatively recognized as political; it is evident in families, child-rearing practices, and cultures of emotion. Bose argues that neocolonial child-rearing manuals popular in turn-of-the-century Calcutta among the urban elites coopted "family" and some older cultural values for use in a new discourse that placed discipline at the pinnacle of a reformulated hierarchy of values. In the new framework, the family was redefined as a private and intimate sphere in which warm but restrained private affective experience produced character for the sake of a disciplined nation. At the same time, nations like India internalized their colonizers' negative perspective on what they considered the colonized people's effeminate emotionalism (Nandy 1983).

While the particular contents of modernist nationalism and the emotions it did or did not value will become clearer below, I wish to state at the outset that global forces of history have been at work changing local discourses, forms of emotional expressivity, ideologies of language, and forms of consciousness of self and collectivity. This chapter has benefited from social constructionist explorations of emotion in culture that find emotion a) inextricably linked with issues of value and thought, b) locally and culturally constituted rather than biologically determined in some unproblematically universal way, and c) historically contingent (Lutz and Abu Lughod 1990; Lynch 1990; Desjarlais and Wilce in press). It goes beyond the works cited, however, in tracing more global constructions of emotion. It also takes "ideologies" — of language, emotion, etc. — to be well-worn paths for consciousness; ideologies are folk constructs, the most hegemonic of which are most formative of consciousness in general, though perhaps least accessible to discursive consciousness (Giddens 1984).

National boundaries have become porous, and anthropology has — somewhat belatedly — acknowledged having reified isolated "cultures" in a way that does not accurately represent today's world. This paper presents evidence for processes that create an increasing amount of homogeneity in the cultural productions of Bangladeshis, Indians, Papua New Guineans, North Africans, and Americans of various origins. It focuses attention on the role of linguistic ideologies (Silverstein 1979; Lucy 1993; Rumsey 1990) in that process. The argument for the influence of the world's distinct languages on local habits of thought and perception associated with Sapir and Whorf is somewhat modified by recent theorists of linguistic ideologies. The Boasians assigned to (mostly unconscious) obligatory grammatical structures a key consciousness-shaping role and consigned speakers' notions of those structures to irrelevance as secondary rationalizations. Recent formulations, however, find linguistic ideologies shaping language use to some extent (Shieffelin, Woolard, and Kroskrity 1998). Thus, if we wish to maintain a Whorfian vision of the consciousness-shaping role of habitual language use — and, here, to argue that traditions of expressive language like lament have sustained unique ways of perceiving and being-in-the-world — we must modify the Whorfian vision to acknowledge the mediating role of linguistic ideologies.

A referentialist ideology of language — conceiving the chief function of language to be reference to an objective universe rather than the performative constitution of realities touching emotion, etc. — is being exported on a massive scale by the industrialized, often English-speaking world. "Export channels" include some literacy movements (Duranti and Ochs 1986; Schieffelin 1995) and the globalization of popular culture. The most effective means by which a referentialist ideology of language spreads, however, is the displacement of indigenous languages like Ungarinyin, which embody radically different linguistic ideologies (Rumsey 1990), by English. The global spread of referentialism cannot fail to change linguistic practice as well as dominant forms of consciousness. Globalization of consciousness proceeds apace.

That is not to say that contrary trends are not also in evidence. They are. Hegemony and resistance are forever coupled. Lament traditions perish in many of the societies surveyed below, but thrive among the Amazonian Warao (Charles Briggs: personal communication, 1996) and might be revived among the Tlingit (Kan 1990). My aim is not to proclaim the irreversible demise of lament and triumph of referentialism through global media mesmerization, but only to point to historical processes that tend in that direction.[2]

Latifa and her Songs of Grief and Protest

Latifa is a 28 year old Bangladeshi woman from a rural family in relatively comfortable circumstances. Latifa and her brothers (in their 30's) had finished high school, making them relatively educated for their generation and more educated than their parents' generation. In 1990 Latifa felt forced to marry an imam (mosque leader), complained about her in-laws, began to love the man, but then saw her brothers beat him and force a divorce. From 1990 to 1992, the year I met and recorded her during her visit to my field home, she lamented almost continually. A local anthropologist and I recorded three laments on three separate days — the first on video, the next two on audio; the first two in the daytime, the last and longest performance at night (Wilce 1998).[3] Example (1) is from the videotaped performance. Examples (2) and (3) — separated only for analytic convenience — are both from the final, nighttime performance.

(1) 1.05 *āmi to kono din kalpanā kar-i •hh i nā:i o go •hh*
I EMPH any day imagine do-I •hh never oh DP •hh
'I never could have imagined, •hh, oh oh oh oh oh •hh'
...

1.13 *(tārpare) āmi to (hay-e nā) (ār ki dure) bujh-i*
(then) I EMPH (become-PRES NEG) (or how far) understand-I
nā •hh, mābu::d •hh
NEG •hh Lord •hh
'(Then) how can I understand it any more, •hh, Lord. •hh'

1.14 *āmāre •hh mābu::d.*
me •hh Lord
'Lord, •hh [what have they done to] me!'

1.20 *(āmāre giyā) kemte: i kar-l-o •hh*
(me going) how this do-PST-3 •hh
'How could they do this to me! •hh'

Thus the singer expresses her bewildered rage at her brothers' treatment of her.

Latifa's performances epitomize lament's tendency to be improvisational, interactively constructed, woman-dominated, and somewhat subversive. Past studies have missed the significance of the jazz-like improvisational character of lament. Latifa's performances improvise variations on a few textual and musical themes. Her musical theme across the three taped days of performance involves a two chord alternation from A minor as tonal center to D minor (tense/"subdominant") and back. Textually, too, Latifa (L) develops and sings variations on a few themes, all of which re-appear in the final, most complete performance I recorded. The refrain of her first performance is "I never imagined [my brothers would do this to me]!" The second performance metaphorically linked her story of suffering (and, presumably, its future evaluation by God) with the day of Hashor, the field where God will enact his fiery judgment. The refrain of Day Three's lament (Example 2, below) was "They murdered me," though the first two idioms reappear as well. That third performance compares with a music reprise; all themes introduced and played with earlier reappear.

(2) Sister, Buji (S): Actually a great aunt, often addressed as "sister"; about 70

2.13 L: *āmi e āgun kemte sahyo go kar-b-o •hh bun go*
I this fire how endure DP do-FUT-1 •hh sister DP
a: a: bun •hh
oh oh sister •hh
'How can I bear this fire, sister o sister •hh?'

2.16 L: *āmāre nā khun-o go kar-s-e •hh*
me NEG murder-even DP do-PERF-3 •hh
'They have murdered me •hh.'

...

2.35 S: *Āllāh-i to /(bharasā)./*
God-FOC EMPH (refuge)
'God himself is [our only] /refuge/.'

2.36 L: */āmār kal[e]jāt/ kemte ghāi-o go di-l-o •hh bun go*
my liver how wound-even DP give-PST-3 •hh sister DP
o o bun •hh
oh oh sister •hh
'/How they/ have hurt my liver, sister oh sister!'

2.37 L: *Āllāh to āmār laigā nāi-o go •hh*
God EMPH my with is.not-even DP •hh
'God is not with me' (or 'God is not there for me')

...

2.42 L: *hāṣar-er-o māṭh-er matan kairā go •hh*
Hashor-GEN-even field-GEN like doing DP •hh
ān-l-o go bun •hh bun go bun •hh
bring-PST-3 DP sister •hh sister DP sister •hh
'They've brought the fire of judgment down, •hh, sister, •hh, sister oh sister •hh'

Improvisation differs from other modes of composition largely in terms of the sort of emergent interactivity evident in Example 2. Latifa's audience(s) included several knots of people in roughly concentric circles from within the house where she sang to some 10 meters away in the courtyard. They spoke during her performances, sometimes timing their utterances to coincide with her sobbing inhalations but often overlapping her sung-wept speech. What is significant about this was the way Latifa interacted with those audiences during her improvisational performance. Although it is true that God's name was never far from Latifa's lips — she invoked Mabud (the Lord) in earlier laments without any obvious "prompting" (1.14 above) — still, on that final night on which I taped her, Latifa seemed to take up God's name from the "sister," Buji, to whom she sang. Buji had urged her to trust God in line 35; Latifa echoed Buji's invocation, but only to say, literally, "God is not even there for *me*" (2.37).

Resistance is gendered, and women have carved out their own spaces and discursive-actional strategies for resistance. In several societies laments are vehicles of choice for women's social protest (Briggs 1992; Holst-Warhaft 1992). Because of their perceived threat to the social order, laments have in various times and places been associated ("strategically," as it were, by male authorities) with madness. Yet such metapragmatic characterizations do not go uncontested; "the poetic expression of grief is perceived by the lamenters themselves not only as an emotional outburst but as a means of mediating that emotion and thereby avoiding the excesses of madness that death might otherwise provoke" (Holst-Warhaft 1992: 28). A Greek woman singing a lament — and, as we shall see, Latifa — would reject the characterizations of her passionate singing as a sign of madness.

According to Veena Das's (1996) account, male violence in neighboring India more commonly inspires silent grief than lament. But Latifa was not silent. Her performances so challenge the authority of her brothers that they literally put her in chains to stop any further performing of the lament beyond the confines of their home. At times, the object of Latifa's resistance is theological orthodoxy (2.37). She also resists (3.83) her family's attempt to label her "mad," as they allude to the possibility that both her ex-husband's love magic and her singing itself are making her head "hot."

(3) Amina (A): Latifa's female cousin, about 25 years old

Caci, "Aunt" (C): one of 3–4 aunts listening to Latifa outside the house.

3.83 L: *āmāre diye pāgal kai-yā kai-te di-l-o nā go •hh*
me with mad speak-PTC speak-INF give-PST-3 NEG DP •hh
'Calling me "mad," they would not let me speak.'

3.84 A: *he Latifa, cup kar-as nạ̄*
Hey Latifa, quiet do-IMV.INT NEG
'Hey Latifa, won't you shut up?'

3.85 A: [to others outside with her]
cheḍi-r māthā ār-o pāgal hay-b-o beṣi.
girl-GEN head more-even mad become-FUT-3 excessively
'The girl's head will get even crazier.'

3.86 C: *māthā-e māthā (bipad āche)*
head-LOC head (danger is)
'(There is danger) to her head.'

3.87 L: *āmāre kemne (x x x x) hay-l-o o o o go* •*hh*
me how (xxx) become-PST-3 oh oh oh DP •hh
'How has [this] happened to me, oh oh oh!'

Latifa's cousin Amina's (A) assertion that Latifa's passionate speech makes her "head even crazier" resonates with a model of madness and sanity linked with humoral heating and cooling. People place their hands on another's head to sense physical signs of overheating believed to accompany excess passions that can make them insane. Still, Amina does not simply draw on her own "cultural models;" she interactively picks up Latifa's mention (line 83) of how her kin exploited the label *pāgal* and throws the label back at her in line 85–but without the verb of speaking, *kaiyā*, and thus without the limiting frame Latifa used. Amina, in fact, speaks the authoritative "direct word" (Bakhtin 1981: 342f). Not only does Latifa's performance become multivocal by incorporating the words of speakers like Buji (2.37, 3.83). Her interlocutors' words (e.g. 3.85) also become tinged with reference to hers, though they fail to engage her in true dialogue; in fact, Amina's line 3.85 perfectly exemplifies the very charge Latifa makes in 3.83, viz., that they are just using the label "mad" as an excuse to stop her protests.

In what follows, I describe Islamization, urbanization, and other faces of modernization that add their pressures to lament in South Asia and elsewhere. It is important to note here, however, that I am not claiming that the suppression of Latifa's particular lament and of her particular use of that expressive tradition were directly motivated by Islamization. When I interviewed Latifa's kin, a male cousin sided with her brothers in silencing her. He underlined the importance of ensuring that the women of one's extended family keep *pardā*, gender segregation. As important as Islam or even religious reputation might be to that family, "keeping one's women in control" is a good (a unit of symbolic capital, Bourdieu 1977) in and of itself. *Pardā* itself as symbolic capital, rather than a more abstract notion like "Islam," is the salient category invoked in defending the suppression of this lament. Nonetheless, the need to control the sexuality, mobility, and free expression of women is akin to the need to control emotionality and genres of emotional expression — needs not unrelated to reformist Islam.

Heightened attention both to *pardā* and to "purifying" Bengali Islam of "riotous" emotional observances felt to be local rather than "truly Islamic" arose during the nineteenth century. As local elites accepted, to some extent, the colonizers' move to identify themselves and their religious, moral, and expressive traditions with rationality, modernist/Islamic reformism was an inevitable response (Geertz 1968). Such reform movements (Ahmed 1981) began to influence the Bengal region profoundly in the nineteenth century, condemning as local impurities such practices as the "riotous reading of *marsiyā* poems on the death of the martyrs" on the day of Ashura in the holy month of Moharram (Mannan 1966: 171). They found in Saudi Arabia a Wahabbi model of Islam more likely to deflect colonial charges of civilizational decline into effeminate decadence. If the Bengali Muslim cult of emotion ("riotousness") among Muslims represented a substrate of resistance to Islam insofar as Islam was once perceived as a religion foreign to Bengal and its values, gaining control of emotionalism was and is understandably a high priority for Middle East-inspired Islamists. Bangladeshi women's status in general is impacted by histories of ideological struggle beginning in the 19th century and lasting into the present.

In what follows, the homologies between ritualization, urbanization, modernization, and religious rationalism in Islam — all of which have an impact on lament in Bangladesh — will become apparent.

Improvisation as Foment

The interactivity of Latifa's performance typifies lament in several other societies, and makes it vulnerable to dismissal, relative to more clearly ritualized discursive forms. Latifa's interactive texted weeping consistently falls toward the right end of the continua laid out by Keith Sawyer (1996).

Sawyer's model bears some comment, though the reader must be referred to that source for a more complete discussion. I will comment only on three categories — ossification/revivalism, the breadth of genre-definitions, and cultural valuation. Sawyer draws the first category from the work of S. Tambiah (1985). Tambiah claims it is inevitable for ritualized performances to lose

Table 1. Ritualized Versus Improvisational Performance. Adapted (with emphasis added) from Sawyer 1996.

Ritualized Performance	**Improvisational Performance**
ossification	revivalism
low creative involvement	high creative involvement
indexically reflexive	indexically entailing
narrow genre definition	broad genre definition
large ready-mades	small ready-mades
low audience involvement	high audience involvement
resistant to novelty	receptive to novelty
changes long-lasting	changes short-lived
high cultural valuation	***low cultural valuation***

semantic content; that is the heart of ossification. In a period of revival, new meanings are attached to ritual forms. Lament in Bangladesh and the Amazon resists ossification through the flexibility with which it "ventriloquizes other discourse genres,"[4] borrowing ever-shifting meanings from a multitude of other events which it indexes intertextually (Briggs 1992). South Asian lament exemplifies broadly defined genres in which "a great variety of performances will be considered … tokens of the same… event type" (Sawyer 1996: 284). Though the labels vary locally (*bhōt* in the Bhojpuri speech community in Bihar, India [Tiwary 1978]; *kānnākāṭi* [crying] or, more precisely, *bilāp* [lament] in Bangla[5] and many other Indo-Aryan languages), the point here is the variety of events that may be thus labeled. Events covered by such terms vary from the wept songs of young brides leaving their families to the angry accusations of those (often women) blaming their kin for failing to provide adequately in Bihar and Bangladesh.[6] Semantic theme as well as melodic structures vary widely in these performances. To draw a stark contrast, relatively fewer events would qualify as "recitations of Surah Fatiha," the opening chapter of the Qur'an, than a "lament" or a "jam session."

The theme of cultural valuation is where Sawyer's model is most in need of revision. Sawyer points to situations of "diglossia" for a parallel to the way performance forms are valued or disvalued in any particular speech community. The problem with his model — and, often, with writing about diglossia — is its essentialization of "cultures."[7] Urban elites often value rural forms only as "quaint" examples they might romanticize as such but whose performers are not part of their reference group. As one stereotypic home of improvisation, we must ask about the cultural valuation of jazz. Estimates of its cultural valuation vary widely. Some ethnomusicologists consider jazz the classical music of the African-American tradition, yet its absence from many great urban concert halls — with the exception of Gershwin's works — indicates it has not achieved that pinnacle of urbane respectability. Improvised rap poetry contests called "freestyle battles" epitomize creativity, but their products are valued primarily by America's urban subalterns.[8] Despite the problematics of "cultural valuation" as a category, its utility is plain in relation to laments improvised by rural Bangladeshi women. Such performances are perishing according to several observers and condemned by modernist Muslim rhetoric (see below), and are no longer being represented in any directly allied written genre as they once were.[9] Thus, though academic folklorists in Dhaka and other cities might rejoice when an anthropologist tapes rural performances of lament, Bangladeshi cultural elites who manage live or broadcasted "cultural performances" happily neglect these forms in order to spotlight more predictable, ritualized songs and dances.

Lament: The State of the Art in Several Societies

It is precisely because improvised discursive forms can lead to more unpredictable and thus uncontrollable criticizing of local powers (Briggs 1992) than do relatively ritualized and entextualized forms (e.g. Greek tragedies, which Holst-Warhaft [1992: 5] argues arose out of traditions of improvised lament) that they more frequently provoke repression. Hence performances like Latifa's tend to elicit violent reactions; she was chained and beaten by the brothers she says "murdered her" (for details, see Wilce 1998). Consistent with my prediction, there is, in fact, rhetoric opposing lament — or, more broadly, women's expressive genres — in a number of societies. Such rhetorical threats to lament reflect a Weberian process of rationalization and a referentialist ideology of language — both in worldwide ascendancy in conjunction with the project of modernity. It was as he described the inexorable process of world-disenchantment or rationalization that Weber wrote, "The genuine Puritan even rejected all signs of religious ceremony at the grave and buried his nearest and dearest without song or ritual …" (Weber 1958: 105). Perhaps Weber had in mind "the songs for the dead that were once improvised at every [European] funeral" (Holst-Warhaft 1992: 6). The purging of "Catholic" elements from European grief observances, I am arguing, is yet another reflection of "the spirit of capitalism" more recently exported to the non-European world along with more obvious trappings of the global economy. Specifically, I argue that in grieving and other cultural domains, emotional discourse and music shaped by precapitalist notions of language and reality are being transformed by the Weberian rationalizing spirit. The increasing global acceptance of the notion that the chief function of language is reference to a preexisting extralinguistic universe is part and parcel of the historical process of "disenchantment" Weber described.

My comparative survey of the "state of the art" of lament starts in South Asia.

Bangladesh, Greater Bengal, and South Asia

Public interviews I conducted *with men* in Latifa's area of Bangladesh in 1996 uncovered a broad agreement that (men feel) lament is not a good thing because: (a) it entails women raising their voices enough to be heard by nonkin, which is itself banned by reformist Islam, (b) mourning a death insults God who has willed that death, and (c) such mourning also inhibits the soul's departure to the next world. (Unfortunately, gender segregation prevented me from conducting parallel interviews with rural women, particularly about lament as protest.) Although it is more than this, such evaluations are at least in part an ideology of language — of how speech performance relates to the social and supernatural world.

A 12 year-old son of a woman who works for a multinational medical aid organization in Bangladesh has, for most of his life, attended elite boarding schools. He and his family have fairly urbanized values though they work or attend school in villages. When I asked the boy about lament, he could scarcely contain a laugh. He said, approximately, "Oh yes, that loud wailing... That's something uneducated rural people do. You won't hear it in the cities." When we link the boy's comments with criticisms appealing to Islam, we are reminded that fundamentalism is a form of modernism — as Geertz (1968) has argued. Urbanizing and Islamizing critiques of lament are cognate.

A rural school teacher described a number of affective and narrative performance genres which he said were formerly common though they were textually bawdy and their prosody transgressed contemporary fundamentalist bans on tuneful self-indexing by the laity. Bangladeshi anthropologists with whom I spoke agreed that women's songs at weddings, along with laments and the narrative, ballad-like genres the rural schoolteacher mentioned — are almost extinct. They attributed the passing of these genres to rapidly increasing Middle Eastern influence on the formerly more open Bangladeshi Muslim culture.

It is important to note that the rural Muslim men with whom I discussed lament as they piloted rickshaws or country boats or stood in stalls in bazaar towns acknowledged the good intent of women who sang laments. That is, they acknowledged laments for the dead as signs of affection. One Madrasah (Islamic school) teacher with whom I spoke in his own book stall at a bazaar said that Islam forbids weeping at the death of one of God's servants (Muslims in general). He agreed, however, with a former student of his who interrupted to say that lamenting nonetheless indicates that the singer *bhālabāse beśi*, "loves [the departed] a lot." Yet *beśi* can mean not just "a lot" but "excessively," and the teacher would have Muslims reserve such zeal for God rather than one's spouse, parents, or children.

This metasentiment is linked with the condemnation I heard, on another occasion, of tuneful praying. "Suleyman" came to my attention after acting "mad," according to his adolescent relatives. Their imitation of his deviant speech was markedly singsong. Indeed, I recorded him on two occasions praying tunefully, chanting his prayers, but never speaking other words in such a chantlike fashion as the adolescents say they heard. When I described that performance to people in rural shops and asked them about melody in the service of religious feeling, Muslims agreed it was shameful. Why? The tunefulness of Suleyman's prayers, they feel, is narcissistic. If his prayers were sincere, why should he draw such attention to himself by praying that way? We must conclude that opposition to tuneful prayers and tuneful text weeping targets not only particular sentiments and words — potentially subversive, as Latifa's example shows — but *speech as performance per se*. Reformist Muslim scruples parallel those of Weber's Protestants who worked, even at gravesides (1958: 105), to replace emotionality with disenchanted expressions of religious seriousness.

Under the right historic circumstances, angry, "blasphemous" lament (Das 1996: 80) in Hindu as well as Muslim communities in South Asia can fall under repressive criticism. Those circumstances have arrived in the form of modernity. Evidence comes from the protagonist of a short story by Indian writer Akhil Sharma in *The Atlantic Monthly* (1995), who says she "sometimes ... hummed along to Lata Mangeshkar or Mohammed Rafi singing that 'grief is no letter to be passed around to whoever wants to read [it].'" The long history of genres for the public performance of grief contrasts with new, media-propagated sensibilities about the privacy of grief. South Asia has recently begun to undergo a privatization of grief paralleling the privatization of feudal lands and, more recently, of India's industries — all cognates of Weber's "spirit of capitalism."

Banerjee (1989) documents the fact that authoritative rejection of women's performance genres in greater Bengal has its roots in colonialism and Victorian mores. Although lament may still be performed in rural Bangladesh, and Raheja and Gold (1994) present a variety of resistive folkloric texts from women in North India, missionaries and colonial administrators did bequeath to the emergent intelligentsia of nineteenth century Calcutta a revulsion toward the public performance of passion. Their attempts to "emancipate" the women of India entailed weaning them from their love of public culture. Why this focus? Emissaries of the British moral order were shocked by the degree to which Indian folkloric productions were dominated by working women recently arrived from the countrysides. Colonial officials and their *bhadrolok* (emerging elite Bengali) allies were even more shocked by the content of the performances. Whereas, in the late twentieth century, some take it for granted that openness in dealing with sexuality betokens "liberation," the would-be liberators of 19th century Calcutta women did not see their performances as liberating.

Banerjee describes nineteenth century *vijaya* songs that domesticated the goddess Durga as a Bengali bride and lamented her departure from her natal family (cf. Raheja and Gold 1994: ch. 3), and *biraha* songs that used "the Radha-Krishna story as a vehicle for voicing women's grievances in contemporary society," often in an erotically playful, frankly sexual idiom (Banerjee 1989: 136). "Significantly contemporary *bhadralok* critics, obviously ashamed of ... uninhibited debunking of Hindu deities, took pains to dismiss [these performances] as the domain of the … 'lower orders' whose base instincts, they said, … [were] tickled by such 'obscene' songs" (1989: 139).

Banerjee helps us historicize the conflict over women's genres. But the ability of women's songs to "debunk deities" is reflected in a recent account of North Indian women's funerary laments which, in Das's own terms (1996: 80), sometimes "blaspheme" the goddess blamed for the person's death. The reality that women's lament can take the form of angry protest (liable to provoke countermeasures from men) is also confirmed by Tiwary (1978). One common occasion for women's lament in Bihar is when they have a grievance against their men and want some change in their behavior. In rural Bihar at the time he described it, *bhēt* songs could still be observed, but change was overtaking them:

> Among the tradition-bound, illiterate village girls, it [departure-weeping after a daughter's marriage] is a universal practice. But it is fast disappearing; it is almost nonexistent among the educated, urbanized girls of these communities (p. 25).

Das describes a different historic shift. She argues that women's *silence* in the aftermath of rape and other forms of attack they suffered during incidents of communal violence marks the divide between contemporary events (in which men violated women) and the heroic deaths of men defending their women and their motherland, events eulogized in classical *bilāp*, "lament". Thus, whereas the forces of urbane rationality combine with Islamization in Bangladesh, Tiwary found modernization and urbanization similarly at work in Bihari girls, at least those not "bound" by Hindu "tradition."

Areas undergoing Islamization and Christian missionization

Outside of Europe and Asia, there are several reports of threat to women's performance genres. In Niger, Susan Rasmussen describes how Tuareg Muslim women's *tende* songs index resistance by their carnivalesque associations, and their marked affect. She writes, "On the one hand, music is much appreciated and has much prestige; on the other, there is also a current of disapproval, which barely tolerates it …. To Islamic scholars and elderly persons in general, a young woman with a beautiful voice is suspect because she, in effect, distracts men from prayer" (Rasmussen 1998: 167).

Lest we think such rhetoric arises only in relation to Islam, Feld reports from the Kaluli of Papua New Guinea: "Lamenting among the Kaluli does seem a bit on the decline mostly due to the forms of emotional repression introduced by evangelical missionaries, and the new ways in which Kaluli struggle with their anger" (Steve Feld: personal communication, 1996). And the rapid social change feared by Navajo elders — including the envisioned death of the lament-like genre which has typified their funeral observances (Thomas Csordas: p.c., 1996) — is hastened by the progress on their reservation of missionary churches and the Native American Church.

The case of Tlingit mourning songs is illuminating for several reasons, among which are the particular role played among the Tlingit by Christianity and even Memorial Day observances, the leading role of Tlingit men in composing and singing mourning songs, and the good records of shifts in the tradition's vitality. These shifts have not all been in a morbid direction, and the future of the genre is somewhat hopeful. Changes in Tlingit mourning practices and potlatch ceremonies are linked in the literature with their acculturation and conversion to Christianity. The potlatch had far more to do with honoring the dead than is often represented in popular accounts.[10] "Songs mourning the dead" were central to the ritual. It seemed for a time that potlatches and related song traditions had died along with other traditions of song among the Tlingit and their neighbors (De Laguna 1972). When potlatches were held in an earlier day and described by ethnographers, they noted that indigenous beliefs had placed some constraints on the amount of weeping for departed souls (ibid.: 523-B). Yet, "to judge by modern custom, the expression of grief was very violent" (533-A). De Laguna considered the mourning songs a help in coping with grief. In her account of a Memorial Day observance after potlatches had gone out of fashion among the Yakutat Tlingit she indicates that the American holiday had taken over some of the functions of the potlatch. Elements of both change and continuity are evident in elders' descriptions of the evolution of the observance of even Memorial Day. Hymn singing under the leadership of a minister had replaced traditions in which songs incorporating Tlingit mythic figures were composed by the bereaved (473-B). What indigenous beliefs about the dangers of excessive grief had not done (eliminate lament) was accomplished with the passing of the generative tradition and its replacement by a tradition (hymnody) which was, *vis-à-vis* earlier Tlingit singing, ossified.

On the other hand, attempts to revive Tlingit potlatch singing might so radically refunctionalize it as to render it offensive to elders. That is what has happened when "Tlingit culture" has been introduced in schools and "Tlingit song traditions" have been performed in public by "children" — the performances have lacked what Silverstein (personal communication) has called "performative oomph." In the words of Sergei Kan (1990), teaching "native culture" in school may "preserve" it, but perhaps at the cost of "the decline of the religious practices' spiritual value in the eyes of many of the younger performers, which hurts the feelings of the older and more conservative people for whom they remain sacred" (p. 355). Secular performances may lack performativity, the notion that the words themselves bring about new realities in the world. However, in one case Kan describes, Tlingit elders attempted both to justify the passing on of the traditions in secular school contexts "while preserving at least some of their sacredness" (356). In words reminiscent of Feld's *Sound and Sentiment* (1990),[11] Kan notes how the elders thanked the young performers for helping them re-experience times gone by while also singing for them the songs capable of "soothing the pain of losing their beloved kin" (360). The final outcome of this experiment is uncertain, though it is a promising example of people resisting "inevitable change" in creative ways that involve at least two generations in a mutually satisfying encounter with a revitalized tradition being made to live. Key to this revival of a lament tradition is the revival of an ideology of language recognizing the performative function of (sung) speech.

Rationalization and Corporate Interests: The State of the Art and the Art of States

In stages, and through many means, modernity impacts grief practices. One such means is commercialization. The rise of commercial cousins to lament entails a profound transformation in the direction of ossified standardization (Smith 1997) — the change being evident, for instance, between Muddy Water's improvisational "Walkin' Blues" and Clapton's version (Hadder 1996). Film, cassettes, and pop culture give new life to genres allied to lament, but also new rigidity suiting mass distribution. The electronic mediation of performance does not necessarily work in conjunction with commercialization as commonly conceived; thus Abu-Lughod (1990) describes how *ghinnawa* (poems of grief over lost love) are now distributed in local networks on home-made cassettes. Still, what has yet to be explored is how that change, which seems to have assured *ghinnawa* of a vital life for some time, has also transformed the meanings of performance, performer, audience, and genre.

In South Asia a paradoxical combination of individuation and nationalization of affect discourse is evident; individuation and corporatization of performances at a higher level than in the past (beyond the domestic unit or village to a national co-optation of "lament") proceed in tandem with each other. We see this split-transformation of affect-discourse in greater Bengal. On the one hand, improvised *choral* women's lament (Devi 1990; cf. Banerjee 1992) is being replaced by individuals performing, as did Latifa, without any choral support, who can thus more easily be shut down. Such individuation likely entails an intermediate stage in the ultimate demise of improvised lament. At a higher level of analysis, improvised domestic performances of lament *must* be replaced by mass-distributed forms over which economies and states can exercise better control if lament-like forms are to serve the interests of nationalism. In fact, Holst-Warhaft argues that this is an ancient process, that the classical Athenian state channeled energies once devoted to lament into "its two great rhetorical inventions, the funeral speech and the tragedy" (1992: 5). This canalization transformed a community-based, face-to-face performance genre that often inspired cycles of revenge[12] into public genres indexically linked with the state's preferred forms of controlled passion and rationality. Obviously predating Protestantism, the association of this change with state-sponsored rationalization — and thus the relevance of Weber — is no less clear.

Jane Goodman (1998) describes what happens when traditional song genres are taken up by Berber nationalists. The latter's ambivalence toward emotional religious songs can be celebrated as resistance to tradition and to Arabic hegemony. On the other hand, it must also strike many in Algeria as a triumph of that rationalization which Weber likened to a cage. Similarly, Good and Good have described how the Iranian Revolution's co-optation of the public performance of grief has led to a crisis of meaning. Iranians must address the issue of what happens to the state of the art of *ta'zieh* (public grieving commemorating the suffering of the Prophet's faithful people) when it becomes the art of the state. When the Islamic Revolution co-opts the performance of *ta'zieh* as a state event, it "raise[s] serious problems at the level of meaning" for Iranians. Distrust of the state runs deep in Shi'a Islam. Suffering as religiously understood — suffering as the key to the moral life in the Shi'ite understanding — has, since the revolution, been turned into a way of understanding the state (as victim of the United States, of Iraq, etc.). At the same time that state is perceived as a failure not only at war but also at ushering in a truly Shi'ite order. These failures

> not only threaten Shi'ism as a tragic social ideology; they also jeopardize the legitimacy of central Iranian cultural forms as frames for organizing the self and emotional responses to discrepancies between the ideal order and social reality (Good and Good 1988: 60).

The case of Iran reminds us that it is just as transformative for a performance genre to undergo state embrace as state persecution. The case also reminds us of the close connections between national self-consciousness and conventionalized forms of expression and emotional consciousness.

In Iran "lament" itself has thus become a trope. In India and perhaps the former Yugoslavia, lament is similarly "entropized" in xenophobic nationalist discourses. In the Hindu nationalist rhetoric of the Indian orator Rithambra, wailing is invoked as a form valued in the past but now enlisted in her cause. The use to which she puts this entropized lament was in depicting the grief she called Hindus to feel in the aftermath of the secular government's attempt to resist her own nationalist followers who were trying to demolish the Babri Mosque. A few attackers were killed some months before a large number of others succeeded in pulling down the mosque. Rithambra stirred up her audience at that time to "listen to the wailing of the Saryu river [site of the government crackdown on her forces, putative drain for the blood of the martyrs Rithambra discursively creates]" (cited by Kakar 1996: 163). News analyses on the former Yugoslavia inform American audiences that metaphorized and reduced tales of grief, death, and collective grievance have served the rhetorical aims of Serb, Croat, and Bosnian nationalists. Note in all these cases the crucial role of emotion-rhetoric — rhetoric that stirs, constitutes, and reflects socially constituted emotion — in creating altered forms of national self-consciousness.

Changing Lament/Lamenting Change: Welcoming and Loathing the Prospect

Clearly lament is no neutral object; its passing or transformation may be welcomed or feared. Elders of the Navajo and of the Yolmo Sherpas of Nepal fear for the future of lament-like genres. Robert Desjarlais (personal communication, 1996) indicates that now only the elders in a Yolmo Sherpa community know how to perform *tser lu* "songs of sorrow." Similarly, Navajo elders who knew the lament-like song genres performed at funerals in the past have, according to "metalaments" about the rapid cultural change Navajos are experiencing, died without apprentices (Thomas Csordas: personal communication, 1996). Navajo consciousness, for elders, entails connections with the past, connections traditionally maintained through performances of grief.

In northern Pakistan, "Paxto" is an ethnic identity that, for women, has traditionally been performed by narrating one's life to other women as one long tale of suffering (Grima 1991). As change comes, however, it leaves some women caught between the past and a future that has yet to arrive, as Grima eloquently describes:

> The perception and organization of life as a chain of crises and stresses is particularly true of rural and older women. In urban centers, among the youngest generations of upper and upper-middle class, educated and working women, there is resentment about perceiving their lives within this framework.

> I often tried to elicit life stories from these young women, but... the schoolteacher's reply [is representative of others]: "I have no story to tell. I've been through no hardships." These women expressed the pressure they felt from relatives in the villages and from their elders in the family, to perform a discourse they no longer identify with.... [One] young upper-class urban mother originally from Peshawar and now living in Islamabad complained to me that she felt pressured by her mother-in-law to tell the story of her children's birth to relatives in terms of the pain and difficulties she had experienced. It angered her because she had, on the contrary, perceived the births as elating. ... [T]he dozen or so urban women I spoke with had responses similar to the ones discussed above and told me they had no story. I could elicit no life narratives. However, they were quick and eager to refer me to an old servant woman or to other women from their family villages who were known to tell the "saddest and most beautiful stories." They appreciated the aesthetic of the *gham* [grief] but did not personally identify with the genre, as if the life story, defined in *paxto* as a story of *gham*, could only be told by those who still molded their existence into the traditional pattern. There is no new model for the Paxtun life story. Thus not having a life story becomes a statement in itself. It may be saying, "I defy the traditional cultural model, but must remain silent until a new one is formed" (Grima 1991: 86f.).

For these women, neither a clear new kind of Paxtun self-consciousness nor a dominant genre of identity-building has emerged.

Urbanizing women are vulnerable to the sort of lonely alienation that is the natural concomitant of modernity as Weber and Durkheim have described it. That alienation, however, pertains to discursive form. Those who are alienated from old genres do not necessarily find new ones, and the gap in which they find themselves can be terrifying, as Crapanzano argues in his analysis of the autobiography of H. Barbin:

> We must, I think, recognize the sometimes desperate desire to succumb to an already warranted narrative of the self. What we can learn from the Barbin manuscripts has less to do with the terror of conformity to a genre, to an already told tale, than to the horror of being deprived of any story whatsoever (Crapanzano 1996: 126).

Latifa finds herself in such a position: her audiences delegitimate her use of old genres, but no new discursive avenues or strategies of political action are immediately available to her in rural Bangladesh. Urban women now march in mass demonstrations and rural men have always had access to public meetings (such as that described in Wilce 1996); Latifa can participate in none of these public speech events, yet also finds the political legs cut out from under her laments. Changes in rural Bangladesh, such as the rapid rise of girls' participation in schooling since the 1980's, have revolutionized expectations (LeVine et al 1993) and changed women's consciousness — without opening new channels for women's political participation.

Conclusion

Nation-states and urbanized populations seem to be succeeding both at effectively challenging metadiscursive strategies entailed in emotional performance and at authorizing referentialist ideologies of language. The relevance of such ideologies to lament is made clear by Urban (1996: 175–6):

> Referential discourse has a way of distancing individuals from immediate affective experience of, and involvement in, the world. It objectifies involvement. Rather than allow individuals to encounter the world with immediacy, discourse blinds experience with the light of consciousness. There is an analogue here to the problem of expression of feeling. In cultures with a developed ritual wailing or lamentation tradition, as in many central Brazilian Amerindian societies, grief is expressed by means of formalized crying. Your stylized weeping tells others of your grief. Contrast this expressive style with one in which an individual says referentially — as is so often the case in American culture — "I'm feeling sad."

This Weberian transformation of cognition, identities, and forms of expressivity is closely linked with so-called rationalization of economies. The link is reflected in the co-evolution of privatization in the spheres of emotion, ritual, and property; in general, these processes of privatization seem to proceed in parallel. Large feudal properties with which a public once felt linked have been privately "distributed" in South India (though perhaps not very widely). The emotional appeals to epidemic-causing spirits that once characterized public ritual paid for by feudal landowners have ceased. Individuals must now pay to visit by rationalized practitioners (rationalized Ayurveds, as it turns out) who have charged patients to be cured during recent epidemic outbreaks (Nichter 1992). Analogously, as funerary rituals in Appalachia (Anita Puckett: p.c., 1996) and among Hmong immigrants (Davis Clay: p.c., 1996) move from outdoors to private, commercial funeral homes, quiet, wordless crying displaces loud public grieving in certain cultural pockets within the United States.

In trying to explain *how* authoritative metadiscourses might effectively repress lament, we should look at the three interrelated processes described by Gal and Irvine (1995): iconicity, recursiveness, and erasure.[13] In this brief chapter I can only touch only on "erasure" of lament by nationalist elites.

Erasure can take the form of enforced forgetfulness in processes of cultural production, displacing even a striking speech phenomenon like lament onto a backstage where tourists and even national officials are less likely to find it. It can also take the form of active attempts to obliterate ways of speaking which come to represent some "alternative, threatening picture" of the society (Gal and Irvine 1995: 975). But erasure of original context and significance also takes place when a state or even a relatively benign school system exercises control over performances and their distribution, as South Asian states tend to do over electronic media. The Bangladeshi state is commited to modernism, and the Bangladesh elite has long been engaged in seeking to "purify" folk practice of its "excesses" of emotion and its "transgressions," from the perspective of scripturalist rationalism (Geertz 1968; Horvatich 1994). Bangladeshi examples of erasure as co-optation include the rationalist-Islamist state's management of the annual performances of Lalan Fakir's songs by contemporary disciples of the nineteenth century Bengali Tantric saint (Salomon 1991),[14] and Bangladesh's state-run television's co-optation of "authentic Garo tribal dances." That which is erased from the public stage is not available as a constituent of modernist national self-consciousness.[15]

Lament is threatened by referentialist ideologies of language. Among other things, such ideologies replace performative models of affect-language with cool reference to emotion; they penetrate families along with global commerce and mass-media. Rural Bangladeshis know that their modernized urban countrymen laugh at their loud, tuneful, texted weeping. Ought analysts put cool objectivity aside and mourn the loss of public texted weeping or facilitate efforts at meaningful revival like that documented by Kan (1990)? Perhaps so, though not because we romanticize the past or essentialize tradition and traditional performance genres as unchanging. My point is rather to uncover global transformations in cultures of affect and cognition, cultures of language — and to argue that no such change serves the interests of all parties involved.

Notes

1. This is a revised and expanded version of a paper presented at the Fifth Annual Symposium About Language and Society, Austin (SALSA V), TX, April 11–13, 1997 and published in the proceedings of that conference. The author is grateful to SALSA participants, and to Geeta Chowdhry, Jill Dubisch, Neill Hadder, Sanjay and Sanjam Joshi, and Gary Palmer for their comments on earlier drafts.
2. Smith (1997), reviewing Babb and Wadley 1995, points with consternation to evidence for "the homogenization of religious symbols, practices, and performances" and the potential for the

"trivialization of discourse and passivization of audiences" arising from the mass media and their influence on religion in South Asia (1997: 221f). Finding some of the contributors to the volume he reviewed naive in their sanguine outlook toward the mass religious media, Smith even holds those media responsible for some of the effectiveness of the spread of the Hindu nationalist movement and religious violence.

3. •hh represents sobbing breaths.
(xx) — Material in parentheses represents uncertain hearings.
a[x]b — Segments in brackets were not phonetically realized but are added to facilitate recognition of the lexemes by area specialists.
The following abbreviations are used:

1,2,3 = person
DP = discourse particle
EMPH = emphatic particle
FOC = focus
FUT = future
GEN = genitive case marker
IMV = imperative
INF = infinitive
INT = intimate verb form (below the "T" level)
LOC = locative
NEG = negation
PERF = perfective
PRES = present
PST = past
PTC = participial marker

4. "The flexible way that [Warao] laments ventriloquize other discourse genres seem to help insure their ability to adjust to historical changes" (Charles Briggs: personal communication, 1996).
5. The people of greater Bengal, including parts of India as well as Bangladesh, are referred to as Bengalis. The language of Bangladesh, currently called Bangla, includes its own standard form, as well as dialects that diverge more markedly from standard Calcutta "Bengali."
6. In addition to Latifa's example of this angry lament, described here, other examples are reported by Doreen Indra (personal communication, 1992) — cases involving women made homeless by the shifting of rivers in northwestern Bangladesh, who then appeal loudly and aggressively to their landed brothers for refuge.
7. For a sustained critique of the concept of diglossia in the sociolinguistic literature and an attempt to transcend its limits, see Herzfeld (1987).
8. Freestyle battles are contests between rappers who are closely monitored by judges as they spontaneously generate rhyming lines before live microphones. Contestants are disqualified if they repeat their own words or those of their opponents (Gagne 1995).
9. Secondary works on just one of the particular forms of written lament (the calendrical lament, known at earlier stages of most Indo-Aryan languages) include Vaudeville 1986, Wadley 1983, and Zvbavitel 1961.
10. "As the potlatch testified to the grief of the living and to the high esteem in which they held their dead, so the giving of the potlatch served to elevate the prestige of the hosts" (De Laguna 1972: 612-A). Popular accounts and even cultural anthropology textbooks like Bohannan (1992) reflect only the second clause of De Laguna's balanced sentence.
11. Feld depicts a reciprocity between Kaluli men and women in Papua New Guinea whereby men's weeping "moves women to song" and women's song "moves men to tears" (1990).
12. It no doubt also sustained a set of what we might call "family values," a form of consciousness fitting a social order that knows no centralized state control.
13. I am indebted to Anita Puckett (p.c., 1996) for pointing out the utility of Gal and Irvine's model for my analysis of the histories of lament genres.

14. Carol Salomon's presentation of Lalan Fakir as subject and object of discourse is rich in cross-cutting meanings. There is no better symbol of shifting, ambiguous identities among Bangladesh's citizens than this nineteenth century figure. Salomon's discussion stresses how, in her ethnographic present (the late twentieth century), Lalan's songs are still performed but either reviled or sanitized. Salomon (1991: 268) writes that "the prevailing attitude of Muslim Bengali society toward Baul songs in general and Lalan's songs in particular, and toward the fakirs who sing them, can serve as a barometer of where it stands at any given time on the question of regional versus Islamic identity." Salomon documents the attempt by "mainstream" Muslim Bengalis to recreate Lalan, the Tantric and mystic, as a folk hero useful to Islamically fervent Bangladeshi nationalism. Though Bangladeshi scholars with Islamicized scruples have changed his name from Lalan *Sā̧i* (<Sanskrit *swāmi*, "lord"; Biswas, Dasgupta and Bhattacharyya 1984: 708) to Lalan *Shah* (Persian, "king"), added an interpolation to the original texts to indicate his birth among the *khātnār jāt* ("circumcised caste," i.e. Muslims), and attempted to drive Lalan's modern disciples, the fakirs, from celebrations designed to co-opt Lalan for orthodox Bangladesh, the Tantric-Islamic message of the songs continues to leak out (Salomon 1991). Those fakirs who brave the government-sponsored "celebrations" of Lalan, whose clothing and long hair mark their rejection of Bangladeshi social norms, certainly add layers of complexity and resistance to the (sanitized) presentations of Lalan's songs.
15. Gal and Irvine make clear that linguists and anthropologists have played significant roles in the processes of iconicity, recursiveness, and erasure. The economic reductionism of much writing about the potlatch (e.g. Bohannan 1992) is an example of how anthropological writing has participated in erasing the ritual significance and the salience of songs of mourning from the potlatch as they have represented it.

References

Abu-Lughod, Lila. 1990. "Shifting politics in Bedouin love poetry". In Catherine Lutz and Lila Abu-Lughod (eds), *Language and the Politics of Emotion.* Cambridge: Cambridge University Press, 24–45.

Ahmed, Rafiuddin. 1981. *The Bengal Muslims, 1871–1906: A Quest for Identity.* Delhi: Oxford University.

Anderson, Benedict R. O'G. 1991. (2nd ed.) *Imagined Communities: Reflections on the Origin and Spread of Nationalism.* London, New York: Verso.

Babb, Lawrence A. and Susan S. Wadley (eds). 1995. *Media and the Transformation of Religion in South Asia.* Philadelphia: University of Pennsylvania Press.

Bakhtin, Mikhail M. 1981. *The Dialogic Imagination.* M. Holquist (ed). Austin: University of Texas Press.

Banerjee, Sumanta. 1989. "Marginalization of women's popular culture in nineteenth century Bengal". In K. Sangari and S. Vaid (eds), *Recasting Women: Essays in Colonial History* New Delhi: Kali for Women, 127–79.

Bohannan, Paul. 1992. *We, the Alien*. Boulder, CO: Westview Press.

Bose, Pradip Kumar. 1995. "Sons of the nation: Child rearing in the new family". In Partha Chatterjee (ed), *Texts of Power: Emerging Disciplines in Colonial Bengal.*

Minneapolis and London: University of Minnesota in conjuction with the Centre for Studies in Social Sciences, Calcutta (*Perspectives in Social Sciences*), 118–144.

Bourdieu, Pierre. 1977 (1972). *Outline of a Theory of Practice*. Tr. Richard Nice. Cambridge: Cambridge University Press.

Briggs, Charles L. 1992. "'Since I am a Woman, I Will Chastise My Relatives': Gender, Reported Speech, and the (Re)Production of Social Relations in Warao Ritual Wailing". *American Ethnologist* 19(2):337–61.

Calhoun, Craig (ed). 1992. *Habermas and the Public Sphere*. Cambridge, MA: MIT Press.

Crapanzano, Vincent. 1996. "'Self'-centering narratives" In M. Silverstein and G. Urban (eds), *Natural Histories of Discourse*. Chicago and London: University of Chicago Press, 106–130.

Das, Veena. 1996. "Language and the body: Transactions in the construction of pain". *Daedalus* 125: 67–91.

De Laguna, Frederica. 1972. *Under Mount Saint Elias: The History and Culture of the Yakutat Tlingit*. Washington: Smithsonian Institution Press.

Desjarlais, Robert and James Wilce. In press. "The cultural construction of emotion". In Veena Das (ed), *The Oxford Companion Encyclopedia of Sociology and Social Anthropology* (Part VII, *The Personal Sphere and Its Articulation*. Oxford University Press: Delhi.

Devi, Mahasweta. 1990. "*Rudali* [The funeral wailer]". In Kalpana Bardhan (ed. and tr.), *Women, Outcastes, Peasants, and Rebels: A Selection of Bengali Short Stories*. Berkeley and Los Angeles: University of California, 206–228.

Duranti, Alessandro and Eleanor Ochs. 1986. In Bambi Schieffelin and Perry Gilmore (eds), "Literacy instruction in a Samoan village". *The Acquisition of Literacy: Ethnographic perspectives*. Norwood, NJ: ABLEX, 213–232.

Feld, Steven. 1990. (2nd edition). *Sound and Sentiment: Birds, Weeping, Poetics, and Song in Kaluli Expression*. Philadelphia: University of Pennsylvania Press.

Gagne, Josh. 1995. "Urban freestyle battles". Unpublished paper. Northern Arizona University.

Gal, Susan and Judith T. Irvine. 1995. "The boundaries of language and disciplines: How Ideologies Construct Difference". *Social Research* 62: 967–1001.

Geertz, Clifford. 1968. *Islam Observed: Religious Development in Morocco and Indonesia*. Chicago: University of Chicago.

Giddens, Anthony. 1984. *The Constitution of Society: Outline of the Theory Of Structuration*. Cambridge: Polity/Basil Blackwell.

Good, Mary-Jo Delvecchio and Byron Good. 1988. "Ritual, the state, and the transformation of emotional discourse in Iranian society". *Culture, Medicine, and Psychiatry* 12: 48–63.

Goodman, Jane. 1998. "Singers, saints, and the construction of postcolonial subjectivities in Algeria". In J. Wilce (ed), *Communicating Multiple Identities in Muslim Communities*. Special issue of *Ethos* 26(2): 204–228.

Grima, Benedict. 1991. "The role of suffering in women's performances of *paxto*". In A. Appadurai, F. Korom, and M. Mills (eds), *Gender, Genre, And Power in South Asian Expressive Traditions.* Philadelphia: University of Pennsylvania Press, 81–101.

Hadder, R. Neill. 1996. "Blues conversations: Notes on practice theory and music-in-interaction". Unpublished manuscript.

Herzfeld, Michael. 1987. *Anthropology Through the Looking-Glass: Critical Ethnography in the Margins of Europe.* Cambridge [Cambridgeshire]; New York: Cambridge University Press.

Horvatich, Patricia. 1994. "Ways of knowing Islam". *American Ethnologist* 21(4): 811–826.

Holst-Warhaft, Gail. 1992. *Dangerous Voices: Women's Laments and Greek Literature.* London and New York: Routledge.

Kakar, Sudhir. 1996. *The Colors of Violence: Cultural Identities, Religion, and Conflict.* Chicago and London: University of Chicago.

Kan, Sergei 1990. "The sacred and the secular: Tlingit potlatch songs outside the potlatch". *American Indian Quarterly* 14(4): 355–66.

LeVine, Robert A., Sarah E. LeVine, Amy Richman, F. Medardo Tapia Uribe, and Clara Sunderland Correa. 1993. "Schooling and survival: The impact of maternal education on health and reproduction in the Third World". In Lincoln Chen, Arthur Kleinman, and Norma Ware (eds), *Health and Social Change.* Cambridge: Harvard University Press, 257–284.

Lucy, John A. (ed). 1993. *Reflexive Language: Reported Speech and Metapragmatics.* Cambridge: Cambridge University Press.

Lutz, Catherine and Lila Abu-Lughod (eds). 1990. *Language and the Politics of Emotion.* Cambridge: Cambridge University Press.

Lynch, Owen M. 1990. "The social construction of emotion in India". In Owen M. Lynch (ed), *Divine Passions: The Social Construction of Emotion in India* Berkeley: University of California, 3–34.

Mannan, Qazi Abdul. 1966. *The Emergence and Development of Dobhāśi Literature in Bengal (Up to 1855 A.D.).* Dacca: Department of Bengali and Sanskrit, University of Dacca.

Nandy, Ashis. 1983. *The Intimate Enemy: Loss and Recovery of Self under Colonialism.* Delhi: Oxford University.

Nichter, Mark. 1992 "Of ticks, kings, spirits, and the promise of vaccines". In C. Leslie and A. Young (eds), *Paths to Asian medical knowledge.* Berkeley and Los Angeles: University of California Press, 224–56.

Raheja, Gloria Goodwin and Ann Grodzins Gold. 1994. *Listen to the Heron's Words: Reimagining Gender and Kinship in North India.* Berkeley, Los Angeles, London: University of California Press.

Rasmussen, Susan J. Forthcoming. "Within the tent and at the crossroads: Travel and gender identity among the Tuareg of Niger". In James M. Wilce (ed), *Communicating multiple identities in Muslim communities.* Special issue of *Ethos* 26(2): 153–182.

Rumsey, Alan. 1990. "Word, meaning, and linguistic ideology". *American Anthropologist* 92: 346–61.

Salomon, Carol. 1991. "The cosmogonic riddles of Lalan Fakir". In A. Appadurai, F. J. Korom, and M. A. Mills (eds), *Gender, Genre and Power in South Asian Expressive Traditions*. Philadelphia: University of Pennsylvania, 267–304.

Sawyer, Keith. 1996. "The semiotics of improvisation: The pragmatics of musical and verbal performance". *Semiotica* 108(3): 269–306.

Schieffelin, Bambi B. 1995. "Creating evidence: Making sense of written words in Bosavi". *Pragmatics* 5(2). 225–244.

Schieffelin, Bambi B., Cathryn A. Woolard, and Paul V. Kroskrity (eds). 1998. *Language Ideologies: Practice and Theory*. New York: Oxford University Press.

Sharma, Akhil. 1995. "If you sing like that for me". *Atlantic Monthly* 275/5 (May): 70–88.

Silverstein, Michael. 1979 "Language structure and linguistic ideology". In Paul R. Cline, William Hanks and Carol Hofbauer (eds), *The Elements: A Parasession on Linguistic Units and Levels*. Chicago: Chicago Linguistic Society, 193–247.

Smith, Brian K. 1997. "Review of *Media and the Transformation of Religion in South Asia* (Lawrence A. Babb and Susan S. Wadley, eds.)". *Journal of Asian Studies* 56(1): 200–222.

Tiwary, Kapil Muni. 1978. "Tuneful weeping: A mode of communication". *Frontiers* 3: 24–7.

Urban, Greg. 1996. *Metaphysical Community: The Interplay of the Senses and The Intellect*. Austin: University of Texas Press.

Vaudeville, Charlotte. 1986. *Bārahmāsā in Indian Literatures: Songs of the Twelve Months in Indo-Aryan Literatures.* Delhi: Motilal Banarsidass.

Weber, Max. 1958. *The Protestant Ethic and the Spirit of Capitalism.* New York: Charles Scribners' Sons.

Wilce, James M. 1998. *Eloquence in Trouble: Poetics and Politics of Complaint in Bangladesh*. New York: Oxford University Press.

———. 1996. "Reduplication and reciprocity in imagining community: The play of tropes in a rural Bangladeshi moot". *Journal of Linguistic Anthropology* 6: 188–222.

Zbavitel, Dušan. 1961. "The development of the baromasi in the Bengali literature". *Archiv Orientalni* 29: 583ff.

Dignity in Tragedy

How Javanese Women Speak of Emotion

Laine Berman
Centre for Cross Cultural Research, Australian National University

Introduction

It is often said that language, power, and status are closely linked in Javanese society such that high-status people actively dilute information, concealing truth, personal opinions, disturbing facts and anything else potentially causing disarray to an interlocutor's thoughts and feelings. Power, in the Javanese sense (see Anderson 1990: 17–77; Brenner 1995), is a kind of divine energy, a mystical, inner strength evidenced by poise, restraint, and equanimity in all social interactions. Disappointment or anger startles, and thus has the potential to dissipate potency and cause hostility (Keeler 1990). The Javanese, particularly those from the court cities of Yogyakarta and Solo, are said to be the most *alus* (refined, calm, smooth) of all Indonesians, while in fact many Javanese have personally and with great pride told me that their people are more refined than any other.

To be *alus* means to actively participate in and work at maintaining harmony and composure through learning to control feelings and weaknesses. Geertz (1960) referred to this avoidance of potential disharmony as the combined values of *iklas, sabar,* and *trimå*. *Iklas* is a detachment from the material world; *sabar* is defined as the absence of eagerness, impatience, and passion; and *trimå* means to acquiesce, referring to the inevitability of fate, class, hierarchy, gender, and event. These three prized characteristics lead to "emotional equanimity, a certain flatness of affect" (1960: 240–1).

Keeler (1990: 132) also describes Javanese refinement as "the behavioral style of potency", which specifically links inner power to "the restraint and calm indicative of disinterestedness and self-control" (1990: 132). Status, according to Keeler, is linked to behavior. He explains that the individual wishing to project high status must express total control discursively and behaviorally through "avoidance of spontaneous or extreme feelings, as evidenced in speech and gesture" (1990: 133). These include suppressing all signs of excitement, anger, jealousy, hilarity, or even hunger, thirst, pain, or exhaustion, what Joseph Errington refers to as "the avoidance or muting of indexically communicative behavior" (1988: 223). In terms of modern Javanese experience, *iklas* means that everything one experiences in life, whether happy or sad, is the will of God and thus, of far greater significance than a mere individual's concerns with feeling, action or effort.[1]

From these descriptions of Javanese language and behavior, we should begin to piece together a picture of a people who value above all else an external display of self as calm and graceful. Yet, these social rules of harmonious order and calm acquiescence already hint at the existence of numerous issues that grind away in silence beneath serene surfaces. As others have stated, "direct disclosure of one's personal innermost feelings is rarely done by use of Javanese" (Wolff & Poedjosoedarmo, 1982: 64). Whether the Javanese people express their emotions or not, what these emotion words really mean within local contexts of meaning, and whether they accomplish these acts in the Javanese or Indonesian languages, are just the tips of a rather deeply entrenched cultural iceberg. This paper begins to challenge a few of the prominent myths and present the basis for further investigations on the Javanese people and language at the discourse level. This analysis of narratives of violence against women provides a means of accessing the factors which shape the actual production of Javanese emotion.

Emotion and Java

To tackle the issue of emotion in Javanese contexts is to begin from the assumption that emotion is a sociocultural construct that is analyzable through its meaning, force, location and performance in the public realm of discourse (e.g., Lutz & Abu-Lughod, 1990: 7). We also assume that people do discuss or at least express their emotions publicly and in a recognizable manner. In terms of Javanese social interaction, this is apparently not the case. Karl Heider's comparative study among the Minangkabau of Western Sumatra and the Central Javanese in the city of Yogyakarta sets out to discover the 'cognitive map of emotion words' by collecting and charting the words used to talk about emotions. Mapping consisted of devising a representation of emotion thought as a two-dimensional lexical map that shows clusters of closely related words as well as the relationships between the clusters (Heider, 1991: 4–5). Heider found that the

Javanese maps were far less unified and reflected much less cultural consensus than the Minangkabau. He thus concluded that since the maps represent informant agreement and cultural consensus, which presumably is a function of explicit use, the Javanese speak much less about emotion than do the Minangkabau (Heider, 1991: 91). In fact, Heider hints that the Javanese are somewhat emotionally confused as a group because of this broad lack of consensus (1991: 93).

Whether or not we accept a notion of 'relative disagreement', Heider's study points out the fact that emotion is not an abstract and detachable 'it' upon which the word is an ostensible representation. Emotion is the ordering, selecting, and interpreting work we accomplish as we manage the fragments of our lives. Most importantly for the social constructionist perspective taken here, emotion, like other aspects of social life, is limited by our linguistic resources and repertoire of social practices (Harré 1986: 4). Thus, analysis of emotion begins by locating how particular emotion words are used and by empirically identifying their basis of usage within the constraints set up by the local moral order. As other constructionists have stated, the meaning of an emotion as its functional significance is to be found primarily within the sociocultural system (Averill 1980 cited in Armon-Jones 1986: 34). Claire Armon-Jones adds, "emotions are regarded by constructionists as functional in that the possession of culturally appropriate emotions serves to restrain undesirable attitudes and behavior, and to sustain and endorse cultural values".

So what does this mean in terms of Javanese contexts? To say a people do not speak openly about their emotions is to say exactly what? These defining statements assist our investigation by explaining how people acquire emotion attitudes as part of their responsibility as social agents to reinforce the social values these uphold. It is generally accepted that emotion obtains much of its social meaning from ethnopsychological knowledge and the role of emotions in mediating social action. Defined then as a response to social events, emotion in Javanese contexts should be located within the types of events that are sure to trigger emotion responses. Emotions arise in social situations and trigger certain types of responses, for which Catherine Lutz has devised a representational format for the emotion schema (Lutz 1986: 293–4; White 1990: 46–47):

SOCIAL EVENT
↓
EMOTION
↓
ACTION RESPONSE

Even in such a scenario with no contextual information, the representation alludes to a type of inferential path and a mode of evaluating and constituting social reality through the mediation of social action and reaction. Emotions are grounded in social interaction and, at least within local contexts, carry known evaluative and behavioral implications (White 1990). Yet, it needs to be kept in mind that the Javanese are known for their emotional reticence meaning 'action' responses may be hidden within patterns of decorum and silence. Thus, it is not just the emotion words of individuals that assist social knowledge, especially since, as Heider has hinted, such words are rarely uttered and display lack of consensus. As Lutz and White (1986) point out, emotions are not just person-centered, rather they are sociocultural *institutions* that depend on interpersonal situations and cultural models that shape emotional meaning and experience. The key, then, to understanding Javanese emotion attitudes may be located within these institutions more than in action responses. Moreover, the actual discursive components of Javanese social interaction have rarely been featured in most of the literature leaving vast areas of natural cultural performance as practice relatively untouched.

Modern research on Javanese language and culture adheres to the traditional categories of refinement and equanimity not just as signs of power, but also as a controlling measure in creating harmony. Meanwhile, these studies often neglect two extremely important aspects of Javanese social interaction:

1. everyday social interactions, and
2. the hierarchical aspects of power that are also *maintained* by harmonious behavior, where those low in the social order humbly adhere to these rigid scales of human worth that for the most part hold no honored place for them.

Ochs (1988: 171) states that all sentences expressed in context have an affective component. Even 'impersonal' styles or those expressing distance reflect personal assumptions about states, events, statuses, norms, and expectations grounded within local values. Thus, from examining the actual stories of personal abuse uttered by working class, urban, Javanese women we can extract a working definition of Javanese affect as the organization of verbal means through which speakers display emotion and their audiences interpret these emotional discourses (e.g., Irvine 1990). Yet, as we will see, contextualizing emotion talk to actual situations of abuse can not always assist us in pinpointing emotion as a discursive event, especially where emotion is represented through silence or reframing. Identifying emotion talk often requires identifying the institution and the cultural values that shape talk. Thus, a particular context needs to be defined from the level of individual response and also from the level of socialized individual as the site where rules, traditions, and social control are inscribed (Bourdieu 1977; Douglas 1982).

To begin at the level of individual response, emotion in a narrative is the affective display located in what William Labov (1972: 366) refers to as *evaluation*: the means used by a narrator to indicate the point of the narrative. Evaluation within narratives is of several types depending on a speaker's purpose in telling the story. External evaluation interrupts the narrative with comments uttered as a means of explaining an aspect of the story to the audience. Internal evaluation preserves dramatic continuity by quoting the sentiment as something occurring at the moment rather than addressing it directly to the listener outside of the narrative (Labov 1972). Intensifiers assist speakers in focusing on an event within a story and emphasizing it. This can be done through adjectives, quantifiers, repetition, reported speech, and many other means which will be discussed as they occur in the stories.

Emotion display will then be further tied to social hierarchy and gender inequality. The aesthetic practices that assist individuals in their quest for the markings of power, i.e., self-control, elegant demeanor, and spiritual potency, are not only assumed to reflect the high status domains of the elite classes called *priyayi*, but they are also assumed to be overwhelmingly male domains. As Suzanne Brenner (1995: 21) points out, this ideological framework for power enforces the widely accepted beliefs that "men have greater self-control than women over their emotions and behavior, suggesting that men are 'naturally' stronger than women in a spiritual sense, and that women should 'naturally' defer to them as a result". Open conflict, then, is often avoided as it can indicate a *man's* lack of potency within his own household. Thus, it is not simply the avoidance of conflict in Javanese interactions that needs to be investigated here but rather the woman's role as insulator or protector of the man's authority (Keeler 1987: 72; Brenner 1995). The questions to be raised here then are, do women *avoid* the expression of emotion (as Heider suggests), are they more emotional and hence less *alus* than men, or do the Javanese have a more subtle system for expressing emotion than has yet been identified by scholarly research?

Based on such broadly accepted ideologies of class, power, and gender roles in Java, women are bound to their social and material domestic contexts, and thus are responsible for the family's daily existence. While women provide the foundations for the necessary attributes of power, i.e., order, peace, and well-being, they gain access only to a derivative form of power. Real power remains the prerogative of men (Djajadiningrat-Nieuwenhuis 1987). Since men are concerned with defining themselves in terms of power and prestige, men are said to speak differently than women. Those that do not lay claim to high status then, i.e., women, low status men, and some transvestites, are relatively freed from the constraints of interactive style and enjoy the freedom they obtain at the expense of status (Keeler 1990: 151–2).

Statements about the elegantly formal processing and monitoring of discursive information in Javanese contexts, such as that which has been discussed thus far, presuppose speakers of *high status* and *males*. On the other hand, comparative statements degrading and devaluing less powerful discourses as simply not quite *alus*, meaning emotion attitudes *are* reflected, reveal how class values are strongly upheld by Javanese and foreign researchers alike. Where Ward Keeler writes “information flows most freely among intimates and to and among people of low status” (Keeler 1990: 137), he alludes to these major discrepancies in class variants via discourse styles. Both the lower classes who cannot adhere to the rules of *alus* and women do not need constant recourse to the controlled expression of status through speech styles deemed critical to the Javanese sense of well-being (Keeler 1990). Furthermore, women do not suppress strong affect and emotion as men do, since they are not concerned with presenting as refined a demeanor (Brenner 1995: 29).

Despite the fact that the Javanese themselves have supported such statements as those above, this chapter aims to challenge some of these class and gender Javanese ideologies. This approach attempts to define human emotion as it is “rationalized and organized in a cultural system” (Irvine 1990: 126) by examining the emotion *within* the cultural system. In Javanese contexts this involves locating and relating the display of emotion to specific cultural constructs and relations of (or expectations about) power. Lutz and Abu-Lughod (1990) claim that embodying emotions in social practice, i.e., locating emotional discourses within situated talk, permits a view of the production of *emotional discourses* as bound up with, and yet distinct from, *discourses on emotion*, i.e., local theories about emotions (1990: 13, my emphasis). Thus, the public use of discourses on gender identity can be taken as the discourses of power within Javanese society and as a foundation from which to show how women’s *emotional discourses* have been shaped by the power relations from which they arise.

This paper examines emotion in natural Javanese contexts. First, I will show how Javanese women actually signal their emotions in everyday talk. In this way, I will show how the Javanese speech levels, despite long being defined as tokens of spiritual potency and respect, actually assist women in evaluating the personal experiences they narrate.[2] Second, I will further contextualize local values in gender roles by elaborating on ‘discourses on emotion’ for the purpose of recognizing how gender roles are constructed. While part one analyzes and defines affect in women's stories of personal pain, part two of this paper then expands the scope of analysis to examine the public discourses that define women's positions in society. From this perspective I will show how ideologies of women's subordination are taken up by women themselves and thus become the means through which they define themselves. Freedom of choice in selecting her own role in society is not really much of an option since Indonesian women are defined relationally to and ultimately dependent on men for their status (i.e. Sears,1996; N. Sullivan,1994). Both ideologically and legally, state discourses position women as dependent wives who exist for their husbands, their families, and the state (Suryakusuma 1996: 98; Sunindyo 1996: 121). In practice a woman must be hard-working and responsible toward all her family's needs, while also silent, passive, and monogamous toward her husband. Thus, through an examination of the public media that defends these narrow roles, we will see that the all-powerful state seems to have no place in its ideology for variations on its concept of the ideal woman. In conclusion, I will argue that the sociocultural institutions that define Javanese behavior actively silence women.

This perspective will ultimately bring us back to the social constructionist definition of emotion and its link with agent responsibility. Since the goal of this Chapter is to show how emotion attitudes and display in everyday talk are shaped by the more powerful discourses of class and gender identity, I will explore the power of the ideological concepts of women's roles by investigating what happens when these ideals are lost. My analysis is based mainly within the Central Javanese city of Yogyakarta, the center of the refinement and hierarchical orderliness that underpins cultural expectations, linguistic standards, and state domination. It is here that I wished to discover how a society that values restraint and harmony above any displays of human emotion permits women to deal with personal tragedies such as rape and other forms of gender violence.

Javanese Speech Levels in Women's Speech

Scholars claim that formal Javanese (*kråmå*) 'protects' its speakers from their "natural inclinations to speak spontaneously" (Siegel 1986: 3–12, see also Dwiraharjo 1991; Soeroso 1990). Within the elegant level known as *kråmå*, are the two highly valued, graceful vocabularies known as *kråmå andhap* which humbles a speaker, and *kråmå inggil* which bestows honor upon an interlocutor or someone spoken about. *Ngoko* (low Javanese), on the other hand, requires no social refinement or abilities. Pure *ngoko* is language void of all sensitivity to status, formality, or the face wants of others (Siegel 1986; Dwirahardjo 1991).

Word selection from within these systems of choice in Javanese is not based upon communicative needs but upon recognition of the social order of things, i.e. "the nature of the world" (Siegel 1986). Dwiraharjo (1991) further states that *worsuh*, or level mixing (what he describes as *krâmâ* moving "downward" toward *ngoko* into the middle realm called *madyå*), usually reflects "emotional" behavior. Emotion here is a type of interference that disturbs the harmony of Javanese etiquette.

My own research on Javanese women's narratives (Berman 1998) has shown that the speech levels function as a type of deictic, very much on par with pronouns, demonstratives, time and place adverbials, all of which anchor an utterance to its context by encoding specific aspects of the context into the utterance itself. As social deictics, speech levels create an additional dimension of hierarchical coordinates of person through respect, age, or through clarifying some other valued or devalued trait. In this respect, speech levels are keys or cues through which evaluational interpretations are clarified.

The shifting of speech levels within a story is an important feature in Javanese because of the wide variations in choice available and the highly evaluative meaning it exposes. As an index of stories, this feature is far more apparent in older speakers' discourse than in texts from younger speakers.[3] Yet, the shifting of speech levels, more than any other feature in elderly speakers' talk, is the contextualization cue that reveals how a story is to be interpreted. As a structuring element in storytelling, it not only places speakers and those being spoken about in the story within a hierarchical social order of rights and obligations, it also assists participants in the interpretation of such events by specifying these social positions.

In the example below, the speaker is Ibu Asmoro[4], an elderly *abdi-dalem* or servant of the royal court. The *abdi-dalem* are noted for their excellent mastery of the rules of decorum and are said to be the models of these stringent behaviors. Ibu Asmoro and I have come to the *kraton* (the Sultan's palace) where we have met Ibu Umaya. Ibu Asmoro began telling a story about her experiences as a singer (*pesindhen*) in the early days of Indonesian national radio (*Radio Republik Indonesia* or RRI). Our focus here is on the way she shifts speech levels to iconically present her positions in relation to the various levels of information she presents:

(1) RRI Violence[5]

106. Asmoro:

menikå kuping di templeki,	our ears were boxed.
wong nyinden kok kåyå kirik kepidak,	the singers were stepped on like puppies.
ha **nikå nåpå-nåpå** nyerik**ken** to,	It was all so painful, y'know,
kulå kendel**ken mawon**..	I just stopped.

	Harjonopawoho **nggih**, wow ..	Harjonopawoho (name) y'know, wow.
	wong sinden kog kåyå tai,	[he treated] the singers like shit.
	dados sami nggodå **menikå**,	While at the same time tempting.
	lajeng kulå manggihi kepala RRI	So I met with the head of RRI
	nyuwun medal.	[and] asked to be released.
107.	Umaya: Wow ..	Wow
108.	Asmoro:	
	Bayar**ipun menikå, kalian** Bu Larasati **mawon**	The pay [I got was the] same as Bu Larasati.
	"**kathah panjenengan sampun kersanipun**…	"There is a lot that you desire.
	artå nikå pundi-pundi wonten timbang **kulå**.."	Where will you get the kind of money I give you?"
	nekan.. nekan mangkel	It was frustrating

In the above story, Ibu Asmoro is explaining why she chose to leave her coveted singing job at RRI, despite, as she states, receiving a salary on par with the most famous singer of the day, Ibu Larasati. This story is part of her *morality* repertoire where she displays her actions as motivated by integrity rather than greed. As in many of her other stories in my corpus, her narratives relate her independence and bravery at dealing with a usually gender-related problem. While the job was tempting financially, she had a firm set of principles which did not include abuse. Her use of varying speech styles serves to index and distinguish levels of self-positioning.

The abusive descriptions appear in *ngoko* through repeating patterns of abusive descriptors:

(2)	wong nyinden kog kåyå kirik kepidak,	the singers were stepped on like puppies.
	wong sinden kog kåyå tai,	[he treated] the singers like shit.

Specific feelings — although not tied to herself as indexed and responsible agent — are presented as external evaluation in *madyă*:

(3)	ha **nikå nåpå-nåpå** nyerik**ken** to,	It was all so painful, y'know,

or in *ngoko*:

(4)	nekan.. nekan mangkel	[It] was frustrating

Meanwhile, her own actions as a responsible and moral agent are described in more respectful *kråmå*. The first utterance in (5) is in a lower *madyå kråmå* than is the second, showing how the speaker shifts social-relational evaluation. The first utterance positions the speaker in relation to her lower-status interlocutor in the story-telling context of the *kraton*, where it clarifies her actions for Ibu

Umaya. The second utterance is in full *krâmâ* and places her in relation with the status-superior head of RRI:

(5) **kulå** kendel**ken mawon**.. — I just stopped.
lajeng kulå manggihi kepala RRI — So I met with the head of RRI

A more explicit use of level shift to mark speaker proximity to her utterance appears below. The vile abuse inflicted by more powerful men upon the women is described through *ngoko* level descriptors. Crude actions are given crude affective words. On the other hand, the internal conflicts the abuse caused the speaker herself appear in krâmâ revealing a pattern of speaker proximity to event and evaluation via speech level shifting:

(6) wong sinden kog kåyå tai, — [he treated] the singers like shit.
dados sami nggodå **menikå**, — While at the same time tempting.

Yet, in the Javanese worlds of ceremonial discourse and rites of giving and receiving honor, Ibu Asmoro uses reported speech to present the words spoken to her from the director of RRI. By shifting back into the story world, Ibu alters her evaluation to reflect idealized internal relative positions. This powerful man is seen here addressing the speaker with *krâmâ inggil* honorifics:

(7) **"kathah panjenengan sampun kersanipun..."** — "There is a lot that you desire..."

This frame shift in the story from external to internal evaluation then permits the speaker to reframe her own status where the powerful man is made to distinguish her as highly respected within an environment that habitually abuses women.

For Ibu Asmoro, the boundaries of the story-telling event permit her the opportunity to co-ordinate specific activities and feelings within a hierarchical grid of social positions and values. Coherence in this story is created through an episodic movement in relational consequences that is fully dependent on speech level functions. From an ego-centric locus, these events are displayed as highly affective evaluations of her reactions to the abuse through symbolic style shifts. Abusive behavior is marked as crude and base through low Javanese (*ngoko*). Feelings not indexing a responsible agent but that describe the awful experiences are in *ngoko* or *madyâ*, middle Javanese. In this case, the style shift is signaling her external evaluation as a movement closer to the speaker, but not too close. It is through the use of internal evaluation, the return to the story-world framing of self and others, that the speaker indexes herself as a responsible agent. Thus, unlike previous studies which claim *ngoko* to be the speech level of emotion and personal experience, Ibu Asmoro's story displays the opposite.

Her personal actions as a responsible agent, depicting her highly principled yet difficult decisions, are in full *krâmâ* (see 6 above). Meanwhile, her reported speech, as the words she herself had spoken:

(8) nyuwun medal, [and] asked to be released.

are in *krâmâ andhap* signaling the formal respect she displayed in spite of the injustice. These speech level variations index at an iconic level the dignity and high Javanese honor she maintained in spite of the cruelty inflicted upon her. Those in power at RRI treated her badly but she still presents herself as addressing them in formal, and humbling, honorifics. Yet she further restores her dignity in the eyes of those that hear the story by presenting the RRI director's words to her in *krâmâ inggil*, the speech level meant to index the most honorific and ceremonial of social relations. As the supposed actual words he spoke to her, Ibu Asmoro's choice of the honorific speech level is displaying how this man in a position of power and as responsible for the abusive situations occurring between his employees, deems her worthy of respect. Thus, it is not so much the abuse, the violence, the loss of job and income, and the loss of face that are at issue here, but the giving and taking of status through indexes of respect and honor.

In terms of Lutz' representation of the emotion schema, we have a narrative that defines a context of personal insult and degradation as the social event and her quitting the job as the triggered response:

SOCIAL EVENT: abuse by male superiors
↓ ↓
EMOTION: pain
↓ ↓
ACTION RESPONSE: quit

The emotion segments of Ibu Asmoro's story are displayed through speech level shifts, which function as a type of deixis to anchor the utterance to its context by encoding specific aspects of her affective evaluation of that situation into the utterance itself. The psychological salience of these speech levels and the propriety they encode are the first 'filters' through which personal abuse is interpreted. In this case, what is being indexed are the personal evaluations of an elderly speaker towards the event, the participants and her own sense of self. Autobiography is being actively filtered through affective evaluation as discourse markers of formality and respect. She does refer to the experience as *painful*, yet *pain* is filtered through the values of dignity as the high status expectation of emotional equanimity. Victimization and abuse are not as bad, providing the victim maintains her dignified composure. This is why she never expresses anger or dismay at the relationally superior male sources of her pain. In this way, those that hear her story are not ‘startled’ and she herself can actively reframe her victimization as a display of her own superiority in terms of high Javanese ideals.

Lutz (1982) defines emotions as statements about the enactment of cultural values, which clarify the cognitive link between the culturally appropriate emotion attitude and the context for which it is a response. Speech levels here are social deictics which create an additional dimension of social rank through respect, age, behavior, or through clarifying some other valued or devalued trait. The culturally appropriate Javanese response to abuse by one’s male superiors as interpreted by Ibu Asmoro then is to increase decorum and with great discursive formality, take one’s leave of the awful environment. Decorum does not simply disguise the hurt but rather functions as a filter through which hurt and degradation can be actively transferred into the highly valued cultural resource called respect both for oneself and, most importantly, from others. Perhaps a more appropriate representation of the Javanese emotion schema may be as follows:

SOCIAL EVENT:	abuse by male superiors
↓	↓
EMOTION:	pain
↓↑	↓↑
PROPRIETY:	refinement
↓	↓
ACTION RESPONSE:	quit

The above schema shows how emotion and sociocultural propriety are linked in a Javanese theory of mind. The symbol EMOTION ↔ PROPRIETY is not used to explicitly represent talk *about* feeling because these women do not openly engage in such speech events. Instead, talk is action which is then taken as evidence of feeling (e.g. Ochs, 1988: 146).

While further discussion of ethnopsychology is beyond the scope of this paper, the data presented here will support the strength of sociocultural contexts and relations of power as controlling factors in shaping Javanese behavior. With Ibu Asmoro’s story as evidence of the autobiographical presentation of self in a context of abuse, the structuring of human emotion as *response* to a distant social event is clearly represented. In this story as in many others in the corpus, speech level variants become more respectful or formal the closer they get to the indexed agent. The clearer the index of agency, the more responsible that agent is for the contents of the story (Mülhäusler and Harré 1990). Thus, the more intimately the speaker indexes herself as agent within the event described, such as through reported speech (as embedded or internal evaluation, Labov 1972), the more formal her words in terms of speech levels. In this respect, shifts in speech levels offer stylistic cues that clarify interpretations of speaker' emotional relationships within their narratives.

Narratives of Shared Victimization

We will now turn to a different style of the story-telling process in this investigation of emotion. The women whose stories we will examine here are young[6] in comparison to Ibu Asmoro and thus reflect a different generation of Javanese speakers. Unlike the situation above where one empowered speaker narrated her personal story to others who did not share these experiences, the three women below have all shared particularly bad experiences as laborers in the Taman Tirto garment factory. Several weeks into the job, salaries were cut to half the minimum wage, the women were required to work more than ten hours per day, come in seven days a week, and they were subjected to verbal and physical abuses as described below. Quitting was not an option as unemployment in Indonesia is high and legitimate job opportunities are scarce. Such treatment of factory workers is illegal, but Indonesia rarely enforces the laws that defend workers' rights. Thus, the discourses analyzed below will show how these young women evaluated their victimized state and how they also used narrative as a means to reinterpret their positions and hence create the only guard against abuse they had available.

The conversation discussed below began as I entered the Budi home and switched on the recorder. Sari and Sigah were talking about others at the factory. In response to hearing the topic of the factory, I asked Sari how her meetings with Depnaker (the Department of Labor) were going. As an observer of the initial steps of resistance to abuse, i.e. the collection and review of Depnaker pamphlets, and as a close family friend, I had good reason to ask out of friendly concern. Turns 38 through 41 show my negotiating for specific information.

The factory management had imposed an overtime requirement on their workers.[7] When this command was issued, management claimed that any worker with a signed letter from a parent stating their objection to working late will be released. In her story (turn 42), Sari claims that she had not intended her letter as a test of the factory policy. But as she approached with the letter, she found that the release policy was a sham:[8]

(9)

37.	Laine: La piye to Mbak nek Depnaker ki.	So how's it going then, Mbak at that Depnaker.

38.	Sari: Sesok selåså	Next Tuesday
39.	Laine: Sesok selåså rep åpå?	Next Tuesday [you] plan what?
40.	Sari: Arep maju protes kuwi.	[We] plan to advance the protest.
41.	Laine: La piye to Mbak	So what's that about then, Mbak.
42.	Sari:*kan* nek anu ki kon *tandatangan pulang pagi* ngono	It's like. if. whatsit. this order to get a signature to go home early
	Yo *kan kebetulan* sing maju ki aku. "*pokoknya saya tak mau tahu*!"	So, y'know, coincidentally, the one who stepped forward was me. "The point is, I don't want to know about it."
	"Lho pak *ini kan* *ada tandatangan dari Bapak!*" "*pokoknya saya tidak mau tahu*,"	"But sir, here, right, there's a signature from my father" "The point is I don't want to know about it."
	nganti sakiki ora dibayar tho…	Up to now, [salaries] haven't been paid.
45.	Laine: Ora dibayar tho?	[You mean salaries] haven't been paid.?
46.	Sari: Okeh.. sik ånå sik kurang slawe ewu	Lots. from before, there's a debt of [rp]25,000[9],
47.	Laine: wow	wow
48.	Sari: Kurang rongpuluh ewu, *padahal* kuwi wong kurang wong telungatus,	A loss of 20,000, but the thing is this loss is for 300 people!
49.	Laine: lho. kok iså.	Oh! How can they do that!
50.	Sari: Mulane dhå metu kabeh!	So that's why everyone will strike!

In story 9, Sari is describing how the management in her factory prevent interaction with their workers. They thoroughly disempower Sari and her coworkers by disallowing any communication: "*pokoknya, saya tidak mau tahu*," (the point is, I don't want to know about it). This speech act succeeds in its purpose as a powerful performative by effectively silencing the workers. I call this utterance a performative because it does not simply describe a state of affairs but actively creates that state (Levinson 1983: 228). In this case, the achieved state is one in which the factory workers are robbed of any dialogue with management. In the acceptably hierarchical (emphasized metaphorically as *paternal*) relations that exist between manager and (female) worker, the felicity conditions for such an authoritarian stance are conventional in Central Java. Sari and the other workers remain silenced as good Javanese daughters would. Their stories display this disempowerment as an absolute manifestation of silence as a norm of politeness vis-à-vis social hierarchy (e.g. Wolf 1996).

Yet, in terms of direct evaluation, Sari's story is based on her internal means of showing that the voice of authority is the voice of lies. While she never actually states this directly, she repeats the words that silenced her twice — *Pokoknya, saya tidak mau tahu* — in Indonesian, the language used by the factory management. She displays her own surprise at discovering the duplicity of the rule, explicitly indexed through *Lho* as she re-creates her own response in Indonesian as reported speech.

42. Sari:

"*pokoknya saya tak mau tahu*!"	"The point is, I don't want to know about it."
→ "Lho pak *ini kan*	"But sir, here, right,
ada tandatangan dari Bapak!"	there's a signature from my father!"
"*pokoknya saya tidak mau tahu*,"	"The point is I don't want to know about it."

Sari is reconstructing the voice of authority as surrounding and stifling her own voice. She can follow the authority's own rules and still lose. Her reconstructed dialogues with the factory are in Indonesian, while her conversations to the cohort are all uttered in Javanese, creating a discursive boundary that separates management from worker. By presenting herself as fully respecting the rule, and completely naïve with respect to its deceit, Sari is highly affective in displaying the underhanded way in which that authority silences her and so many like her. She will repeat this silencing performative frequently throughout her narratives to identify from a purely internal perspective the boundaries of the power play she is fighting, a boundary made further salient through code-switching. Thus, while she never utters a direct evaluation or external emotion attitude in this situation, she frequently repeats their words as reported speech.

The use of reported speech was for Bakhtin ([1934]1981) a crucial sign of the heteroglossic nature of all social discourse. He has shown how the multiple voices writers give to speakers in their texts index how others are to interpret the meaning or significance of that text. In the women's oral narratives, they repeat the words that oppress them to create a formulaic rallying cry through which the ugliness of their own suffering is brought to life in a way they are able to control, or at least denounce. Through reported speech, Sari has discursively created a dichotomous arena within which this power-play involving survival and safety for factory women is to be fought fairly.

Sari's story, then, takes on a different significance. Unfamiliar with the discourses of outward conflict or protest as those low in the social hierarchy must be, the women create their own through invoking what they assume are the locally appropriate ways and means of talking resistance. Within such a discourse, external evaluations of anger or threats are rare, replaced by the use of internal evaluation as the cohort reconstruct their dialogues with the factory managers. Through repeating the authority's words, their positions of power are displayed as unjust and immoral. In comparison, the workers present themselves as a unified band of silenced, but morally right victims, who may use emotion words such as *sedih* (sad) and *enek* (sickening), but never as indexed to an individual as singularly responsible agent. As seen above in Ibu Asmoro's story, externally descriptive adjectives evaluate the misuse of power, not the personal or individual feelings of the victims. Thus, as their decision to wage protest solidifies, the cohort's styles of interacting as a group also solidify into a unitary self.

Story 10 shows how repetition of the same disempowering performative we heard in story 9 dramatically enhances the immorality of the scene. The harsh cruelty of imposed silence is highlighted as the women face a locked door when they try to leave the factory at closing time:

(10)

272. Sari:	
jarene "*saya nggak mau tahu*"	*They said "I don't want to know".*
mbayangke we sedih åpå.	*Can [you] imagine the sadness, heh,*
enek, sing nglakoni [ha ha ha...]	*[it's] sickening what was done [hahaha].*
direwangi nangis-nangis ora entuk mulih.	*All that crying and still not allowed to leave..*
273. Sigah:	
Ha.a. nangis neng ngarep lawang,	*that's right, crying in front of the door,*
ora entuk bali tetepan	*and still not allowed to leave*
275. Endang:	
nganti jam telu	*up to 3:00*
ngantek aneng kantin anu	*there in the canteen, uhm.*
"kowe ki sekå ngendi wae tå ?"	*"What are you doing in here?"*
"ngelih pak" ngono.	*"[we're] hungry sir" it was said.*

This story combines both internal and external evaluation to describe through implication an unspecified group of women standing by the locked door, hungry, frightened, crying and wanting to go home. They were answered with a firm "I don't want to know about it". The repetition of the voice of authority established an intertextuality at several levels, one being its link to earlier stories of abuse and cruelty, as well as those yet to come. It also evoked the memories and fears of the recent events at the factory. Far from the actual scene, repetition here empowered the women by presenting them with an adversary that can no longer silence them.

Sigah's allo-repetition, or the repetition of each other's words, in 273 shows her support for Sari's external description of crying workers wanting to leave. Sigah adds the location and emphasizes the refusal to allow the crying women to leave. Endang's turn 275 moves the stage to the canteen where some workers had hidden. Endang repeated for her cohorts the words that were spoken there, repeating and clarifying the diverse roles between powerful and oppressed. In her story, the empowered are angry because those in the role of victim stopped work to eat, even though lunch was already three hours late. Yet none of these scenarios clarify what happened next. Did the women all return to their work stations, still crying and hungry?

All the stories in this corpus reject notions of individual agency as nearly all avoid revealing who had taken part in these scenes. All subjects are left ambiguous, or apologetically down-played, as in story 9 where Sari reports that *coincidentally* (kebetulan) it was she who stepped out in opposition to the voice of authority. The dichotomy of *we* and *they* positions this creates, strengthens the women's positions as a *group* of righteous victims separated from the authority along clearly delineated moral grounds. These stories construct inclusive story frames so all are equally subjected to the injustice, where unity in the stories is symbolic of the empowering strength needed to voice resistance. Yet only in the safety of secret resistance could the women take a stand against their enemy — however immoral this enemy may be.

In terms of affective display of emotion, these stories demonstrate the use of repetition for two essential functions: allo-repetition confirmed the cohort's unity by verifying their like-mindedness. Reported speech, or repeating the words uttered by factory management, strengthened the cohort's position by distinguishing them from this immoral and unjust voice of authority. The women then, enact their protest by repeating the words of their oppressors which, within the safety of their stories, they were empowered to condemn. Thus, very much like Ibu Asmoro's story, the evaluative elements of the narrative permit the active reframing of social positions within abusive contexts along moral grounds.

Returning to the emotion schema, the social event here is also abuse by superiors, and the adjectives used were 'sadness' and 'sickening'. Propriety as the cultural value through which emotion is filtered was previously measured by refinement, but the younger Javanese women do not resort to the same type of refinement. Where Ibu Asmoro saw refinement as the dignified presentation of self within hierarchically structured scales of giving and receiving status and respect, these women seem much more accepting of their disempowerment. They do cry, they do mock others, and they do want to honor the rules of their superiors. The issue here is that the superiors refuse to abide by expectations of fair-play that even Ibu Asmoro received as she asked to withdraw from her position. These women expect the righteous, moral order of status and worth to hold and that is why they attempt to protest rather than quit. They are not attempting to challenge the social hierarchy, but rather they are hurt by their superiors' refusal to behave in a manner befitting those in positions of power. In this scenario, the emotion schema reveals the sadness evoked by events that expose discrepant beliefs in the social roles and behaviors of those in power.

SOCIAL EVENT:	abuse by superiors
↓	↓
EMOTION:	sadness
↓↑	↓↑
PROPRIETY:	expectations of fairness
↓	↓
ACTION RESPONSE:	protest

Had the workers realized the futility of their efforts, they never would have protested. Their error was in assuming the social order in modern Java was still based upon a righteous and moral order of worth.

Despite a clear and moral purpose underlying their unified voice in the performance of these 'protest' narratives, it is in the evaluation stance that major differences of character appear. Their styles of personal evaluation expose the discursive areas of social and cultural difference vis-à-vis propriety among these younger generations. Like Ibu Asmoro, Sari's preferred strategy for evaluating the ugliness of the scene is to use reported speech, especially the repetition of the line she evaluates as most cruel, most unjust:

Sari:	"*pokoknya saya tidak mau tahu*"	"The point is, I don't want to know about it."

Reported speech is often said to raise questions about the experience and the reports of experience. The truth of a direct quote is not at issue but rather the action it is brought to serve within the narrative. Whether or not the quote is constructed (cf. Tannen 1989), or the faithful rendering of a past utterance, its frequency and its purpose in the narratives show that the women wave it like a banner of affect. The women have appropriated the voice of their own oppressor in order to fight back (Bakhtin 1981). The voice of authority is the voice of lies, injustice and immorality from which the cohort's just and moral voices can be better heard. Yet, individually, socially, and at work the cohort are silent. Only through this collective voice, uttered in isolation from more powerful others, and at a distance from the authority can they escape the reach of their oppressors.

Where Sari uses reported speech, Sigah turns to other evaluative strategies:

(11)

82.	Sari:	
	→ Ånå ning wis "*nggak mau tahu..*"	→ There are who just "don't want to know".
	"*pokoknya.*"..piye wingi kae jawabane,	"The point is," how'd that go yesterday, that response?
	"*peraturan itu dapat diubah?*"	"The regulations can always be changed"?
83.	Sigah:	
	Mana yang diemut	What can be done
	kalau peraturan-peraturan diubah-ubah!	if the regulations are repeatedly changed!

Sigah confirms Sari's recall of the immoral words as she repeats, and expands to increase the impact by externally evaluating it (turn 83). Sari repeats the oppressive words while Sigah emphasizes their effectiveness. The women's words function interdependently where one turn is not nearly as affective without the other. Sari's reported speech is an internal marker that evokes the words that wound, while Sigah's contribution functions to externally evaluate it, to express the depth and pain of the wound. She repeats Sari's quoted words *peraturan* (regulation) and *diubah* (be changed) in the reduplicated forms to show how her participant role is to externally evaluate through expanding, enforcing, and emotionally intensifying Sari's disimpassioned, internally evaluated utterances. Their complementary styles may be a reaction to the other, or a part of personal style, or a part of the cooperative strategy of unity. To construct equal responsibility, one must be equally positioned and equally involved in the story.

Yet, a potential conflict arises where Sari and Sigah show their differences with regard to rude, aggressive language. Sari and her family have definite urban *priyayi* values despite their poverty, whereas Sigah is more able to express emotion and anger. When Sigah blurts out crude names in reference to one of the bosses, Sari agrees but does not use the same styles of language:

(12)

59.	Sigah: Kae wong Batak	that [woman] is a Batak[10]
60.	Laine: såpå kuwi	who's that?
61.	Sari: Bu Meri kuwi	that Bu Meri
63.	Sigah: Singkek jenenge	[like a] Chinese[11] its called

64. Sari: **Enten <u>ngangge</u>** kok ging kok, kok, → *<u>saya ngak mau tahu</u>*	There are [who] use, [false start?], → "I don't want to know"
65. Sigah: Singkek ki elek-elek uwis!	These Chinese, they're disgusting, and that's that!
66. Sari: Rådå ora penak he Dik, nyambut gawe neng kono ki	Its rather not very nice, is it Dik, working over there.

Sari cannot repeat Sigah's vulgar references. In her turn 64, she style switches to *Madyå* Javanese, but all that comes out is *kok ging kok, kok*. This has no meaning beyond a surprise and disbelief, *kok* being what Errington (1988) calls a psycho-ostensive of surprise. Sari falls back on her internal style of evaluation by repeating her formulaic reported speech: *saya enggak mau tahu*, made more poignant by knowing this is the most anger Sari is capable of displaying. Where Sigah is able to use highly affective words such as *Singkek*, the derogatory word for ethnic Chinese, and *elek-elek*, the reduplicated emphasis for disgusting, Sari responds through vastly understating the experience as "rather not very nice" in her turn 66.

The following story text (13) shows Sari, Sigah, and Endang repositioning themselves in relation to another boss, Meri, a Philippine woman who they describe as crude, loud, and ill-mannered. This text shows how the Javanese social values of refinement and elegance are evoked — not for its role in disempowering the cohort but for the purpose of reviving their self-esteem:

(13)

169. Sari: nek <u>ngomong banter-banter</u> iyå *Mbak* Len?	when [she] speaks, it's so loud y'know, Mbak Len?
170. Laine: iyå….pådhå wae…	o yea, same [as me]
171. Endang: <u>omong-omonge keras</u> suarane….	[her] speaking voice is so crude
172. Sigah: kåyå <u>eneng gunung</u> kae. <u>ora duwe tånggå</u>, hahaha….	like up in the mountains, with no neighbors, hahah
174. Sari: kae ki, kae ki, <u>wong ndeså</u>.	That [woman], that [woman], no class,
<u>neng</u> Filipina <u>gunung</u> <u>ora duwe tånggå</u>,	these Philippine mountain [folk that] have no neighbors,
nek <u>ngomong bengok-bengok</u> neng arep lawang	when [she] speaks [she] screams in front of the door.
[hahaha]	

In the above text, the women link their utterances into one unified narrative by repeating and allo-repeating their insulting descriptions of their boss, Meri, co-constructing a cohesive story, rich with imagery of vile, ill-mannered behavior. This co-constructed story vividly demonstrates how these victims of the social order are ready to use any means at their disposal to classify and persecute another. Meri's visible frustration and anger with what she sees as the ignorance and incompetence of her workers (see below) become a tool for ridicule because a 'proper' Javanese adult must never call such attention to herself. Yet, the public display of social elegance as a celebrated and measurable badge of in-group membership is denied the cohort by virtue of their own low status as factory workers. Not only is Meri branded vile through her lack of refinement, so are the *wong ndeså* or rural peasants that Meri is compared to.

The cohort co-construct these humorous pictures of an inappropriate model of power by taking up each others' contributions, repeating, and expanding them to achieve their own superior status as refined, Javanese urban dwellers:

(14)

331. Sigah:	
mbanting lawang	slamming the door
nggåwå gitik kae	carrying that whip (?)
njuk nek nesu	so when [she's] angry
sikile diunggahke kae [hahaha]	[she] raises her leg like that [hahaha]
332. Sari:	
la ngomong basa inggris yå ora dong!	and speaking that English, can't understand any of it!
333. Endang:	
Tony yo judek yo!	That Tony is really hopeless right!
nesu-nesu nganggo båså inggris yå?	[when she's] furious [she] uses English right?
mbuh ora dong maksude åpå deke ngomong	haven't a clue what she's saying
ning akhire lungå dewe [hahah]	in the end, [she] just goes away [hahaha]
la ora dong ha ha aku ..	I just haven't a clue ha hah
såpå wae	who ever
la masalahe åpå ora dong. Hahahah	the problem [I] don't get it hahahah
334. Sari: Sit.Sit.Sit.! åpå kuwi,	shit, shit, shit! What's that,
ndremimil kae le ngomong *bahasa* Inggris	She really does run off at the mouth in that English.
aku ora dong yå..![hahahaha....]	I can't understand any of it! [hahahaha....]

335. Sigah:	
bola-bali bilang "no-gut" kae njuk *pergi*	back and forth saying "no-good" then, go away
336. Laine: jahitane på elek?	Is it that the sewing is bad?
337. Endang: ya *karena* elek *itu*!	yep, because it's bad!
338. Sigah:	
karna dia tidak memperhatikan kita dadine jahitane elek	because they don't pay attention to us we mess up the sewing

A good manager ought to "pay attention" to the workers in order for them to produce, as Sigah informs us in turn 338. Not only is their behavior shockingly inappropriate, the managers display none of the paternal attentions expected from someone in power. It seems extremely likely then that a manager who is Javanese, male, and refined could easily achieve everything that Meri and Tony could not (see also Wolf 1996).

If we examine more closely how the cohort manage their self-esteem under these difficult conditions, we can extract a scale of social worth based on negative behaviors and classifications. Individuals displaying loud or crude actions, as described in 13 and 14 above, are referred to as *ndeså*. To refer to another as *wong ndeså* or 'peasant' is highly insulting, but not *crude* as was Sigah's use of racist terms *Singkek* and *wong Batak*. As we can see by the cohort's use of ethnic and class slurs in a highly derogatory manner, they certainly do view their own refinement as superior to others', permitting them the recourse to negatively evaluate other ethnic groups and powerful individuals, as well as the lower classes, for their crudeness.

While the cohort are aware of their own victimized state, their perception of that oppression is shaped by the 'natural' order through which they understand their world[12]. Thus, the cohort tightly grasp the same system for measuring social worth that permits their own abuse in a cyclic order of oppress and be oppressed. Through the evocation of these Javanese scales of refinement in their stories, we can observe the women actively evaluating and redefining their own and others' social status markers. Meri and Tony, marked as the immoral oppressors, are ridiculed for *lacking* the attributes that should ideally mark their positions of power and *not* for representing power or even abusing it. The oppressiveness of the social hierarchy is not at issue here, but the behaviors appropriate for occupying positions of power are.

In the safety of their band of conspirators, far from the oppressing realities of the Taman Tirto factory, these women are able to find humor in the behaviors and words that cause them pain. By ridiculing those that ridicule them and by intentionally sewing badly whenever a fore person is not watching, the workers get their little revenges. These two stories show the women co-constructing a slap-stick comedy routine where their Philippine bosses in the starring roles are ranting and raving, kicking doors, and screaming in a language as well as a behavior none of the workers understands, since she would never behave in such a bold manner. The stories consist of each participant's involvement in a coherently similar turn that contributes to the whole of the discourse. None of the cohort stands out as separate and none places themselves into the story in any exclusive manner. None of this sufficiently empowers them to overcome their problems either. This type of empowerment is enacted through affective display for day-to-day survival and self-esteem. But in terms of their relative 'real world' positions within the Javanese social order, the cohort are actively reproducing the very behaviors and discourses that marginalize them.

Yet, within a different social context, Sari can be seen telling her factory story in a much more affective manner. In story 15 Sari is now speaking with Sri, another factory worker, her father, and Sri's father. In this context, the factory story is told specifically from the perspective of forced overtime and the serious problems this causes the women. Meanwhile, within cross-gender and hierarchical contexts of interaction, none of the abusive scenarios are related:

(15)

33.	Sari: **nikå mawon**	And what's more,
	ingkang ndalemipun tebih-tebih njih,	those whose homes are far away y'know,
	judek **nikå**.	[they're] desperate.
	arep nangis ora iså.	[They] want to cry but [they] can't.
	sampun mboten komanan bis,	The buses have already stopped running,
	ingkang dalemipun mBantul,	those whose homes are in Bantul,
	nikå lho Pak.	what about [them] sir?
34.	Pak Sri: la **enggih.**	Oh yes.
35.	Sari: **dalem**e adoh kog. Pak,	Their homes are so far y'know sir.
	makane njuk malah trimå	so that's why it's just accepted.
	malah **mboten** dhå mlebu esuke,	even so no one will go in tomorrow
	rak dhå malah anu. to	everyone even, whatsit, [false start]
	mesakke.	its a real shame.
	yen sesuk muni nglembur	when tomorrow [they] say overtime
	njuk malah **mboten** dhå mlebu.	then no one's going to take it.

In comparison to her earlier stories with Sigah and Endang, Sari now uses an entirely different style of affect in her storytelling. Since her purpose in telling is very different than in the previous context, her evaluation uses none of the reported speech she most often used with her cohort. Here, her goal is to present a clear perspective on the serious implications of the overtime issue, that of being stranded at the factory in light of the shared knowledge regarding women traveling alone at night. Her affective strategies are the repetition of phrases stressing the distance these women will need to travel from the factory:

33.	Sari:	nikå mawon	And what's more,
→		ingkang ndalemipun tebih-tebih njih,	→ those whose homes are far away y'know,
		judek nikå.	[they're] desperate.
		arep nangis ora iså.	[They] want to cry but [they] can't.
		sampun mboten komanan bis,	The buses have already stopped running,
→		ingkang dalemipun mBantul,	→ those whose homes are in Bantul,
		nikå lho Pak.	what about [them] sir?
35.	Sari:	→ daleme adoh kog. Pak,	→ [Their] homes are so far y'know sir.

Her repetition grows more affective as she moves from general, reduplicated *tebih-tebih* (far away) to the more specific naming of the area many of the workers live in, and thus more involving, *Bantul*[13]. Finally she utters the simple, direct almost plea-like: ***dalem**e adoh kog. Pak* (their homes are so far away y'know. sir,) in *ngoko*, which contrasts with her general *tebih-tebih* in *krâmå*. Yet regardless of the speech level used for the adjective describing the distance, Sari maintains the *krâmå inggil* term **dalem** (home) as highly honorific of the women she is referring to. Honorific terms address others, never the speaker. This shows that Sari has taken on the role of spokesperson, yet excludes herself.

Sari describes the women's predicament through adjectives such as the various terms for distance above, and the encoded frustration below. The second idea unit is also marked by a dramatic level shift into *ngoko*, while only the particle *nikå* maintains *madyå*, yet indexed to no responsible agent:

judek **nikå**.	[they're] desperate.
arep nangis ora iså.	[They] want to cry [but they] can't.

The women are desperate, in fact, so desperate that they cannot even cry. The issues here of travel and safety for women *are* serious, so serious in fact that the Department of Labor requires all factories that keep their female workers after dark to supply them with transportation home. Again, a necessary and humanitarian law exists but is not enforced by anyone with the power to do so. But, because their homes are so far away and:

sampun **mboten** komanan bis,	The buses have already stopped running,

the women are thoroughly trapped again. They cannot go home at night because they cannot afford the expense of the other modes of transportation available, they cannot afford the gossip that brands women who move around at night, and they are afraid of the potential disasters that await women on the streets. Yet, of these three very good reasons for refusing overtime work at the factory, not one is actually mentioned in the story. Silence rarely means insignificance. Here the silence marks shared community knowledge that needs no repetition. Look at what the women had said last week while recording the conversation between Sari, Sigah, and Endang:

(16)

280.	Endang: tur nek bengi, yå ora wani Mbak	so then at night, y'know [we're] not brave [enough to go home] Mbak
281.	Laine: He.ee.	right.
282.	Sigah: ngko nek ditemu uwong, piye?	So later if we meet someone [on the streets] then what?
283.	ALL: [hahah cilåkå.] He.ee.	[hahaha disaster] right.
284.	Endang: yå nek sik nemu apik ora åpå-åpå. Nek sik nemu elek,	So if [we] run into someone good no problem. If [we] run into one who's bad,
285.	Sigah: E.e. Nek sik nemu mulih nesu yå?	Right. If [we] run into one going home in anger, then what?

In more private contexts within which the women are positioned as equally subjected to the dangers of predatory male sexuality, the fear of violence is mentioned. Topics such as this rarely arise in conversation, although they are alluded to where ever women need to negotiate travel at night. With all this in mind the women are forced to accept their plight:

makane njuk malah trimå	so that's why it's just accepted.

Sari's use of the word *trimå* is symbolic of Javanese acquiescence to one's fate. In terms of Sari's affective stance, and in its co-occurrence with overtime, distance, lack of buses, and the unmentioned cause of it all, *trimå* strongly marks the women as victims, subjected to the tyrannical, and shockingly unfair authority of Taman Tirto management.

With their victimized status firmly established within terms that no father could possibly reject, Sari now shifts her footing to that of the fighter. Her grounds for protest are inarguable so she can now evaluate, again through repetition, her new confrontational stance:

35.	Sari:	malah mboten dhå mlebu esuke,	even so no one will go in tomorrow
		rak dhå malah anu. to	everyone even, whatsit, [false start]
		mesakke.	its a real shame.
		yen sesuk muni nglembur	If tomorrow [they] say overtime
		njuk malah mboten dhå mlebu.	then no one's going in.

Sari's narrative uses external evaluation through her stance as direct, to the point, and displaying a strong conditional, *yen* (if):

→ yen sesuk muni nglembur	→ If tomorrow [they] say overtime,
njuk malah mboten dhå mlebu.	then no one's going in.

While Sari shows no agent responsibility through linking a predicate to an "I", she is, in fact, thoroughly empowered within this context because she has constructed for herself a fully ratified group voice just as seen in the stories told with the cohort. She uses the abbreviated form of the plural marker *pådhå*, or *dhå,* (turn 35) to signal the group but to not specify what part of the group or how large it is. As argued earlier, unity is empowering and by invoking a unified group, the protesters actively empower themselves.

In turn 35 Sari's stance is that of the self-assured fighter, the activist and leader who is perfectly aware of her choices and is prepared to take them. She is showing her empowered stance, especially in defiance of those who attempt to wrongfully hurt her and her cohorts. Her knowledge of her own rights is magnified by her change of frame where she steps out of her defiant stance to externally utter *mesakke* "its a real shame." No one should have to endure the indignities thrust upon them, so now, *if* provoked once more, they will fight.

Sari's status as the sole animator within this context, has offered her much more freedom here than she had above where equality and sharedness were the rules. Sari herself lives rather close to the factory and rides a bicycle there in less than 10 minutes, so she does not share the problem of being stranded at the factory at night. But here she is very affective in presenting the group position, specifically mentioning those that live in Bantul, the village south of Yogyakarta. While not directly inconvenienced by being stranded, she speaks with what seems like a figure's direct involvement:

33.	judek **nikå**.	it's desperate.
	arep nangis ora iså.	[SUBJ] want to cry but can't.

She explains the desperation and tears and she lowers her speech style to *ngoko*, the speech level assumed to signal emotional involvement. Yet, as we saw above in story 1, *ngoko* was used to describe awful situations, whereas personally indexed behaviors appeared in other styles. While far more work needs to be done to clarify broader patterns of affect in Javanese, as described above, the speaker's own position in relation to her narrative requires explanation. Is she a concerned outsider, a mere animator, or is she including herself as figure? Since Javanese requires no pronominal indexing or subjects, the question needs to be answered from the perspective of participation and the responsibility it implies.

Sari utters no first person pronouns, but she uses the word dalem to reference home, others' homes and not her own. She is speaking about other people's experiences more so than her own and she uses external evaluation rather than the internal she used above. Where does the speaker fit into her discourse in terms of emotion display, agency and responsibility? Sari's participant role is now one of full responsibility for the discourse because she too is a woman and fully subjected to the social rules underlying the entire conversation as framed here. In such a speech situation as this, Sari's ability to get home at night is irrelevant. While there are no first person pronouns to index her stance within the story as agent or even to index the stories as personal experience, the fact that she is the sole animator indicates her responsibility for that agent position (cf. Mühlhäusler and Harré 1990). As Duranti (1988) states, describing a fact about the world has performative ends, and, in terms of the consequences for an utterance, the speaker is fully responsible.[14]

This direct implication between participation and responsibility functions for all speakers where all those present are responsible for the shaping and defining of these utterances. Participation is a collective involvement where meaning requires uptake. Sari can be bold in her story, however, because she has taken on the responsibilities of her gender. She speaks from 'we' not 'I'. Thus, experiences are framed as those of the group and emotion words describe shared states in response to the unfairness. It is a given that women must not travel alone at night and with its forced, sudden overtime, the factory management never permits women to arrange to be picked up ahead of time. While this reference to their fear of traveling at night is never uttered, it nevertheless underlies the entire story as it was framed for the fathers. These emotion states reveal how the broader community and its rules for women's behavior have shaped the workers' very legitimate concerns for their own safety and reputations as illustrated by the emotion schema:

SOCIAL EVENT:	unfairness by superiors/forced overtime
↓	↓
EMOTION:	desperate
↓↑	↓↑
PROPRIETY:	rules about women traveling at night
↓	↓
ACTION RESPONSE:	protest

Thus, as stated elsewhere (Lutz and Abu-Lughod 1990), emotional discourses in Javanese are highly dependent on the discourses on emotion which never need to appear in the stories because of the socialization processes that teach all members of society its rules of inclusion. These are the *givens* that underlie women's discourses and their displays of emotion. Javanese women are positioned by the wider society as a means of contextualizing their emotional discourses within the social values that shape the discourses of emotion (Lutz & Abu Lughod 1990). We shall pick up on the theme of abuse raised by these young women in order to better understand how these emotion discourses are framed by gender relations in Javanese society. The display of emotion will be linked to relations of power through the social hierarchical aspects of Javaneseness. It is here that language has the greatest potential for constituting discrimination as social practice (Fairclough 1989; Freeman & McElhinny 1995).

Controlling Female Identity

Javanese institutions are hierarchical in their means of shaping all aspects of social interactions from local conversations to the structures of the community and the very circumstances of culture itself. Since conversation is not separable from the larger social order that frames it, issues of *control* and particularly *self-control* are basic to recognizing Javanese ways and means of negotiating social meaning (Berman 1998), and hence, displaying emotion. Social interaction is the arena in which speakers display their shared mental strategies and representations as a basis from which they can monitor the production and interpretation of their discourse (i.e., exercise their *self-control*). The aim of much of this current line of research then is to develop a strategy for recognizing presupposed beliefs shared by speech participants and to identify how such knowledge affects the structure of discourse (van Dijk 1994: 108). Hierarchical positioning as a broad-reaching and highly constraining aspect of Javanese society already organizes all social interactions, whether in the family or in the public sphere. It also sets up the perfect foundation of power through which to impose attitudes and actions while restricting reflection and choice, what others have referred to as 'psychological violence' (Ellul 1973).

Yet, Brenner shows how these dominant gender ideologies obscure the subtler ways in which people think and talk about gender as day-to-day practices (1995: 41). For example, women's behavior and speech styles are described by men as lacking the qualities Javanese deem worthy of respect (Keeler 1990: 130). Meanwhile, it is the woman who is responsible for teaching her (male!) children the linguistic and social etiquette she supposedly does not master. Furthermore, Brenner explains that historically, as in the post-colonial era, it is widely expected that Javanese women should manage their husbands' income, because the mundane domains of family business, markets, and any concerns with money are seen as *kasar* (unrefined, crude, uncivilized). The dominant gender ideologies, as the "official" views on gender distribution of roles, state that male concerns with prestige and potency prevent them from bargaining or dealing with petty financial matters. This is why women inhabit the domains in which the 'boisterous', hence demeaning, behaviors are common. However, as Brenner shows, an alternative reason for women to hold on to the money is because men cannot control their desires as women can and that given financial control, men will fall victim to their 'passion-ridden nature' through sex, gambling, extravagant consumption, and more. Does such behavior undermine the ideology of male self-control and potency? No since males are expected to be *nakal* (naughty), they may take great pride in their "unquenchable lust". Brenner (1995: 35) reports "that the positive associations of sexual potency and of generally "manly" behavior offset any shame that might accompany their inability to exercise self-control".

Most important then, "women's control over their own desires serves to compensate for men's lack of control, and by so doing preserves the assets that should properly be used to ensure the family's security" (Brenner 1995). Thus, it is the woman's responsibility to guard her husband's tendency to *manly* behavior, protect the family's resources, protect his dignity and status, and, since he is the recognized head of the family and the means through which she achieves her own status, she must protect him in order to defend her own status and that of her children.

Since a woman's nature is to be loving and giving, she must accept natural male weaknesses, including responsibility for his misdeeds and the loss of harmony in the family without demanding his support, or her own power and prestige in return (e.g. Brenner 1995). Hence, it is precisely these silences, the widespread neglect of her identity and aspirations, and the blatant inequality of ideological roles that remain the dominant factors in this ideological framing women.

In January 1996, I began regularly visiting the Women's Crisis Center in Yogyakarta. With good publicity through a Sunday advice column in the local press (Kedaulatan Rakyat, KR) publicly silent women send their letters of pain and suffering to the center, although none have ever appeared in person requesting shelter or assistance. Of five letters received from young rape victims that January, all described similar patterns. Each had been raped by a friend, neighbor, or relative, and they all used the same vocabulary to describe their reactions. Since none became pregnant from the ordeal, the women state that they had never told anyone about the rape including members of their own families, and it was only now with their discovery of the center through the Sunday press that they found a means to seek help. All the women used the term *dinodai* (stained or disgraced) to describe themselves, and they described their loss of virginity as being destroyed for life (*menghancur* or *merusak masa depan*).

En: Lima tahun yang lalu saya diperkosa oleh teman sendiri. Saat itu saya tidak berani bercerita dengan siapapun termasuk orangtua karena takut. Baru saat inilah saya baru sadar bahwa ternyata perbuatan teman saya itu sangat menyakitkan dan merusak masa depan saya

Five years ago I was raped by my own friend. At that time I was afraid to tell anyone including my parents because of fear. Only now have I become aware that obviously my friend's actions were very painful and destroyed my future.

Kadiyem: Saya tak bisa mengungkapkan masalah ini kepada siapapun juga termasuk keluarga saya sendiri.

I cannot speak of this problem to anyone at all including my own family.

Gadis: Saya menyimpan sakit lair batin karena dinodai majikan lelaki (alias Bapak)

I am concealing an internal and external pain because I was disgraced by my male boss (alias Sir)

Semarang: Sampai sekarang belum ada yang mengerti. Saya juga belum bilang sama orang tua saya. Karena takut jatu ke tangan polisi.

Up to this time no one knows. I also have not yet told my parents because I am afraid it will fall into the hands of the police.

While the pain and defilement of rape that each of these women is forced to bear alone and in silence is hideous enough, what I want to focus attention on are what each interprets as the social consequences of her rape. Since, in most of the cases documented here, the actual sex act occurred many years ago, long before she was fully aware of the consequences, the trauma and its resulting anti-social behavior began much later:

Yogya Utara: Saat itu umur saya 7 tahun, sehingga belum begitu sadar akan akibatnya.	At that time I was 7 years old, so [I] wasn't yet aware of the consequences.
Rasty: Saya waktu itu kan belum ngerti apa-apa. Akhir-akhir ini terlintas dalam benak saya.	At that time [I] didn't know anything. Lately this has been on my mind.
En: 5 tahun yang lalu saya diperkosa oleh teman sendiri. ... Baru saat inilah saya baru sadar bahwa ternyata perbuatan teman saya itu sangat menyakitkan dan merusak masa depan saya.	Five years ago I was raped by my own friend. ... Only now have I become aware that obviously my friend's actions were very painful and destroyed my future.

The trauma is caused by the women becoming aware of what Sen (1994) described as 'awakened sexuality'. In these terms, awakened sexuality refers to any physical state beyond that of *suci* (pure). In some cases, the woman confessed to having touched herself. Socialization, however, teaches her that such thoughts, emotions or acts are disgusting, wrong, and unforgivable. When an unmarried woman's body becomes sexualized through whatever means, she is forced to accept the guilt. Yet, similar to the speech situations described in the stories above, women respond to their victimization, not through releasing their emotional excess and requesting help or support from loved ones, but rather through displaying the idealized, silent, restraint expected from those with power.

In the letters, the women state that they feel horrible remorse for their awakened sexuality to the extent that they avoid social contact. Their is no anger toward their victimized state, but rather acquiescence toward the social values that shape their evaluations. These low status women then, actively dilute information, concealing truth and disturbing facts that have the potential to cause disarray to their family's or friends' thoughts and feelings.

Kadiyem: Selama ini saya slalu menghindari teman-teman yang bermaksud bersahabat lebih dekat dengan saya. Saya menghindari dengan berbagai alasan. Saya cuma tak ingin menyakiti dan mengecewakan apa lagi orang-orang yang saya cinta. Karena saya merasa sudah tak perawan lagi saya ngak mau menyakiti hati mereka, maka lewat rubrik ini saya berharap bisa menemukan jalan keluarnya.	Up till now I always avoid friends with good intentions to become more intimate with me. I avoid them with all sorts of reasons. I just do not wish to offend or disappoint anyone especially people I love. Because I am no longer a virgin I don't want to hurt them, so through this column I hope to find a way out.
Rasti: saya takut dan menyesal sekali atas semua kejadian yang menimpa dan telah saya lakukan. Saya merasa kotor, najis, menjijikkan, rendah. Saya tidak berani membina hubungan dengan orang lain (baik dalam taraf pertemanan atau pacaran)	I am afraid and very much regret all that happened to me and the things I have already done. I feel dirty, defiled, disgusting, and low. I am afraid to develop relationships with other people (either as friends or boyfriends).
Yogya Utara: saya ingin sekali bisa bergabung, bergaul bersama teman-teman sebaya seperti halnya gadis lain, namun saya betul-betul merasa tidak bisa karena saya sudah kotor, tak suci lagi. Rasanya semua orang bisa melihat keadaan saya yang sesungguhnya.	I really wish I could gather, socialize with friends my own age like the other girls do, but I truly feel I cannot because I am dirty, no longer pure. It feels as if everyone can see my real state.

For each of these five young women, an experience of sexual abuse led directly to silence and withdrawal. It is the consequence of the act, the fear that knowledge by others most certainly leads to rejection, that silences these women. Violence lies not only in the actual rape, but the personal responsibility she must assume for the rest of her life and the fear she must suffer in isolation, lest anyone discover her secret. Loss of virginity for young women like Kadiyem is "offensive". Rasty and Yogya Utara avoid social contact because they know that as someone who is unmarried but no longer pure (*suci*), they are dirty (*kotor*), bear the stigma of their stain (*noda*), and hence, force upon themselves the consequences of permanent rejection. Each of the young women states that she can no longer bear the suffering and has no where else to turn for help.

In terms of the emotion schema then, we find that because of the event called rape, each of these women has responded publicly with silent acquiescence. The emotion they mentioned most was disgust, but it was not aimed at their rapist or their friends and family who could not help them. The disgust was aimed inwards at the victim because this is where they have learned that the responsibility lies.

SOCIAL EVENT:	rape
↓	↓
EMOTION:	disgust
↓↑	↓↑
PROPRIETY:	ideal woman
↓	↓
ACTION RESPONSE:	silent acquiescence

These five young women, between the ages of 17 and 20 years, have all mastered the dominant discourses which brand them as responsible because of their low status and gender. As among the factory cohort, there is no expression of anger or questioning of the hierarchy that imposes these standards. Instead, all suffer in the passive silence of the dominant fantasy of ideal femininity that here passes for high cultural values. In four of the cases the rape occurred when she was very young, and each states that it was only later that she became aware of the consequences of the act. In these cases, it was not so much the rape that had traumatized her but her failure to live up to the dominant fantasy of ideal femininity that society imposes upon her. The fear and self-disgust emerge from her awareness that she is *stained*, no longer acceptable to others, and that she alone is responsible for bearing the guilt of male weaknesses. Thus, she has taken it upon herself to suffer in silence rather than burden others with the knowledge of her crime.

Conclusions

These various forms of narratives of violence against women, from the workplace stories of abuse in the distant past to those of the present, those of rape, first-hand experience through anonymous letters, about sexual violence, have permitted us a very intimate look at gender roles in Indonesian society. By comparing all of these narratives by and about women's experience, consistencies that assist us to define the genre emerge. This chapter traces the ways in which social hierarchy and its resultant inequality have a major role to play. Not only have other scholars described how Javanese women accept and uphold gender inequality and the values, expectations, and responsibilities it demands. This paper has also shown how an elderly woman, young factory workers, and five young rape victims have responded to their experiences of violence by voluntarily accepting their ideal woman roles.

In order to understand the relationship between emotion, gender identity, culture, and power, the state with its control of discourse structures needs to be recognized as an active means of constructing social meaning while constraining agency and choice. We have just seen several cases in which I have tried to show how narrative analysis reveals not just the violent act itself but how the telling reflects speaker's evaluation of these acts. These narratives, then, reveal the constraints placed on women's permissible responses to acts of violence. This chapter has examined some of the speech styles of affect in women's talk about personal violence, and argued that these displays of emotion are channeled through sociocultural rules of propriety that are based upon a hierarchical ordering of gender and power positions over specific personal perspectives or feelings. I have also argued that we need a clearer understanding of the social values that shape how women learn socially appropriate manners of speaking.

As a means of examining Javanese women's identity, I focused on emotion in natural contexts to show a) that Javanese do indeed express their emotions, b) what form these expressions may take, and c) how these expressions are shaped by sociocultural values of hierarchy, respect and power. Not only did we see how Javanese women express emotion within narratives of personal abuse and pain, but we also saw that in these stories, all of the suffering was caused by men and relations of unequal power. In none of these interactions, however, did a speaker express blame or anger toward these inequalities or the social systems that defend them. On the contrary, the narratives show how each of the victims attempted to deal with her suffering through displaying the ideal Javanese woman as she strongly defends the notions of formality and power that oppress her. Expectations of silence, refinement, and avoidance of disturbing information guided each of these speakers through her difficulty. The factory workers' narratives in particular showed how they did not reject the inequality, just the behaviors of the empowered that did not conform to their expectations of fair play.

In this way, I expanded the traditional definitions of speech levels as tokens of spiritual potency, emotional equanimity, and respect to show how they actually assist women in evaluating the personal experiences they narrate.

Evaluation as display of emotion was firmly based on the speech levels and other indexes of hierarchical positions. All emotion discourses reflected formality and respect as the right and true order of things. A speaker could 'fight the system' so to speak by showing how empowered individuals may have abused her, but in each case, her fight involved a reframing of self from victim to respected person by describing herself as responding to her indignity with perfect propriety. If she were truly *alus* (refined, calm, smooth), she would show in her narratives how she behaved with appropriate refinement and was ultimately treated with respect. Yet, in none of these cases did she receive any compensation for her heavy loss. In addition to shifting speech levels, it was also shown how code-switching from Javanese to Indonesian to even English was an additional marker of affective stance, capable of defining and particularly, *re*defining relative positions, again permitting victimized speakers the opportunity to confront and challenge their oppressors through a means that would never challenge or even dent the rigidity of the system.

The types of evaluation used suggest that different styles of evaluation achieve different functions. Within this corpus, reported speech appeared in stories where contextual constraints required careful self-monitoring or where speakers shifted from general description to self-indexing. In situations which were more emotional and less guarded, evaluation was of the external type with adjectives, intensifiers, and frequent frame breaks to inject comments in Javanese *ngoko*. Yet, in terms of agency and self-indexing, face-to-face conversations show how these Javanese women vary in their abilities to self-index. The elderly speaker used more respectful speech levels to mark utterances that indexed her own words and those who spoke to her. In this respect, speech level shifts are seen as stylistic cues through which personal interpretations of social relationships are clarified, and as such, they are an integral part of the Javanese strategy for expressing an emotional self. The younger speakers, on the other hand, all reveal strong tendencies to not index themselves at all as responsible agents. In these stories, as in many others in the corpus, subjects tended to remain ambiguous or to refer to others, i.e., not the speaker, or the group as a whole. Responsibility for the contents of the story is then divided among many. These variations in the distribution of agency and responsibility affect styles of evaluative speech. In terms of the conversational data, reported speech as an internal marker of affect seems to be a less aggressive and more refined type of evaluation than the external use of adjectives and intensifiers. In this corpus, the more involved the speaker, the more external evaluation she will use, the opposite of what Labov (1984; 1972) and Tannen (1989) claim for American speakers. This becomes clearer when placed in conjunction with the social constraints on storytelling.

Reported speech indexes a speakers' words and thus functions to involve a speaker with her community of others in the story. External evaluation indexes the current speaker and her immediate context, and thus makes a point about both. It is this variation in group and self-indexing in terms of the social values of emotion and propriety that deserves further investigation.

The emotion schema, adapted from Lutz (1986), was helpful in recognizing how the social event and emotion response were shaped by propriety as the cultural values through which the emotion is filtered. Charting response helped to reveal how Ibu Asmoro saw refinement as the dignified presentation of self within hierarchically structured scales of giving and receiving status and respect, whereas the younger generation of factory women seemed much more affective in their response, what I argue was evidence of their acceptance of oppression. They do cry, and they do mock their superiors (unlike Ibu Asmoro), but they also do want to honor their rules, expecting the righteous, moral order of status and worth to hold. In none of these narratives are women attempting to challenge the social hierarchy. The emotion schema helps to reveal the pain evoked by events that expose discrepant beliefs in the social roles and behaviors of those in power. In comparison to the crude and irresponsible behaviors of the (mostly) male superiors, women's victimization and abuse are not as bad, providing the victim maintains her dignified composure. In this way, those that hear her story are not 'startled' and she herself can actively reframe her victimization as a display of her own superiority in terms of high Javanese ideals.

Through the rape victims' silence and the factory workers' evocation of Javanese scales of refinement in their stories, we can observe the women actively evaluating and redefining their own and others' social status markers. Emotion display is then channeled through the descriptions of *others* who can be ridiculed for *lacking* the attributes that should ideally mark their positions of power, and *not* for representing power or even abusing it. The oppressiveness of the social hierarchy is not at issue here. But the behaviors appropriate for occupying positions of power are.

In concluding, statements about power and gender in Java need to be reinterpreted beyond generalizations that claim women and other low status people enjoy more freedoms from the heavy constraints and demands of Javanese sociocultural values. It is not just high status males who maintain the behaviors that are emblematic of divine energy and mystical inner strength and evidenced by poise, restraint, and equanimity in all social interactions. Women, and particularly women as victims, also behave in these exemplary manners. But as this study attempted to show, their reasons were very different. While men are said to avoid emotional behavior in order to maintain a facade of power, women have no such claims to power. They avoid emotional display in order to maintain the facade of propriety that empowers men at their expense.

Notes

1. Personal communication from Romo Barsana Condrapurnama, a well-known local paranormal, abdi-dalem [servant of the royal court], and expert in local philosophy, gamelan, and history. Romo was the director of Museum Sonobudaya until his retirement. He now runs the Paku Alaman museum.
2. To achieve this end, I present private discourses of working class urban women within their own natural networks of friends and family to show how women express affect in their narratives of personal experience. The fieldwork from which this information comes was carried out in 1991–1993, and again in 1995–6 in the city of Yogyakarta, Central Java for a study of conversational narrative among working class women. For their trust, thanks are due to the women whose voices were represented here. In addition, thanks are due to Rifka Annisa, Krido Mardowo, Kedaulatan Rakyat.
3. Atong (a teenager, see Berman, forthcoming) and Sari (below), shift into Indonesian in addition to and often rather than different levels of Javanese, a change typical of the younger generation of Javanese speakers no longer able or willing to master the complexities of kråmå. There are other reasons too. Since Indonesian is the language of education, ideology, and mass media, level switching re-constructs the styles associated with such domains.
4. Ibu Asmoro was 78 years old at the time of the recording. She was still the respected elder of the palace singers (*pesindhen*) after over 64 years of faithful service as a servant (*abdi-dalem*) in the sultan's palace. These servants receive very little in terms of financial compensation for their dedication. Thus, most servants needed to find alternative resources. Radio Republik Indonesia was the only lucrative alternative employment for musicians within the era Ibu Asmoro discusses. Ibu Asmoro's story refers to the late 1930s or early 1940s before Indonesian independence from the Dutch.

    Ibu Umaya is also an *abdi-dalem* and *pesindhen* but she is at least 35 years younger than her interlocutor here. I am also present and recording this interaction, but had remained silent during this story.
5. Key to transcriptions:

    In order to clarify speech level shifts, the following key is used:

    Javanese *ngoko* is in plain font;
    madyo style is in simple bold;
    basic *kromo* is in bold font with underline;
    kromo honorifics, either *kromo inggil* or *kromo andhap* are in bold with double underline.
    Indonesian appears in italics.

    . falling intonation and noticeable pause.
    ? rising intonation and noticeable pause.
    , slight rise and slight pause.
    : lengthened syllable
    // interrupted turn
    [ ] words in brackets are not direct translations but added to assist interpretation.

    Orthographic representations are all consistent with modified Javanese spelling with few exceptions. Truncated words are presented phonetically and final a, pronounced /ɔ/ as in *law*, is spelled å. Final k is pronounced /ʔ/ but spelling remains standard.

6. The data examined here are from a 45 minute conversation in Javanese and Indonesian I recorded in Yogyakarta, Central Java in early 1993. I had been recording talk in this urban, working class family home for over a year and was a well-established part of daily life. Sari, aged 26, was the second daughter in the Budiharjo family. She was joined by Sigah and Endang, two of her co-workers at the factory. Sari was the eldest but not by much. All of these women were unmarried.
7. Since these stories have no specific temporal markers, only relational, it is impossible to know when the overtime and the pay cuts had begun. Scanning previous transcripts with Sari does not help as the factory is never mentioned. She did not speak about events such as these that conflict with social norms and expectations.
8. See the key to transcription. There is no *kråmå* speech in this conversation so underlining refers to repetition here, one of the most frequent forms of affective marking. As usual, Indonesian language is in italics.
9. While this only amounts to roughly US$12., this is a month's salary in Central Java — but still not enough to live on. To put it into clearer focus, this amount is more than double Ibu Asmoro's palace salary.
10. The Bataks are an ethnic group from Northern Sumatra. The Bataks, according to Javanese wisdom, are loud, aggressive thieves that lack refinement.
11. Singkek is a derogatory that refers to a Chinese immigrant that maintains Chinese habits (Echols & Shadily 1989).
12. Paolo Freire's *Pedagogy of the Oppressed* offers a possible explanation for the role of authoritarian control in the cognitive and behavioral development of the peasant classes or *wong cilik*. Freire described this relationship as one of *prescription* since it "represents the imposition of one individual's choice upon another, transforming the consciousness of the person prescribed to into one that conforms with the prescriber's consciousness. Thus, the behavior of the oppressed is a prescribed behavior, following as it does the guidelines of the oppressor (Freire 1993 [1970]: 28–9)". We need to dwell deeper on an oppressed model of humanity to better understand why, as Freire also states, "the oppressed [...] tend themselves to become oppressors (Freire 1993 [1970]: 27–28)."
13. Bantul is a rural village just south of Yogyakarta and roughly 8–10 kms. from the factory.
14. In the end, and without any notice, all the women who were involved in the 'protest' were suddenly fired through military intervention at gunpoint. See Berman (forthcoming).
15. PKK is the primary channel through which the state filters its official ideologies to women (see Sullivan 1990, 1994; Suryakusuma 1996; Djajadiningrat-Nieuwenhuis 1987; Weiringa 1992.)
16. In fact, the hierarchical structure mirrors the position of each member's husband, i.e., women acquire position *because* of their husbands, not because of their own capabilities (N. Sullivan 1994).
17. I have recently been told that the five points called *Panca Darma Wanita* have been superseded by the 10 points of PKK. PKK's 10 central points are seen everywhere: on signs in front of every government office right down to the level of village heads called RW and RT, and in relief on gateposts (across from Pancasila) at the entrances to every village and village sub-section throughout the country. The 10 points are: 1. to experience and spread Pancasila, 2. take part in community work activities (gotong-royong), 3. take responsibility for food, clothing, and housing, 4. keep order in the household, 5. be concerned with education, 6. possess skills, 7. be

knowledgeable in health issues, 8. develop a cooperative lifestyle, 9. preserve the environment, 10. possess healthy intentions.

18. As N. Sullivan (1994: 146) notes, most women will go to enormous trouble to avoid causing their menfolk loss of face. Even the wives of the laziest and most useless men will not talk openly about their lack of responsibility to the family.
19. 'Self-censorship' is also the term used to understand the reproduction of elite ideologies and perspectives in the print media. See Hill (1994) and Sen (1994).
20. Emphasis for all these texts is presented exactly as it was in the original article.
21. I had hoped to check with court records to compare length of jail term with details such as virginity, etc., but could not get permission from local courts.

References

Anderson, Benedict. 1990. *Language and Power: Exploring Political Cultures in Indonesia.* Ithaca: Cornell University Press.

Armon-Jones, Claire. 1986. "The thesis of constructionism". In Rom Harré (ed), *The Social Construction of Emotions.* Oxford: Basil Blackwell, 32–56.

Bakhtin, Mikhail. [1934]1981. *The Dialogical Imagination.* Caryl Emerson and Michael Holquist (eds and trans) Austin: University of Texas Press.

Berman, Laine. 1998. *Speaking through the Silence: Narrative, Social Convention and Power in Java.* Oxford Series in Anthropological Linguistics. New York: Oxford University Press.

Blackburn, Susan. 1994. "Gender Interests and Indonesian Democracy". In Bourchier, David and John Legge (eds), *Democracy in Indonesia 1950s and 1990s.* Monash Papers on Southeast Asia No. 31, Centre for Southeast Asian Studies. Melbourne: Monash University.

Bourdieu, Pierre. 1977. *Outline of a Theory of Practice.* Cambridge: Cambridge University Press.

Brenner, Suzanne. 1995. "Why women rule the roost: Rethinking Javanese ideologies of gender and self-control" In Aihwa Ong and Michael Peletz (eds) *Bewitching Women and Pious Men.* Berkeley: University of California Press, 19–50.

Burke, Kenneth. 1969. *A Rhetoric of Motives.* Berkeley: University of California Press.

Cameron, Deborah. 1990. *The Feminist Critique of Language: A Reader.* New York: Routledge.

Djajadiningrat-Nieuwenhuis, Madelon. 1987. "Ibuism and Priyayization: Paths to power?" In E. Locher-Scholten and A. Niehof (eds), 43–51.

Douglas, Mary. 1982. *Natural Symbols.* New York: Pantheon.

Duranti, Alessandro. 1988. "Intentions, language, and social action in a Samoan context". *Journal of Pragmatics* 12: 13–33.

Dwiraharjo, Maryono. 1991. *Tingkat tutur dalam bahasa Jawa cerminan adab sopan santun berbahasa.* Paper presented at Kongress Bahasa Jawa: Semarang.

Ellul, Jacques. 1973. *Propaganda: The Formation of Men's Attitudes.* New York: Random House.

Errington, J. Joseph. 1984. "Self and self-conduct among the Javanese priyayi elite". *American Ethnologist* 11: 275–290.

———. 1988. *Structure and Style in Javanese.* Philadelphia, PA: University of Pennsylvania Press.

Fairclough, Norman. 1989. *Language and Power.* London: Longman.

Freeman, Rebecca & McElhinny, Bonnie. 1995 "Language and gender". In Sandra McKay and Nancy Hornberger (eds), *Sociolinguistics and Language Teaching.* Cambridge: Cambridge University Press, 218–280.

Geertz, Clifford. 1973. *The Interpretation of Cultures: Selected Essays.* New York: Basic Books.

———. 1960. *The Religion of Java.* NY: The Free Press.

Gramsci, Antonio. 1971. *Selections from the Prison Notebooks.* Edited and translated by Quintin Hoare and Geoffrey Smith. London: Lawrence and Wishart.

Hanan, David. 1993. "Nji Ronggeng: Another paradigm for erotic spectacle in the cinema". In Virginia Matheson Hooker (ed), *Culture and society in New Order Indonesia.* Kuala Lumpur: Oxford University Press, 87–115.

Harré, Rom. 1986. "An outline of the social constructionist viewpoint". In Rom Harré (ed) *The Social Construction of Emotions.* Oxford: Basil Blackwell, 2–14.

Heider, Karl. 1991. *Landscapes of Emotion.* Cambridge: Cambridge University Press.

Hellwig, Tineke. 1987. "Rape in two Indonesian pop novels: An analysis of the female image". In E. Locher-Scholten and A. Niehof (eds), 240–254.

Hill, David. 1994. *The Press in New Order Indonesia.* Asia Paper No. 4, University of Western Australia Press.

Irvine, Judith. 1990. "Registering affect: Heteroglossia in the linguistic expression of emotion". In Catherine Lutz and Lila Abu-Lughod (eds), 126–185.

Keeler, Ward. 1987. *Javanese Shadow Plays, Javanese Selves.* Princeton: Princeton University Press.

———. 1990. "Speaking of gender". In Jane Atkinson and Shelly Errington (eds), *Power and Difference: Gender in Island Southeast Asia.* Paolo Alto, CA: Stanford University Press, 127–152.

Labov, William. 1972. "The transformation of experience in narrative syntax". *Language in the Inner City.* Philadelphia: University of Pennsylvania Press, 354–396.

———. 1984. "Intensity". In Deborah Schiffrin (ed), *Meaning, Form, and Use in Context: Linguistic Applications.* Washington DC: Georgetown University Press, 43–70.

Levinson, Stephen. 1983. *Pragmatics.* Cambridge: Cambridge University Press.

Locher-Scholten, E. and a. Niehof (eds). 1987. *Indonesian women in Focus.* Dordrecht-Holland: Foris Publications.

Lutz, Catherine. 1982. "The domain of emotion words in Ifaluk". *American Ethnologist* 9: 113–28.

———. 1986. "Emotion, Thought, and Estrangement: Emotion as a Cultural Category". *Cultural Anthropology* 1: 287–309.

———. 1990. "Registering Affect". In Catherine Lutz and Lila Abu-Lughod (eds), 126–61.

Lutz, Catherine and Geoffrey White. 1986. "The Anthropology of Emotions". *Annual Review of Anthropology* 15: 405–36.

Lutz, Catherine and Lila Abu-Lughod (eds). 1990. *Language and the Politics of Emotion.* Cambridge: Cambridge University Press.

Mead, George H. 1934. *Mind, Self, & Society: From the Standpoint of a Social Behaviorist.* C. Morris (ed). Chicago: University of Chicago Press.

Mühlhäusler, Peter and Rom Harré. 1990. *Personal Pronouns.* Oxford: Basil Blackwell.

Mulvey, Laura. 1975. "Visual pleasure and the narrative cinema". *Screen* 16(3): 6–18.

Ochs, Elinor. 1988. *Culture and Language Development: Language Acquisition and Language Socialization in a Samoan Village.* Cambridge University Press.

Sears, Laurie (ed). 1996. *Fantasizing the Feminine in Indonesia.* Durham: Duke University Press.

Sen, Krishna. 1994. *Indonesian Cinema: Framing the New Order.* London: Zed Books Ltd.

Siegel, James. 1986. *Solo in the New Order: Language and Hierarchy in an Indonesian City.* Princeton: Princeton University Press.

Smith-Hefner, Nancy. 1988. "Women and politeness: the Javanese example". *Language in Society* 17: 535–554.

Stark, Frank. 1996. *Communicative Interaction, Power, and the State: A Method.* Toronto: University of Toronto Press.

Sullivan, Norma. 1994. *Masters and Managers: A Study of Gender Relations in Urban Java.* Women in Asia Series, St Leonards, NSW: Allen & Unwin.

Sunindyo, Saraswati. 1996. "Murder, gender and the media: Sexualizing politics and violence". In L. Sears (ed), 120–139.

Suryakusuma, Julia. 1996. "The state and sexuality in New Order Indonesia". In L. Sears (ed), 92–119.

Tannen 1989. *Talking Voices: Repetition, Dialogue, and Imagery in Conversational Discourse.* Cambridge University Press.

Tiwon, Sylvia. 1996. "Models and maniacs: Articulating the female in Indonesia". In L. Sears (ed), 47–70.

Van Dijk, Teun. 1994. "Ideological Discourse Analysis". Unpublished ms.

Weiringa, Saskia. 1992. "Ibu or the beast: Gender interests in two Indonesian women's organizations". *Feminist Review.* No. 41, Summer.

White, Geoffrey. 1990. "Moral Discourse and the Rhetoric of Emotions". In Catherine Lutz and Lila Abu-Lughod (eds), 46–68.

Wolf, Diane. 1996. "Javanese factory daughters: Gender, the state, and industrial capitalism". In L. Sears (ed), 140–162.

Wolff, John and Soepomo Poedjosoedarmo. 1982. *Communicative Codes in Central Java.* Data Paper #116 Southeast Asia Program. Ithaca: Cornell University Press.

Public and Private Voices

Japanese Style Shifting and the Display of Affective Intensity

Cynthia Dickel Dunn

Theories of Japanese Selfhood: *Ura* and *Omote* as Behavioral Modes[1]

The Japanese sense of self has long been described as contextual, neither fixed nor absolute, but rather shifting in accordance with the social situation. Research on the Japanese construction of self has posited contrasts between two different modalities of interactional behavior, one of which is controlled, restrained, and disciplined, the other more open, spontaneous, and emotionally expressive (Lebra 1976; Doi 1986; Rosenberger 1989 and 1994; Bachnik 1992; Tobin 1992; Cook 1996a). Often these contrasts are described with the Japanese terms *omote* and *ura*. *Omote* literally means outside, front, or surface; more metaphorically, it implies the world of appearances and a mode of behavior which is public, onstage, or on display. In contrast, *ura* is that which is back or hidden, not on public display. Thus *omote* behavior is more restrained and concerned with social appearances, while *ura* behavior involves the freer expression of both positive and negative affect. The contrast is well exemplified by the Japanese as they are most often seen, and indeed stereotyped, by foreigners as unfailingly polite, stiff, and formal, and the perhaps equally stereotypical image of Japanese drinking parties where people sing and dance, joke with each other, play games, and end the evening singing Auld Lang Syne with their arms clasped around each other's shoulders.

Such contrasts have also been related to a distinction between the behavior appropriate to *uchi* 'in-group' or *soto* 'out-group' situations (Lebra 1976; Bachnik 1992). Emotional spontaneity is associated with intimacy and in-group situations. The open display of affect both asserts and presumes an emotional closeness, while one is expected to be more restrained in the face one shows *soto*, the 'outside' world. These associations between in-group and spontaneity or out-group and restraint are not absolute. Groups such as a family, school, or workplace allow varying degrees of emotional expressivity across different activities, and hierarchical roles may mean greater restraint for lower status members even in intimate situations (e.g., Rosenberger 1994). Nonetheless, the open display of affect is an important means for building a sense of in-group belonging and rapport.

Although certain modes of behavior are normatively associated with particular groups, activities, or situations, it is not simply the situation which determines the extent of affective expression. Different actors may display varying degrees of emotional intensity or restraint even in the same situation, thus constructing different types of relationships and styles of self-presentation. *Ura* and *omote* are not inherent features of a situation but are constructed in and through actors' behavior. It is this construction of *ura* and *omote* styles of behavior and the shifting along a continuum between the two that I wish to examine here.

Anthropological research on emotion has demonstrated both the culturally constructed nature of emotional experience and its links to local understandings of personhood and social relationships. Recent research in this area has examined not only how emotions are conceptualized and described in particular cultures, but also how emotion is displayed and enacted in discourse. In addition to considering lexical items and talk *about* emotion, linguistic anthropologists have begun to investigate the linguistic means conventionally used to *index* affect in a variety of languages and cultures (Irvine 1982 and 1990; Ochs and Schieffelin 1989; Lutz and Abu-Lughod 1990; Besnier 1990). Such investigations of how people perform as well as describe emotion add another dimension to our understanding of the cultural construction of emotion within and across different societies.

In this chapter, I contribute to a growing body of research on the linguistic indexing of affect through an investigation of how emotional intensity is communicated in Japan. As Ochs and Schieffelin (1989: 14–15) note, linguistic forms which index intensity of affect appear to be more numerous than those which specify the type of affect. Such affect intensifiers display the speaker's degree of emotional involvement in what he/she is saying. Ethnographic and linguistic research in areas such as Java (Geertz 1960), Samoa (Shore 1982), Senegal (Irvine 1982 and 1990), and Iran (Beeman 1986) has shown that the indexing of degrees of emotional involvement or restraint is an important means for the definition of social situations and roles in a number of different cultures.

In the following analysis, I examine how Japanese speakers shift along a culturally-meaningful continuum from more emotionally expressive to more emotionally distanced or restrained speech styles. Discussions of *ura/omote* in the literature almost invariably mention patterns of language use as a distinguishing feature of these two behavioral modes. Yet existing studies have not provided an analysis of how particular linguistic features are used in context to create a more *ura* or *omote* situational atmosphere. Through the analysis of actual instances of discourse, I examine how a variety of linguistic features are used to construct more affectively engaged or distanced styles and how such styles, in turn, become cultural resources for the presentation of self and construction of social relationships. I follow Bachnik (1992) in arguing that *ura* and *omote* are best understood, not as binary oppositions, but as a continuum; behavior is always more expressive or more restrained compared to some other point on the continuum. I further argue that the nature of this continuum is best demonstrated through the micro-analysis of situated linguistic practice. The present analysis focuses on speeches given by two Japanese college students at a meeting of a student speech club. I show how, within the same context, one of the speakers shifted into an emotionally engaged style which built rapport with her audience, while the other remained more distanced and impersonal. The analysis shows how the linguistic form and content of the speeches worked together to create different rhetorical effects and index the speaker's affective stance towards the audience. Such a micro-analysis of actual instances of discourse illuminates the process of shifting along the *ura-omote* continuum and allows us to see how these cultural categories are created in and through individual behavior.

Linguistic Indices of Affective Engagement in Japanese

Japanese is rich in surface-segmentable forms which function primarily to index social relationships, situations and the speaker's affective and epistemological stance. A great deal of research has focused on structural descriptions of these linguistic systems, including extensive work on honorifics (Martin 1964; Minami et al. 1974; Harada 1976; Ide 1982; Shibatani 1990) and interactional particles (Uyeno 1971; Tanaka 1977; Tsuchihashi 1983). Most such studies are implicitly normative, taking a rule-governed approach to the phenomena in question and elucidating abstract patterns of use or the meanings of forms in isolation. Only recently have researchers begun to investigate the use of such forms in the context of actual spoken or written discourse (e.g., Ikuta 1983; Cook 1990a, 1990b, and 1996a; Maynard 1993).

My purpose here is not to repeat earlier structural studies of particular linguistic indices, but rather to show how speakers creatively use such forms in context to create cultural meanings. I analyze the use of a variety of linguistic forms in the two speeches described above, showing how these forms were combined with particular rhetorical strategies to index varying degrees of emotional intensity or restraint. My approach combines a quantitative analysis of the frequency of particular linguistic variables in the two speeches with a discourse analysis showing how these variables were used to produce particular rhetorical effects. In the remainder of this section, I briefly introduce the linguistic variables to be considered.

One of the most salient indicators of the speaker's stance towards the situation and addressee in Japanese is the form of the predicate. The Japanese predicate involves an alteration between *direct* and *distal* forms in which distal forms are marked by the *desu* form of the copula or the addition of *-masu* to the verb stem.[2] For example, both of the following sentences can be used to mean 'I'm going,' but one is direct and the other distal:

(1) *Iku.* Direct form
go

(2) *Iki-masu.* Distal form
go-DIST
'[I'm] going.'

Direct forms are the first forms acquired by young children within the family and are thus associated with intimacy and spontaneous self-expression. Distal forms are acquired later, as part of a more disciplined, socially aware (*omote*) style of behavior which children learn to use in dealing with the outside world (Cook 1996a). The use of distal forms expresses interpersonal distance, respect, and a public, outward-facing social persona while direct forms index a greater degree of intimacy, empathy, and open or spontaneous self-expression (Ikuta 1983; Cook 1996a). As the norm for conversation among intimates, direct forms do not in and of themselves index emotional intensity. However, a shift from distal to direct or the interjection of direct forms into primarily distal discourse can indicate empathy and rapport with the addressee or the speaker's spontaneous emotional reaction.

A second indicator of affective stance is the use of a group of particles variously referred to as sentence particles, 'final particles' (*shuujoshi*), or interactional particles (Maynard 1993). These particles do not directly affect the referential content of a message, but rather index the speaker's epistemological and/or affective stance towards that content. Interactional particles discussed here include *ne*, *yo*, and *no*. *Ne* is used to request or assert agreement, indexing alignment and common affective ground between speaker and addressee (Uyeno

1971; Cook 1990a; Maynard 1993). *Yo* is used for emphatic assertion of the speaker's statement (Uyeno 1971; Maynard 1993). *No*, which also functions as a nominalizer, indexes presupposed group or common knowledge; it can indicate explanation, emphasis, and the building of rapport or common ground (McGloin 1980; Cook 1990b). Such particles are very common in conversation and provide an affective frame or comment on what the speaker is saying.

A final linguistic feature to be considered here is the use of postposing or right-dislocation. Standard Japanese word order is SOV. The postposing or right dislocation of elements after the verb can be used as a type of repair, but may also function to add emotional emphasis (Hinds 1982). The use of right and left dislocation for affective emphasis has also been noted in other languages such as French (Blyth 1995), Italian (Duranti and Ochs 1979), and Wolof (Irvine 1982). When postposing is used in Japanese, the focus is on the predicate, with the specifications of who, what, or how following afterward. This pattern can strengthen or emphasize propositional statements and directives.

In the following sections, I show how these various forms are combined with such discourse-level strategies as reported speech or thought, representations of emotional states, assertions of empathy, and various forms of directives to index the speaker's emotional engagement and build rapport with the addressee(s).

The Ethnographic Context: Officers' Reports in the Speech Club

The data to be considered here are drawn from a larger ethnographic and sociolinguistic study of speech styles and style shifting among Japanese college students. All of these students were members of an English speech and debate society at a women's college in Tokyo. During seven months of fieldwork, I observed and participated in various club activities including practice sessions for working on speeches, organizational meetings for conducting club business, speech contests, and socializing at bars and restaurants. The event on which I focus here was an end-of-the-semester meeting at which the club officers were giving reports to the membership. Approximately thirty club members were seated at desks arranged in a square, with the officers all seated along one side. The president opened the meeting and asked each of the officers to give a report on the year's activities and also to provide comments or reflections (*hanseiten*) on how the year had gone.

Compared with daily practice sessions and socializing, the club meeting was a relatively formal, *omote* situation. The size of the group, the predetermined speaking order, the monologic nature of the speeches themselves, and the fact that people spoke from their positional identities as officers all contributed to this formal atmosphere (cf. Irvine 1979; Atkinson 1982). Forms of address and reference were more official and socially distant than usual. In other club activities, members most often addressed each other with personal names plus the endearing suffix *-chan* or the more respectful *-senpai* 'senior' for students older than the speaker. During the meeting, however, fellow members were carefully referred to by full name, family name, or their title as officer, all followed by the respectful suffix *-san* (roughly equivalent to English 'Mr./Ms.'). Distal forms were used more often than in ordinary conversations among same-age club members, and there were fewer uses of interactional particles and other markers of affective engagement. As an example of this contrast, Tables 1 and 2 compare the frequency of distal use and interactional particle use in the officers' reports with the use of these forms in a social conversation between two of the same club members (Akiko and Ritsuko).

Table 1. Percentage of Predicates in Distal Form: Meeting and Conversation[a]

	Meeting	Conversation
Kiyomi	55/183 (30%)	NA
Toshiko	45/65 (69%)	NA
Ritsuko	32/73 (44%)	0/163 (0%)[b]
Akiko	74/103 (72%)	4/99 (4%)[b]

[a] See Dunn 1996 for a detailed description of how the variables were defined and operationalized. Chi square figures at the bottom of each table include the Yates Correction which is recommended for small sample sizes or small expected frequencies. The algorithm used was $\Sigma(|O - E| - 0.5)^2/E$ where O = Observed Frequency and E = Expected Frequency.

[b] $p < .001$

Table 2. Percentage of Clauses with Interactional Particles: Meeting and Conversation

	Meeting	Conversation
Kiyomi	1/157 (0.6%)	NA
Toshiko	0/104 (0%)	NA
Ritsuko	2/89 (2%)	48/239 (20%)*
Akiko	0/122 (0%)	25/125 (20%)*

* $p < .001$

In general, the officers' reports were impersonal and information-oriented, listing the different club activities and who had participated, the members who had competed in speech contests, which funds had been spent for what purposes, etc. In their comments and reflections on the past year, however, some of the officers shifted to a more personal tone as they talked about the need for members to put more effort into club activities. Ritsuko and Kiyomi, in particular, displayed a greater degree of affective intensity in the persuasive rhetoric of the second part of their speeches than in their earlier, more factual reports. In the following section, I analyze an excerpt from this part of Ritsuko's speech to demonstrate how various linguistic features were combined to display affective involvement and build rapport with the audience. I then compare Ritsuko's speech with that of another officer, Akiko, who also attempted to encourage greater participation in club activities, but who used a more distanced and affectively restrained voice to do so.

Ritsuko's Speech: The Display of 'True Feeling'

Ritsuko began her speech with a description of the different speech contests, which members had participated, and who had won prizes. After providing this information about the semester's activities, she announced, "A word from me" (*Atashi kara hito koto*). After this framing of her speech as a personal comment, Ritsuko began encouraging everyone to work harder at writing speeches and participating in contests. In this section of the speech, Ritsuko's use of distal forms decreased dramatically. This can be seen in Table 3 which compares her frequency of distal forms and interactional particles before and after the comment "*Atashi kara hito koto*" (Parts A and B respectively). Note that in the first part of her speech, Ritsuko's rate of distal use was not dissimilar to the overall rates of other officers such as Akiko (72%) and Toshiko (69%). In appealing to the members for greater efforts, however, she shifted to a much greater use of direct forms. Her use of direct forms displayed the strength of her emotional involvement in what she was saying and emphasized her in-group solidarity with other club members.

Both the form and the content of the later part of Ritsuko's speech functioned to build an emotional rapport with the audience. She repeatedly asserted empathy with their feelings while also expressing her own enthusiasm and affective engagement. In addition to the increase in direct forms, she began using interactional particles, postposed elements, strong directives, and quotations of what her audience might think or feel in a particular situation. The following

Table 3. Frequency of Selected Linguistic Variables in Ritsuko's Speech

	Part A	Part B
Percentage of predicates in distal form	27/42 (64%)	5/31 (16%)[a]
Percentage of clauses with interactional particles	0/49 (0%)	2/40 (5%)[b]

[a] $p < .001$
[b] $p = .39$

excerpt from the second part of Ritsuko's speech shows how the different linguistic and rhetorical forms worked together to build a sense of emotional intensity.

Excerpt 1: Ritsuko's Speech at Student Meeting[3]

1. *Maa./ I-kooki./ ippon kaki-ageru*
well final-semester one write-give
no ga kihon na-n da keredomo, /3.0/
NOM SUBJ standard COP-NOM COP but

'Well, one—, the standard is to write one speech
during the second semester but,'
2. *Nn./*
nn
'Nn.'
3. *Zehi,/ kyoo kara,/ hajime-te*
definitely today from begin-and
kudasai./ Supiichi o kaku koto./
give(H+) speech DO write NOM
'Please definitely begin today. Writing speeches.'
4. *Ra—ze—rainen no zenki ni muke-te./*
next-year GEN first-semester to meet-and
'for nex— for the first semester next year.'
5. *Mo—/ ano—/ kyoo kara,/ hajime-nai to,/*
um today from begin-not if
'If you don't begin today,'
6. *mata kitto haru ni na-tta toki ni,*
again surely spring to become-PAST time at
chokuzen ni na-tte, aa kai-te-nai tte
just-before to become-and aa write-and-not QT

koto ni/ zettai kurikaeshi-te shimau node,/
NOM to certainly repeat-and end-up since
'then when spring comes, at the last minute, you'll just end up, Oh I haven't written it yet! all over again so,'

7. *kyoo kara/ hajime-te kudasai./*
today from begin-and give(H+)
Risaachi demo./ Benkyoo demo./
research even study even
'please begin today. Doing research. And studying.'

Ritsuko began by stating the general standard for writing speeches, and then issued her first directive in line 3. Here she used the intensifier *zehi* which has a meaning of insistence: 'by all means' or 'be sure to'. The descriptions of what the audience was to begin (writing speeches) and the purpose (for the next semester) were postposed after the imperative (Please begin today). This postposing made the directive sound more direct and forceful, although it was also mitigated with the polite *kudasai* (literally the honorific imperative form of 'give'; roughly equivalent to 'please'). In lines 5–6, Ritsuko went on to specify what happens when people don't prepare in advance. Her direct quotation of a person's "inner speech" in this situation ("Oh I haven't written it yet!") invited her audience to enter imaginatively into the hypothetical scenario she created. Rather than stating that they would be in a panic, she enacted the experience of panic. Line 7 is another directive, with the specifying elements again postposed to foreground the imperative force.

In the next part of the speech, Ritsuko continued to offer directives and talk about her audience's emotions when giving speeches.

Excerpt 1 continued

8. *De,/ supiichi to iu no o kaki-age-te,/*
and speech QT say NOM DO write-finish-and
'And, finish writing your speeches and,'

9. *de,/ purezenteeshon shi-te,/*
and presentation do-and
'and present them and,'

10. *hajimete,/ sono omoshirosa/ toka,/*
first-time that interest such-as
'for the first time, things like the fascination and,'

11. *Sugoi kowai mono na-n da kedomo,/*
very scary thing COP-NOM COP but
'It's very scary but,'

12. *Demo,/ nanka sono kaikan tte iu ka,*
but somehow that pleasurable-feeling QT say QM
suteeji ni tatsu kaikan toka ga
stage on stand pleasurable-feeling such-as SUBJ
wakaru to omou no ne./
understand QT think NOM IP
'But, somehow I think you'll understand that wonderful feeling, that, how can I put it, things like that wonderful feeling of being onstage.'

Here Ritsuko referred again to her audience's emotional experience, expressing her understanding of how scary it can be to perform in public in a foreign language, while also hoping that they would be able to experience the thrill of doing so successfully. The sentence-final forms in line 12, "… *omou no ne*," contribute to the building of emotional rapport with the audience. The verb 'I think' is in the direct form (*omou*) which can communicate intimacy, empathy, or strong feeling. The particle *no* adds an explanatory tone (*because* you will have this wonderful feeling…) and also frames Ritsuko's statement as shared group knowledge within the speech club. Finally, *ne* asserts common affective ground with the audience, soliciting their understanding and agreement with Ritsuko's projection of their future emotional state. The combination of forms thus signals an affective reaching out to the audience.

Similar linguistic and rhetorical features can be observed in the next several lines. These include statements that Ritsuko really does understand how the audience feels (lines 14–15) and the use of intensifiers such as *honto* 'really' or 'truly' and *zehi* 'definitely' (lines 14, 15, and 16).

Excerpt 1 continued.

13. *De chikara mo nobashi-te/ ikeru to*
and strength also extend-and can-go QT
omou-n da kedomo,/
tthink-NOM COP but
'And I think you can succeed in developing your skills and,'

14. *Ippon kaki-ageru/ tte iu no wa*
one write-finish QT say NOM TOP
honto ni sugoi taihen na koto/ de
truly very tough thing and
'Completing a speech is really difficult and,'

15. *atashi mo honto ni yoku wakaru-n da kedo,/*
I also truly well understand-NOM COP but
'I really do understand but,'

16. *De sono kabe o,/ hontoo zehi norikoe-te,/*
and that wall DO true definitely overcome-and
'you really have to overcome that difficulty and,'

17. *Mazu ippon,/ toriaezu,/ Moo donna*
first one for-now already any
mono demo ii kara,
thing even good because
'for now, just one speech, anything's okay so,'

18 *kaki-age-te,/*
write-finish-and
'finish it up and,'

19 *De, ironna hito ni mi-te-mora—/(u)*
and various people from look-and-receive
no ne?/ Jibun yori umai hito./
NOM IP oneself more-than skillful people
'and have various people look at it, okay? People who are more skilled than you.'

In line 15, Ritsuko used the first-person pronoun *atashi* in "*Atashi mo honto ni yoku wakarun da kedo*," 'I really do understand.' Because the sentence subject can be and often is omitted in Japanese, Ritsuko's use of the pronoun emphasized her personal involvement and understanding of her audience's experience: 'I too, I myself, really understand...." Line 19 contains both a directive with postposed elements and another use of the *no ne* sequence of interactional particles. In the remainder of her speech, Ritsuko continued to issue directives and encouragement until the very end where she shifted back to a more *omote* mode and used a very formulaic honorific phrase to thank everyone for their participation (*Otsukare sama deshita* which uses honorific forms to refer to causing someone fatigue).

In contrast to the informational focus of the first part of Ritsuko's speech, in the second half she referred directly to the affective experience of her audience and exhorted them to put forth greater effort. In doing so, she used a variety of forms which emphasized group solidarity and emotional involvement including direct forms of the predicate, interactional particles, quoted speech/thought, postposing, personal pronouns, and forceful directives. Her use of these stylistic forms marked a shift in the second part of her speech from an official, impersonal voice to a style that was more intimate and emotionally expressive, building an affective rapport with her audience.

Several months after the meeting, I discussed the tape and transcript with Ritsuko. I asked specifically about her use of the distal forms. Ritsuko told me she had not been consciously aware of her lower frequency of distal use in the later part of her speech. She said, however, that this section contained ideas she felt very strongly about and most wanted to communicate to the younger members of the club. In discussing this, Ritsuko used the term *honne*, meaning one's true, personal thoughts and feelings. *Honne* is frequently contrasted with *tatemae*, the socially agreed-upon principles that must be upheld in public. *Tatemae* belongs to the 'outward-facing' world of *omote*, while *honne* can be expressed within the in-group, in *ura*, or 'backstage', contexts. Ritsuko's use of direct forms and other markers of emotional intensity framed her speech as the expression of *honne* 'true personal feeling'. She felt strongly about what she was saying and, whether consciously or not, she choose linguistic and rhetorical forms which communicated that strength of feeling to her audience.

Through her use of directives, references to personal experience, and displays of affect and intimacy, Ritsuko constructed a stance that was simultaneously authoritative and caring. In doing so, she stepped into a culturally sanctioned role as an experienced senior providing guidance and advice to her juniors. Her behavior here bears a resemblance to what has been described as a "motherese" strategy in which Japanese women use language which simultaneously communicates both power and intimacy to create a characteristically feminine authority (Smith 1992; Sunaoshi 1995). Although Ritsuko communicated 'personal feeling', she did so in culturally conventionalized ways, drawing on a repertoire of speech styles and social roles available to her as a young Japanese woman in a position of authority in the club.

Akiko's Speech: Communication through Emotional Restraint

Although all of the club officers were asked to reflect on the year's activities, not all of them displayed the same affective intensity as Ritsuko. Her shift to a more emotionally engaged style contrasts with the behavior of another officer, Akiko, who remained in a more impersonal, *omote* mode throughout her speech. Akiko's speech was marked by a consistently high frequency of distal forms (72%) and by a complete absence of interactional particles, postposing, or reported speech. In one sense there is nothing to be explained here; Akiko simply remained within the formal, public mode established at the beginning of the meeting. I hope to show however, that her choice to remain within this impersonal mode was no less strategic and meaningful than was Ritsuko's choice to shift styles.

Akiko began her speech by reporting on the annual speech contest organized by the club, giving the lists of participants, sponsors, and prize-winners. Akiko had been quite disappointed by a general lack of help and participation in organizing the contest. Following her report, she, like Ritsuko, began exhorting the younger members to work harder on club activities and stressed the importance of everyone's participation. Yet her speech style remained quite distanced and formal. In the following excerpt, for example, note the high frequency of distal forms (glossed as DIST and underlined for ease of identification).

Excerpt 2: Akiko's Speech at Student Meeting

1. *Toku ni, ichinensei/ no kata wa,/*
   Especially first-year-student GEN people(H+) TOP
   ano,/ kotoshi hajimete desu node,
   um this-year first-time COP(DIST) since
   'Because this year was the first time for the freshman in particular,'
2. *amari—/ wakara-nai mama ni, /2.5/*
   not-much understand-not state in
   kyooseiteki ni,/ han-kyooseiteki ni,/
   coercedly, half-coercedly
   tetsudawasare-te,/
   made-to-help-and
   'they were coerced, half coerced, to help without really understanding and,'
3. *shingai da-tta ka mo shire-mas-en keredomo./*
   regrettable COP-PAST QM also can-know-DIST-not but
   'that may have been unpleasant.'

4. *Kore ni tsuite wa, motto,/ yoku,/ setsumei o*
this to about TOP more well explanation DO

suru beki da-tta. to hansei o
do should COP-PAST QT reflection DO

shi-te -i -masu. /2.0/
do-and-be-DIST

'Concerning this issue, I regret that we didn't do a better job of explaining things.'

5. *Kore wa,/ ima sara/ iu yoo desu keredomo,/*
this TOP now again say manner COP(DIST) but

'I know this sounds like crying over spilt milk but,'

6. *moo zutto,/ juuyonenkan mo,/ rainen*
already all-the-way fourteen-years even next-year

wa juugokaime de,/
TOP fifteenth-time and

'it's already been fourteen years, and next year will be the fifteenth time so,'

7. *zutto tsuzuite-ki-te-iru/ (to iu)*
all-the-way continue-come-and-be QT say

taikai (na) node,/
contest COP since

'since it's been such a long-running contest,'

8. *kore kara mo zehi, tsuzuke-te*
this from also definitely can-continue-and

hoshii node,/
want since

'and since we really want it to continue from now on,'

9. *sugoku daiji ni, /omo—/omo—/*
very importantly

omo-tte hoshii to omoi-masu kedomo./
think-and want QT think-DIST but

'I hope everyone will think of it as important.'

10. *Minna de,/ hiraku taikai na node,* /2.0/
everyone by open contest COP since

'Since it's a contest we all put on together,'

11. *kore ni tsuite wa,/ mata, /2.5/*
this to about TOP again
kore mo,/ shikkari hikitsui-de,/
this also soundly pass-on-and
'this is something [I really want to] pass on properly and,'

12. *mina-san ni,/ igi (no),/ rikai*
everyone-TI from significance GEN understanding
o,/ fukame-te hoshii to omoi-masu./
DO deepen-and want QT think-DIST
'I hope everyone will deepen their understanding of its significance.'

Although Akiko encouraged everyone to work harder on future contests, she expressed her disappoint with their previous lack of effort only indirectly (lines 1–4). Rather than issuing directives like Ritsuko, Akiko framed her requests in lines 9 and 12 with the mitigating phrase "… *hoshii to omoimasu*," literally 'I think I/we want…,' or 'I hope that…'. In fact, Akiko did not actually request that people work harder on the contest, only that they "think of it as important." She even took the blame on herself for not sufficiently explaining the importance of their efforts to the younger club members.

When I later played the tape for Ritsuko and Akiko, Ritsuko commented on how angry Akiko had been at the lack of help in organizing the contest. Akiko laughed and admitted that she had not expressed her criticisms fully or directly at the meeting. She commented,

Excerpt 3: Akiko talking with Cyndi and Ritsuko

Hontoo wa,/((laughs))*/*
true TOP
Anata-tachi, motto,/ igi o,/
you-PL more significance DO
rikai,/ shi-te yo./ tte ii-taka-ta./
understanding do-and IP QT say-want-PAST
'Actually, ((laughs)) what I wanted to say was, You have to understand the importance of this!'

In commenting on what she "really wanted to say," Akiko used the unmitigated directive *rikai shite yo* 'understand this!' Here *yo* is another interactional particle which serves like a verbal exclamation point to emphasize what the speaker is saying. Akiko also used *anata-tachi* 'you-plural', a relatively direct and blunt form of second-person reference. This strong directive contrasts sharply with the indirect phrasing Akiko used in the actual meeting: *Minasan ni igi (no) rikai o fukamete hoshii to omoimasu* 'I hope everyone will deepen their understanding of its significance.'

We see here the contrast between the *omote* of public expression and the *ura* of the feelings expressed more directly to me and Ritsuko. Yet Ritsuko clearly recognized the anger even in Akiko's more public and indirect form of expression. Depersonalized or affectively muted speech need not imply an *absence* of affect, but rather its culturally conventionalized restraint or control. Indeed it was quite possible that Akiko's indirectness actually made the younger club members feel more guilty than if she had scolded them directly. Furthermore, the use of extremely polite language with intimates or a shift from more casual towards more formal language is itself one conventionalized way of expressing anger in Japan. Thus Akiko's seeming indirectness and emotional restraint may actually have communicated her feelings quite clearly.

The comparison of Ritsuko's and Akiko's speeches shows that *ura* and *omote* speech styles are not straitjackets of linguistic conformity nor automatic behavioral responses to a particular situational context. Rather, they exist as cultural resources which are used in individual creative acts of meaning. Recent work by Johnstone (1996), Kiesling (1996), and the "California Style Collective" (Arnold et al. 1993) reminds us to understand speech styles, not simply as a function of age, sex, ethnicity, and context, but as creative acts in which speakers draw from a cultural repertoire of indexical signs to construct individual identities. In the examples discussed here, both Ritsuko and Akiko drew on conventionalized cultural meanings, roles, and linguistic signs, yet they used these resources to communicate very different stances towards their audience. The differences in this context may have to do with the rather different messages the speakers chose to communicate, and specifically with Akiko's resentment about the speech contest. Yet such stylistic choices are also a part of these speakers' on-going presentation of self across different contexts and audiences. In other situations as well, Ritsuko often came across as more open and enthusiastic, Akiko as more poised and restrained. When first meeting me, for example, Ritsuko shifted very quickly to direct forms despite our age difference, while Akiko continued to use mostly distal forms with me for quite some time. Thus it is not simply the case that *ura* expresses while *omote* hides the "true self". Both of these behavioral modes are cultural resources for the presentation of self and construction of social roles and relationships.

Honne and *Tatemae*: Social Functions of Affective Display

The analysis of Ritsuko's and Akiko's speeches shows that both *ura* and *omote* styles of behavior involve culturally conventionalized forms of expression and that both are important as a means of self-presentation. The ethnographic literature on Japan has frequently emphasized contrasts between *ura* and *omote*, *honne* and *tatemae*, personal feeling and the constraints of social duty. Yet equally central to Japanese cultural behavior is the ability to create strongly-felt affective bonds which promote group solidarity and group effort. As Rosenberger (1989) notes, the energy of emotional spontaneity can be either inner-oriented towards individual gratification or outward-oriented to create empathy and group harmony. Ritsuko's speech at the meeting was framed as the expression of *honne* 'real personal feeling', but it also clearly supported the publicly-approved principles (*tatemae*) of hard work, perseverance, and group effort. Her speech style provided an affective reinforcement of the social ideals she espoused.

Ritsuko was not alone in her use of an affectively charged style to build group solidarity and promote social ideals. Later in the same meeting, following the officers' reports, the president asked the graduating students to each say a few words about their experiences in the club. Speaker after speaker stood up and spoke about times when she had felt discouraged and thought about quitting the club, talked about how older students and other club members had encouraged her to persevere, and finally explained how much she had learned and benefited from being in the club. Although each speaker recounted her individual feelings and experiences, their personal narratives all seemed to be telling the same story. Furthermore, the speakers employed many of the same stylistic devices Ritsuko had used in her earlier speech. In comparison with the officers' reports earlier in the meeting, there was much less use of distal forms (frequencies ranged from 20% to 36%). Several of the speakers used interactional particles, and many of them used reported speech or thought to enhance the affective immediacy of their narratives. Like Ritsuko, they drew on their personal experience and made affective appeals to the audience in order to support broader moral principles. Statements of social norms concerning perseverance, self-development, and group loyalty were thus strengthened and reinforced through affective display. In these speeches, the public and private faces of the self come together as *honne* 'personal feeling' is put in service of *tatemae* 'social principles'.[4]

In their acts of self-presentation, Japanese speakers use a range of stylistic features which mark speech as *omote*—public, formal, and restrained—or as allowing one to glimpse *ura*, the underneath, by indexing intimacy, spontaneity, and emotional expressiveness. Yet the analysis presented here shows that the boundaries between these modes of expression are not always as sharp as analytic convenience might have them be. *Honne*, the open display of true feeling, can itself be quite conventionalized and serve to emotionally reinforce socially-approved behavior. Conversely, the seeming impersonality and self-restraint of a formal speech style may clearly communicate the speaker's personal emotional stance. *Ura* modes of expression are indeed culturally conventionalized, although they may well be perceived and experienced as spontaneous and natural. And a speaker's more formal, *omote* mode is also one facet of his/her individual self-expression. Although it is easy to dichotomize the contrasts between them, both *ura* and *omote* need to be understood as complimentary aspects of socially constructed yet uniquely individual selves.

Notes

1. Funding for this research was provided by the National Science Foundation, the Japanese Association of University Women, the Woodrow Wilson Fellowship Foundation, and the University of Texas at Austin. I am grateful to Tomoko Watanabe for help with transcription and to Risako Ide for checking the translations. I would also like to thank Debra Occhi, Miyako Inoue, and Hari Kanta Ogren for helpful comments on previous drafts.
2. These forms are also sometimes referred to as *plain* and *polite*. The *direct/distal* terminology is from Jorden and Noda 1987. Direct forms are also the norm in some written genres where they signal an informational focus to the exclusion of social considerations. As argued by Maynard 1993 and Cook 1996b, distal forms show a social awareness of the addressee. The use of direct, as opposed to distal, forms may mean that the social identity of the addressee is irrelevant (as in expository writing), that strong emotion has overridden consciousness of the addressee's status, or that the relationship is sufficiently intimate (or the addressee of such low status) that face considerations need not be a concern. The intended meaning of any particular instance of the direct form is sometimes ambiguous even for participants.
3. Transcription conventions are as follows:

   / Pause-Bounded Phrasal Units (see Maynard 1989). Pauses of greater than one second are given to the nearest half second between slashes, e.g., /2.5/.
   . Final fall.
   , Continuing intonation.
   ? Rising intonation (questioning or appeal)
   — Cut-off word or phrase.
   ( ) Uncertain hearing.
   (( )) Non-verbal noises and transcriber's comments.

   Abbreviations used in glosses: DIST Distal Form; COP Copula; DO Direct Object Marker; GEN Genitive; H+ Subject Honorific; IP Interactional Particle; NOM Nominalizer; PAST Past Tense; QT Quotative; QM Question Marker; SUBJ Subject Marker; TI Title; TOP Topic Marker; VOL Volitional.

4. It is not my intent to suggest that affective displays always function to support the status quo. Affectively charged speech can also be used to arouse outrage, resistance, or rebellion against the existing social order.

References

Atkinson, J. Maxwell. 1982. "Understanding formality: The categorization and production of 'formal' interaction." *British Journal of Sociology* 33:86–117.

Bachnik, Jane M. 1992. "The two faces of self and society in Japan." *Ethos* 20:3–23.

Beeman, William O. 1986. *Language, Status, and Power in Iran*. Bloomington: Indiana University Press.

Besnier, Niko. 1990. "Language and affect." *Annual Review of Anthropology* 19:419–51.

Blyth, Carl. 1995. "*Cest bon, ca!!!*: Conventionalized displays of affect in French." In *Texas Linguistic Forum* 34 (Proceedings of SALSA II). Austin: Dept. of Linguistics, University of Texas at Austin, 130–42.

California Style Collective (Jennifer Arnold, Renee Blake, Penelope Eckert, Melissa Iwai, Norma Mendoza-Denton, Carol Morgan, Livia Polyani, Julie Solomon, and Tom Veatch) 1993. "Variation and personal/group style." Paper presented at NWAVE 22, University of Ottawa, Canada.

Cook, Haruko M. 1990a. "The sentence-final particle *ne* as a tool for cooperation in Japanese conversation." In Hajime Hoji (ed), *Japanese/Korean Linguistics*. Stanford: Stanford University Center for the Study of Language and Information, 29–44.

———. 1990b. "An indexical account of the Japanese sentence-final particle *no*." *Discourse Processes* 13:401–39.

———. 1996a. "Japanese language socialization: Indexing the modes of self." *Discourse Processes* 22: 171–97.

———. 1996b. "Collocation of indexical signs: Social meanings of the plain form in Japanese." Paper presented at the Fifth International Pragmatics Conference, Mexico City, Mexico, July 4–9.

Doi, Takeo. 1986. *The Anatomy Of Self*. Trans. by M.A. Harbison. Tokyo: Kodansha International.

Dunn, Cynthia Dickel. 1996. *Style And Genre In Japanese Women's Discourse*. Unpublished Ph.D. dissertation, University of Texas at Austin.

Duranti, Alessandro and Elinor Ochs. 1979. "Left-dislocation in Italian conversation." In Tamy Givon (ed), *Syntax and Semantics Vol. 12*. New York: Academic, 377–416.

Geertz, Clifford. 1960. *The religion of Java*. Glencoe, IL: Free Press.

Harada, S.-I. 1976. "Honorifics." In M. Shibatani (ed), *Syntax and Semantics, Vol. 5: Japanese Generative Grammar*. New York: Academic, 499- 561.

Hinds, John. 1982. *Ellipsis in Japanese*. Carbondale IL: Linguistic Research Inc.

Ide, Sachiko. 1982. "Japanese sociolinguistics: Politeness and women's language." *Lingua* 57:357–85.

Ikuta, Shoko. 1983. "Speech level shift and conversational strategy in Japanese discourse." *Language Sciences* 5:37–54.

Irvine, Judith T. 1979. "Formality and informality in communicative events." *American Anthropologist* 81:773–90.

———. 1982. "Language and affect: Some cross-cultural issues." In Heidi Byrnes (ed), *Contemporary Perceptions of Language* (Georgetown University Round Table on Languages and Linguistics 1982). Washington D.C.: Georgetown University Press, 31–47.

———. 1990. "Registering affect: Heteroglossia in the linguistic expression of emotion." In Lutz and Abu-Lughod, 126–61.

Johnstone, Barbara. 1996. *The Linguistic Individual: Self-Expression in Language and Linguistics.* New York: Oxford.

Jorden, Eleanor Harz and Mari Noda. 1987. *Japanese: The Spoken Language.* New Haven: Yale University Press.

Kiesling, Scott. 1996. "Power roles and cultural models in the language of fraternity men." Paper presented at the Fourth Berkeley Women and Language Conference, April 19–21.

Lebra, Takie Sugiyama. 1976. *Japanese Patterns of Behavior.* Honolulu: University Press of Hawaii.

Lutz, Catherine A. and Lila Abu-Lughod, eds. 1990. *Language and the Politics of Emotion.* Cambridge: Cambridge University Press.

Martin, Samuel E. 1964. "Speech levels in Japan and Korea." In Dell Hymes (ed), *Language in Culture and Society.* New York: Harper and Row, 407–415.

Maynard, Senko Kumiya. 1989. *Japanese Conversation: Self-Contextualization through Structure and Interactional Management.* Norwood, NJ: Ablex.

———. 1993. *Discourse Modality: Subjectivity, Emotion, and Voice in The Japanese Language.* Philadelphia: John Benjamins.

McGloin, Naomi Hanaoka. 1980. "Some observations concerning *no desu* expressions." *Journal of the Association of Teachers of Japanese* 15:117- 49.

Minami, Fujio *et al.* 1974. "Keigo no taikai" (The system of honorifics). In Shiro Hayashi and Fujio Minami (eds), *Keigo Kooza, Volume 1: Keigo no Taikei.* Tokyo: Meiji Shooin, 47–178.

Ochs, Elinor and Bambi Schieffelin. 1989. "Language has a heart." *Text* 9:7- 25.

Rosenberger, Nancy R. 1989. "Dialectic balance in the polar model of self: The Japan case." *Ethos* 17:88–113.

———. 1994. "Indexing hierarchy through Japanese gender relations." In Jane M. Bachnik and Charles J. Quinn (eds), *Situated Meaning: Inside and Outside in Japanese Self, Society, and Language.* Princeton: Princeton University Press, 88–112.

Shibatani, Masayoshi. 1990. *The Languages of Japan.* Cambridge: Cambridge University Press.

Shore, Bradd. 1982. *Sala'ilua: A Samoan Mystery.* New York: Columbia University Press.

Smith, Janet S. 1992. "Women in charge: Politeness and directives in the speech of Japanese women." *Language in Society* 21:59–82.

Sunaoshi, Yukako. 1995. "Your boss is your 'mother': Japanese women's construction of an authoritative position in the workplace." In *Texas Linguistic Forum* 34 (Proceedings of SALSA II). Austin: Dept. of Linguistics, University of Texas at Austin, 175–88.

Tanaka, Akio. 1977. "Joshi" (Particles). In *Iwanami Kooza Nihongo 7: Bunpoo II*. Tokyo: Iwanami Shoten, 339–434.

Tobin, Joseph. 1992. "Japanese preschools and the pedagogy of selfhood." In Nancy R. Rosenberger (ed), *Japanese Sense of Self*. Cambridge: Cambridge University Press, 21–39.

Tsuchihashi, Mika. 1983. "The speech act continuum: An investigation of Japanese sentence final particles." *Journal of Pragmatics* 7:361–87.

Uyeno, Tazuko Y. 1971. *A Study of Japanese Modality—A Performative Analysis of Sentence Particles*. Unpublished Ph.D. dissertation, University of Michigan.

Cognitive Approaches

From *Hiren* to *Happî-endo*

Romantic Expression in the Japanese Love Story

Janet S. (Shibamoto) Smith
University of California, Davis

The Japanese are not widely known in the Pacific as the Romeos of the Rim. In fact, it is generally thought that, at least in their marital lives, Japanese men and women do not hold romantic love but rather practical considerations and complementarity within family units to be at the core of the bond between them. In 1993, Iwao claimed that "…marriage in Japan, in contrast to the United States with its emphasis on romance and love, is generally contemplated in objective terms based on practical considerations (e.g., economic stability, social status, and family relations). Unlike most Americans — who marry as long as they feel they are in love, regardless of age — Japanese (except perhaps today's youth) tend to think that marriage and falling in love (*ren'ai*) are two different things" (Iwao 1993: 61). Coleman also notes that, in Japan, sexually coupled pairs tend to be recognized less in terms of their interpersonal relatedness than in terms of their gendered unity within a family unit (Coleman 1991: 174–6). Nonetheless, in the post-War era, women (and to some degree men) are in the process of re-evaluating the husband-wife relationship (Hendry 1981: 29). In particular, they are in process of reconsidering its value as an affective bond vis-à-vis the more traditional primary affective bond between the parent and child.

Of interest here is one piece of this re-evaluation process. In this paper, I report preliminary results of an analysis of *ren'ai shôsetsu* (romance novels) published between 1971 and 1995. The analysis is aimed at elucidating the properties of "ideal love" (Kövecses 1988), at least for the Japanese female reader of romance fiction, in an attempt to understand contemporary formulations of a cultural model of the Japanese emotion ***AI* 'LOVE'**.

AI

In discussing the prototypical loving relationship in the Japanese case, Wierzbicka invokes *amae*, a dependency concept based on the bonds between the infant in relationship to its mother (Wierzbicka 1992). This relationship forms the prototypical "love" bond. Her claim is supported by the Japanese literature, which details the history of the concept *AI* as originally describing 1) feelings from superior to inferiors and 2) as being closely related to Buddhist and Confucian notions of pity or compassion (see (1a, d) below). Ôno (1981) states that the term *ai* began to be used with the meaning *koi* 'love between a man and woman' (stressing the physical expression of that love) in the early Meiji era (1868–1912) as the result of a search for a euphemistic term for *renbo* 'love attachment', which had taken on somewhat vulgar connotations. The use of *ai* to refer to the thoughts about and treatment of a cross-sex other as an equal, however, only became marked under Western influence.[1]

We have, then, two competing terms for LOVE concepts, *ai* and *koi*, which combine to form the modern term *ren'ai* 'love', as in *ren'ai kekkon* 'love marriage' and *ren'ai shôsetsu* 'love novel'. *Ren* is the Sino-Japanese reading, or pronunciation, of the character for *koi*, and is the reading commonly used in compound words. See (1–2) for an indication of the range of meanings associated with each term (Morohashi et al. 1982: 21, 43; defining terms listed in order of appearance, translations from Katsumata 1954 or by author).

(1) *ai* 'love, affection, fondness, attachment'

a.	*itsukushimu*	'love, be affectionate to; pity, take pity on'
b.	*taisetsu ni suru*	'take care of'
c.	*jô o kakeru*	'to have feelings for'
d.	*awaremu*	'pity; feel compassion for'
e.	*shitashimu*	'to be intimate with, be friendly toward'
f.	*kawaigaru*	'love, pet, make a pet of'
g.	*hiiki o suru*	'favor, patronize'
h.	*shitau*	'yearn for; adore, idolize; follow'
i.	*koisuru*	'love, have tender passion for'

(2) *koi* 'love, tender passion'

a.	*omou*	'think of, be interested in, feel tenderly toward; wish, want'
b.	*shitau*	'yearn for; adore, idolize; follow'
c.	*danjo ga tagai ni omoi o yoseau*	'a man and a woman feel mutual interest, tenderness'

It is the use of these (and associated) terms, and the narratives within which they appear that concern us here.

Japanese Romance Fiction

The Japanese romance novel may be characterized as category literature. Radway (1984) defines category literature as fiction which exhibits single-minded reliance on a "recipe" that dictates the essential ingredients to be included in each version of the form and which has consistent appeal to a regular audience. There are three major subgenres of Japanese romance category fiction: 1) hyper-serious novels, ending in *hiren* 'blighted love'; 2) light or ironic novels with a *happî-endo* 'happy ending'; and 3) translations of Harlequin-type western romance novels. This analysis concentrates on the latter two subtypes.

One might challenge the inclusion of translations of western love stories, wherein the protagonists are western men and women in foreign settings. Harlequin translations have, however, been an immensely popular version of romance fiction since their first translations appeared in bookstores in the summer of 1981. In a *Yomiuri Shinbun* article in the summer of 1996, marking the fifteenth year of Harlequin translations into Japanese, one of the women interviewed for the piece reported that she read about twenty of these novels a month and that she had, in fact, taken ten of them on her honeymoon. I suggest, therefore, that they have a significant effect on how the readers of this particular category of popular fiction construe "true love".

True Love: A Model

My examination of Japanese romance fiction analyzes differences in the use of the two terms *ai* and *koi* in denoting "true love". I begin the analysis with a contextualization of love in Japanese romance novels in terms of selected elements of Kövecses' language-based folk model of American ideal love. Kövecses commences his examination of the American folk model(s) of romantic love with the assertion that linguistic models give important clues to our romantic feelings.

> One reflection of our conceptual system is language. Thus the examination of the linguistic expressions that have to do with love should prove a fruitful approach to the study of the conceptual model of love.[2] (Kövecses 1988: 12)

The model of ideal love developed by Kövecses after an extensive survey of "conventionalized linguistic expressions"[3] in English is presented in (3).

(3) 1. True love comes along.
The other attracts me irresistibly.
The attraction reaches the limit point on the intensity scale at once.
2. The intensity of the attraction goes beyond the limit point.
3. I am in a state of lack of control.
Love's intensity is maximal.
I feel that my love gives me extra energy.
I view myself and the other as forming a unity.
I experience the relationship as a state of perfect harmony.
I see love as something that guarantees the stability of the relationship.
I believe that love is a need, that this love is my true love, that the object of love is irreplaceable, and that love lasts forever.
Love is mutual.
I experience certain physiological effects: increase in body heat, increase in heart rate, blushing, and interference with accurate perception.
I exhibit certain behavioral reactions: physical closeness, intimate sexual behavior, sex, loving visual behavior.
I experience love as something pleasant.
I define my attitude toward the object of love through a number of emotions and emotional attitudes: liking, sexual desire, respect, devotion, self-sacrifice, enthusiasm, admiration, kindness, affection, care, attachment, intimacy, pride, longing, friendship, and interest.
I am happy.

(Kövecses 1988: 58–59)

Within this ideal model of love in English, there are two submodels, one constituted by complex metaphorical concepts, the other by metonymical concepts such as physiological reactions (Kövecses 1988: 86). The elements of the supermodel that I address are drawn from both the submodels. Among the metaphorical concepts constituting the first submodel, I explore the notion of love reaching and exceeding a limit point on a scale of intensity: "The attraction reaches the limit point on the intensity scale at once. The intensity of the attraction goes beyond the limit point. I am in a state of lack of control".

Associated metaphorical concepts are, e.g., 'love as fluid in a container', 'love as insanity', 'love as fire, magic, rapture'. Specifically, I ask whether Japanese true love is seen as necessarily exceeding limit points on scales of intensity or, rather, as something that can, perhaps even should, be contained. Second, I ask whether love guarantees the stability of a relationship in the Japanese case or whether circumstantial stability guarantees true love: "I see love as something that guarantees the stability of the relationship". Associated metaphorical concepts are 'love as a nutrient [need]' and 'love as a unity', which leads to the belief that a true love is irreplaceable.

The second submodel is a set of metonymic concepts involving physiological reactions ("I experience certain physiological effects: increase in body heat, increase in heart rate, blushing, and interference with accurate perception") and loving behaviors ("I exhibit certain behavioral reactions: physical closeness, intimate sexual behavior, sex,[4] loving visual behavior"). I examine the physiological reactions of true love and the verbal and visual behavior attendant upon it. Loving behaviors take on particular importance in light of the claim that, although Japanese freely report *experiencing* emotion, emotion regulation and control in Japan is viewed as a more mature, socialized trait and skill, leading to a lesser degree of emotional *expression* (Matsumoto 1996: 90).[5]

The Characters

Kôji and Sayaka are a young couple who meet at the airport as both are about to leave for Hawaii; they are immediately attracted to one another, but Sayaka is a much-loved and protected only daughter (and younger sister) — a *hakoiri-musume*, lit., 'a daughter kept in a box' — and Kôji's family situation is a complicated and difficult one. Kôji and Sayaka are my Japanese *happî-endo* romancers, drawn from the novel *Kekkon no Toki* by Hiraiwa Yumie.

Theo and Jane(y),[6] from *Umi no Mieru Ie* by Robin Donald (tr. Katô Shiori), are my western pair; Theo is older, in his early thirties, highly successful and overwhelmingly masculine, while Janey is very young, under twenty, and, like Sayaka, something of a *hakoirimusume*. These four typify the Japanese and western lovers in my sample and will be used throughout for illustrative purposes.

Love — Off the Scale or Containerized

The thoughts and feelings that Kôji and Sayaka have for one another are shown in Table 1.

Table 1. Thoughts and feelings of romantic love, Kôji and Sayaka

Kôji	**Sayaka**
Positive feelings	
omoi- dasu think put out 'to recollect'	*ai tai ki ga* meet DES feeling SU *shikiri ni suru* incessantly/eagerly do 'constantly wish to see X'
shikiri ni omou constantly/eagerly think 'to think of constantly'	*kokoro o kasumeru* heart DO skim, graze 'to skim across [one's] heart
kokoro ni ukabu heart to float 'to float into [one's] heart'	
ai o jikaku se- zaru o enai love DO be aware of be forced to 'to be forced to be aware of love'	
aishi-dashi-te iru love begin GER PROG *jibun no kokoro ni kizuku* self GEN heart to become aware of 'to become aware of [one's] feelings of beginning to be in love'	
kokoro o hik- areru heart DO to draw,pull PASS 'to be drawn to'	
amazuppai mono ga sweet-sour thing SU *mune o yogiru* chest DO go across 'a sweet-sour feeling runs across [one's] chest'	

Negative feelings

nayamu 'to suffer'	*kanashimu* 'to feel sorrow'
i- te mo tat- te mo be GER even stand GER even *ir- are- nai ki ga suru* be POT NEG feeling SU do 'to feel restless'	*katei no fukuzatsusa ni* family GEN complexity at *hirumeru* (sic) flinch 'to flinch at the complexity of [someone's] family'
aisuru koto o tamerau to love thing DO hesitate, vacillate 'to hesitate to love [someone]'	
kokoro ga mijime heart SU wretched, miserable *de aru* is 'to be wretched, miserable'	
kokoro no naka wa heart GEN inside TOP *(akikaze no yô na)* autumn wind GEN like *wabisha ga aru* desolation DO have 'to have in [one's] heart a desolation (like the autumn wind)	

First, we see some new expressions of feelings of love, or love's beginning: *omou* 'think', *kokoro ni ukabu* 'to cross one's mind' (lit., 'to float into one's heart'), *kokoro o hikareru* 'to be drawn to' (lit., 'to have one's heart attracted'), etc. Notice that nowhere is there reference to feelings overflowing, bursting out of, or in any way exceeding the capacity of the heart, chest, or mind to contain them, a point to which I return below. Kôji is quite aware of his feelings for Sayaka, which he terms *ai* 'love'. There is a down side to Kôji's love: he is aware of the impediment that his family situation represents and worries about Sayaka's plans for an *o-miai* 'meeting with a view to marriage' with a rival. He suffers (*nayamu*) but hesitates about whether he should/can love Sayaka (*aisuru koto o tamerau*). Sayaka, for her part, also thinks of Kôji: she constantly wishes to see him (*aitai ki ga shikiri ni suru*) and he "skims" across her heart (*kokoro o kasumeru*). She, too, however, is concerned about her feelings for Kôji; specifically, she falters at the complexity of his family situation (*katei no fukuzatsusa ni hirumeru*). Here I suggest that the impediment to her romance, and an impediment is necessary in romance fiction or love stories would be very short indeed, is one that gives us significant clues to the Japanese ideal love scenario. In the Japanese case, the heroine's concerns about her beloved are typically not about the beloved's personal infidelities or cruelties nor his coldness and indifference, but about his family (or other *uchi* 'in-group') situation. Note that in Sayaka's case this is not a concern about his family vis-à-vis hers (his family did not do her family a wrong), but simply the situation on its own terms. The issue is this: is his family a suitable container for their love? Sayaka is concerned as well about whether her family will be comfortable if she married into a "complicated" family situation; in other *happî-endo* novels, paternalistic bosses, supportive (often stably married) networks of (usually female) friends, etc., may substitute for the family. But the bottom line is that the "container" must be suitable for true love to flourish; a love that overflows, explodes, or escapes the container (i.e., passes the "limit point" on an intensity scale of attraction) cannot be successful. An appropriate "container", moreover, is essential to the relationship's stability; rather than the love Kôji and Sayaka experience guaranteeing the stability of the relationship, we find the stability of the relationship's container guarantees the love.

The Harlequin novels, on the other hand, focus on individual rather than external impediments, and the resolution of the difficulties between a romancing pair involves the overflow of feeling out of its container, which causes all impediments to be swept away in the ensuing flood of emotion. The 'container' is often the seemingly indifferent or hostile male member of the pair who has, up to the climax of the story, kept his feelings in check by exerting his iron self-control. Other 'containers' may be the hero's conviction that he is somehow irredeemably flawed (by past actions, for example), the heroine's conviction that the hero is interested only in sex, etc. In the case of Theo and Janey, the impediment is the great difference in their ages and Janey's lack of education and experience. The 'containers' that keep the pair's emotions in check are Theo's self-control and Janey's pride. Janey does her best to hide her feelings because she, like many Harlequin heroines and unlike most Japanese heroines, is convinced (and bothered by her conviction) that Theo's approaches to her are prompted by lust rather than by true love (4). And it is not, in fact, the case that Theo has given Janey no reason to feel this way (5).

(4) Janey's thought:
Teo [*Theo*] *wa, tatoe sasayaka na aijô o kanjita to shite mo, sore ga kare ni totte nan no kachi mo nai koto o sugu ni satotta hazu de aru. Kare hodo keiken yutaka na otoko ga, utsukushiku mo nai komusume-gotoki ni, seiteki miryoku igai no nani o kanjiru to iu no darô.*

Even if Theo *had* felt [some] small affection [for her], he surely must have immediately realized that it had no value for him. How could one imagine that a man of his great experience would feel anything except sexual attraction for [someone] like a young girl who isn't even beautiful?

(*Umi no Mieru Ie*: 139)

(5) Theo to Janey:
Koi no amai kizu kai? Boku wa sô wa omowanai. Koi to iu yasashii sakkaku to, ima bokutachi ga kanjite ita tannaru yokubô to wa marukkiri betsumono sa.

[You think what you are feeling] is the sweet hurt of love? I don't think so. The gentle illusion of love and the mere desire that we were feeling just now are completely different things.

(*Umi no Mieru Ie*: 85)

Note that Janey uses the term *ai* (*aijô*) in reference to Theo's feelings in (4); in fact, she uses *ai* and *ai*-related compounds throughout. Theo, in contrast, uses *koi* in (5) and throughout, even when he is referring to his own feelings, feelings which he views as 'true love'. This difference in use by (fictional) men and women of *koi* vs. *ai* to denote true love requires further analysis.

To continue the story, despite his great (albeit unexpressed) love for Janey, Theo leaves her for a two year period. During this time, she grieves for her lost love, but gets an education and a job, travels extensively, and is courted by other men, who she, however, rejects as she is unable to forget Theo. At the end of their story, they are both irresistably drawn back to the town where they met. They are reunited and their mutual love is revealed. When Janey asks why, if they loved each other, they had to go through such painful months of separation, Theo replies that she had been too young, too inexperienced, and that he could not be satisfied with the kind of childish love that caused a woman to lose her head over the first attractive man she meets (6).

(6) *Kimi wa mada akanbô datta n da yo. Boku wa kimi ga hoshikute tamaranakatta. Kimi ni koi o shita n da. Shikashi, mite kure no yoi otoko ni hajimete atte noboseagaru yô na, sonna osanai ai dake de wa boku wa manzoku dekinakatta.*

> You were still a baby. I wanted you unbearably [much]. I fell in love (*koi*) with you. But I couldn't be satisfied with the kind of childish love (*ai*) in which [a women] loses her head over the first attractive man she meets.
>
> (*Umi no mieru ie*: 167)

Again, note Theo's use of *koi* for his own feelings. For the love of a women for a man, he uses *ai*.

Once Janey had cleared up her personal defects, however, Theo was waiting since — as Kövecses' model specifies — the object of love is irreplaceable. This provides considerable contrast to the case of Sayaka and Kôji, as Sayaka seriously considered marrying the young man with whom she had the *o-miai*, on the grounds that the "container" (that is, the other suitor's family) was highly suitable to a successful loving relationship, and that, even without great, throbbing (*tokimeki*) passion, once they married, a quiet love (*shizuka na ai*) would develop (*sodatsu*). For Sayaka, then, the love and the appropriate interpersonal container for that love are in delicate balance.

The Physiological Effects of Love

Kövecses' model of ideal love suggests that lovers experience certain physiological effects, such as increase in body heat, increase in heart rate, blushing, etc. Theo and Janey do: they respond to each other physiologically in a number of ways. Their breathing is impaired (*iki ga tomarisoo*), they throb (*dôki ga hageshiku myakuutsu, shinzô ga kuruidashisoo ni naru*, etc.), their blood boils (*chi ga wakitatsu*), they feel like they're melting (*tokeru*). They also shake, and Janey blushes. See Table 2. The Harlequin novels also describe "violent passion flaring up", "hot hearts", bodies "burning" (with passion), and "electric" feelings, all consistent with Kövecses' predictions.

Table 2. The Physiological Effects of Love: Harlequin Translations

Breathing	*iki ga tomari-soo* breath SU stop seems '[it] seems like [my] breath would stop'
Throbbing	*mune no tokimeki* chest GEN palpitation 'throbbing of the heart' *dôki ga hageshiku myakuutsu* throbbing [of the heart] SU violently pulse '[one's] pulse beats violently' *shinzô ga kurut- ta yô ni myakuutsu* heart SU go crazy PST as if pulse '[one's] heart beats as if it had gone crazy' *shinzô ga kurui- dashi-soo ni naru* heart SU go crazy begin seems DAT become '[one's] heart comes to seem as if it were beginning to go crazy' *kekkan no naka o uzuki ga* blood vessel GEN inside DO throbbing [ache] SU *kakemawat-ta* circulate PST '[a] throbbing ache began to circulate' *shinzô ga takanaru* heart SU sound loudly '[a] heart begins to beat loudly'
Seething/boiling	*chi ga wakitatsu* blood SU seethe 'blood seethes'
Melting	*zenshin ga mizu no yô ni toke-te* whole body SU water GEN like melt GER *shimai-soo ni naru* finish like DAT become '[her] whole body seemed like it was completely melting like water'
Shaking	*piripiri furueru* violently tremble 'tremble violently'

Blushing	*kôchô shi-ta kao* flushing do PST face '[a] flushed face'
	kao o akarame-ta face DO redden PST '[someone] blushed'
	kao no hoteri face GEN glow/heat 'blushing'
Heat & electricity	*gekijô ga futatabi moeagaru* violent passion SU again burn up '[their] violent passion once again flared up'
	atsui kokoro hot heart '[a] hot heart'
	mi ga kogareru body SU burn '[one's] body burns'
	karada- jû ni denryû ga hashiru body throughout in electric current SU run '[an] electric current runs throughout [her] body'

What about the physiological effects of love on Kôji and Sayaka? Well, they do a little shaking and blushing, but metaphors of heat and descriptions of throbbing, boiling, melting and the like are absent. In their place are descriptions of loss of balance, triggering leaning and clinging desires and/or behaviors. See Table 3. I submit that this is a part of the Japanese ideal model of love that taps a traditional, cross-generational (or status-asymmetric), *amae*-centered concept of love that continues to have a powerful effect on how Japanese women construe "true love".

Loving Visual Behavior

Kövecses' model claims that romantic pairs of men and women will exhibit "loving visual behavior" and analysis of both Japanese "happy-ending" and Harlequin translations yielded some clues as to what visual behavior is/can be taken as markers of true love. Kôji, Sayaka, Theo, and Janey each provide visual

Table 3. The Physiological Effects Of Love: The Japanese Novels

Shaking	*karada ga furueru* body SU tremble '[one's] body trembles'
Blushing	*aka-ku naru* red ADV become 'to blush' *tereru* feel/be shy 'to be embarrassed'
Leaning/balance effects	*ama- ku yorikakaru* sweet ADV lean against 'lean against [someone] sweetly' *heisei o ushinau* composure DO lose → *motare- te aruku* lean against GER walk 'to lose [one's] composure [and thus need to] walk leaning against/supported by [one's lover]' *sugaritsuku* cling to 'cling to' *hisshi de sugaritsui- te kuru* desperation with cling to GER come 'cling to [someone] desperately'
Heart tickles	*kokoro ga ama- ku kusugu-rareru* heart SU sweet ADV tickle PASS '[one's] heart is sweetly tickled'
Contentment	*manzoku suru* contentment do 'be content'

displays aside from blushing which signal affect. Theo and Janey look at each other a lot, not always in a loving fashion, it is true, but always in a way that signals one or another stage in the progress of a romance. Theo, in particular, looks at Janey composedly (*yûzen to*), with a sharp, cutting gaze (*surudoi manazashi de, sasu yô na shisen*), and sometimes in ways suggestive of passion (*mabuta no okusoko ni hageshii jônetsu no honoo ga yadoru*); see (7) and (8).

(7) Theo: composed and sharp looks

a. *Yûzen to J o nagameru.*
composure with J DO gaze at
'[He] looks at J composedly.'

b. *J no kao o jitto nozokikon- da.*
J GEN face DO intently peek/peer at PST
'[He] peered at J's face intently.'

c. *Surudoi manazashi de mitsumeru.*
sharp look with stare at
'[He] gives [her] a sharp look.'[7]

(8) Theo: passionate looks

a. *Kare no shisen wa J no kata no arawa*
he GEN gaze TOP J GEN shoulder GEN open/public
ni nat- ta suberaka na hada o samayot- ta
DAT become PST smooth skin DO rove/wander PST
ageku mune no fukurami ni ochi-ta.
as the final outcome chest GEN bulge to fall PST
'His gaze, after wandering across the smooth skin of her bare shoulder, fell to the swell of her breast.'

b. *Mabuta no okusoko ni hageshii jônetsu no*
eyelid GEN bottom at violent passion GEN
honoo ga yadoru.
flame SU lodge/dwell
'In the depth of [his] eyes was the flame of violent passion.'

Janey looks back at Theo less often, but sharply (*kitto*) when necessary (9). She, perhaps significantly, looks up (*aogu*) when directing her gaze at Theo and sometimes he has to cause her to do so (*aomukaseru*, lit. 'cause to turn one's face upward'). More often, however, Janey looks down or away (*somukeru, fuseru*), until the end of the novel when she can — at last — see love in Theo's face (*ai ni oboreta amai hyôjô o misete iru* '[T] was showing [her] an expression drowned in love'), as all impediment to their romance has been cleared away verbally.[8]

(9) Janey

a. *Kitto kare o mitsume-ta.*
sharply him DO stare at PST
'[She] stared at him sharply.'

b. *T o aogu.*
T DO look up[9]
'[She] looks up at T.'

c. *Kao o somukeru.*
face DO look away
'[She] looks away.'

d. *Kao o fuseru.*
face DO turn down
'[She] looked down.'

Other visual behaviors which signify the blossoming of emotion between Janey and Theo are what I call "lip behaviors". Theo gives ongoing[10] cues to his feelings through his lip gestures: he smiles in various ways (teasingly, grinning broadly, sarcastically, and icily)(10a-d). He also firmly compresses his lips, as if to hold back emotion (see 10e, f). In response to Theo's compressed lips, Janey typically bites hers (11).

(10) Read My Lips: Theo

a. *itazurappo- ku hohoemu*
mischievous ADV smile
'to smile teasingly'

b. *niyaniya warau*
grinning laugh
'to grin'[11]

c. *hinikuppoi kuchibiru*
sarcastic lips
'[a] sarcastic smile'

d. *kôritsui- ta yô na hohoemi*
freeze PST like smile
'a frozen smile'

e. *hageshi- ku musub- are- ta T no kuchimoto kara..*
violently ADV tie PASS PST T GEN mouth from
'from T's firmly compressed lips…'

f. *Kata- ku musun- de i- ta kuchibiru o futto*
hard ADV tie GER PROG PST lips DO suddenly[12]
yawarege-ta.
relax PST
'[He] suddenly relaxed his lips, which had been tightly compressed.'

(11) Read My Lips: Janey
a. *kuchibiru o kamu*
lips DO bite
'to bite [one's] lips'
b. *kuchi o kamu*
mouth DO bite
'to bite [one's] lips'

Kôji and Sayaka exhibit considerably less loving visual behavior. For them, in fact, true love is exhibited more by less (visual behavior, that is). At the beginning of their romance, it is true, Sayaka responds to what she takes as slights by glaring (*niramitsukeru, niramikaesu*) at Kôji; otherwise, they look away from one another at significant moments. Kôji looks straight ahead (*shômen o muku, zenpô o miru, mae o muku*); Sayaka, like Janey, looks down (*utsumuku*). On the one occasion — meeting after a separation of several weeks — that Sayaka reads something in Kôji's eyes, it is neither cutting sharpness nor violent passion, but rather *natsukashisa* 'fondness'. Finally, as their love story progresses, these two look at each other and smile (*kao o miawasete bishô suru*).

Matsumoto (1996) suggests that the rules of display for Japanese emotions are different from those of Americans or Europeans; Japanese display rules, for example, dictate that persons of higher status should be cautious in showing the emotions of joy and happiness. This, Matsumoto claims, is related to "the underlying Japanese philosophy that, in order to be able to endure intense, emotional events of life, one must learn to resist the temptation to become emotional about them — to have inner strength. The control of one's emotions is central to achieving a higher status in the Japanese way of thinking" (Matsumoto 1996: 58–9). This does not mean that Japanese people are unemotional. In fact, Japanese report emotional experiences as occurring more frequently than do either Americans or Europeans. But in Japan, control of emotions is viewed as a sign of maturity. There, Japanese tend to be less self-revealing than Westerners, particularly in the use of expressions of intimacy and personal feeling. We are not surprised, then to find significant affect expressed in facial expressions. Affect can be read openly in the romantic partners eyes in the Harlequin translations and in more subtle, yet significant shifts of gaze in the Japanese corpus. The loving visual behavior is quite different in the two subgenres.

Ai Vs. Koi: Putting The *Ren* In *Ren'ai*

Finally, I would like to turn to the question of how our lovers declare their love. Do they declare *ai* or do they declare a more physically passionate *koi* ? Is reading the Japanese romance different from reading the translated Harlequin?

Yes, and no. Sayaka and Janey feel, and in the end declare, their *ai*. No matter how they recognize the more sexual aspects of their loving feelings, the phrase they use to express their feelings is *aishite imasu* 'I love you'; in other novels, an occasional heroine whispers (*sasayaku*) *suki desu* 'I like (really like) you', but romantic heroines do not, in my corpus at least, declare anything remotely remsembling lust (the *koi*-related terms). Japanese men engaged in true love, as well, seem to avoid lustful specificity. Kôji declares his love for Sayaka (both to her and to her brothers) in terms such as (to her brother) *Suki da, kekkon shitai to omotte iru* 'I love her and want to marry her', and (to Sayaka) *Kekkon shite kurenai ka. Suki nan da.....Aishiteru n da* 'Won't you marry me? I love you.....I love you'. He refers to a past, failed and not "true" love as *koi*. Other Japanese male protagonists avoid even the terms *suki da* and *aishiteru*. Theo and his Harlequin companions, on the other hand, are more various in the assertion of their feelings; Theo says (to Janey): *Boku wa kimi ga hoshikute tamaranakatta. Kimi ni koi o shita n da.* 'I wanted you hopelessly. I fell in love with you.' Although Theo does not use *ai* -related terms to Janey, other Harlequin novel males do; always, however, mixed with terms such as *koisuru*, *horeru*,[13] and the like. For the Japanese reader of Harlequins, these men put the *ren* in *ren'ai* in ways their Japanese romance novel heroes do not.

Conclusion

Clearly, the model of ideal love in the Harlequins differs from that narrated in the Japanese *happî-endo* novels. The Harlequin model is one of *tsunoru omoi* (thoughts/feelings grown violent/intense), *wakitatta jônetsu* (seething [lit., bubbling up] passion), and *moeagaru yokubô* (desire bursting into flames). The *happî-endo* model speaks of mutual dependency expressed in leaning (*yorika-karu*) and clinging (*sugaritsuku*), properly contained (contra the Kövecsesian model of American love as something that escapes or overflows its container) within the respective relevant *uchi*-units of the romancing pair. In either case, Japanese women reading the two subgenres of romance fiction addressed in this presentation are "reading" romantic narratives built around the husband-wife pair bond as individually loving and successful — i.e., with the *happî-endo* of marriage or prospective marriage. In an era when Japan is concerned about women's delay in entering into marriages and their reluctance to undertake childbearing and the effect of these on population stagnation, in an era when not only Japanese news media but such news magazines as Newsweek can write articles headlined "Take a Hike, Hiroshi" (Newsweek: 38–39, August 10, 1992) — suggesting that Japanese men may be less than full participants in the re-evaluation of the husband-wife affective bond — it may be important to understand how Japanese women are construing love and marriage in the late twentieth century. I suggest that a close examination of the narratives of successful love found in romance fiction may be one small aspect of that understanding.

Notes

1. Wierzbicka (1992) provides a "bare-bones" definition of LOVE.

   love (X loves person Y)

   (a) X knows Y

   (b) X feels something good toward Y

   (c) X wants to be with Y

   (d) X wants to do good things for Y

   She suggests that the modern European concept of *love* (*amour, Liebe, amore*, and so on) — around which this model is constructed — is particularly important and that the emergence of this concept in Western folk philosophy constitutes a significant stage in the development of human ideas and values. She also notes that, at least in the Japanese case, it leaves a fair amount out.
2. Kövecses stresses, however, that this is only one approach; a study of the conceptual metaphors characterizing love can neither assess the psychological validity of the resultant conceptual models nor accommodate the various social variants that may affect their understanding (Kövecses 1988: 13).
3. E.g., 'I'm madly in love'; 'he's crazy about you'.
4. As Kövecses notes, sex and intimate sexual behavior are related but not synonymous (1988: 30); our heroes and heroines often confuse the two (at first), although their confusions are handled differently in the domestic *vs.* the translated romances.
5. Although I dispute Matsumoto's assertion that "the emotion lexicon of the Japanese places an added burden on the individual Japanese, who must weigh the consequences and meanings of the expression of important, personal feelings to social relationships. The differential degrees of social meanings to the Japanese, via their language, make it much more difficult for them to express emotion or feeling; they have neither the social freedom nor the vocabulary to express such things in the way that Americans can, who speak freely about their emotions in

the rich English language with its many shades of meaning" (Matsumoto 1996: 127). That Japanese social actors (or any social actors within their own cultures) feel themselves burdened by their own cultural constructions is certainly a dubious claim at best, and the assertion that English is a more nuanced language than Japanese betrays a profound misunderstanding of the nature of language(s).

6. Jane is called Janey — her childhood nickname — by her family, her friends, and Theo most of the time; when Theo is talking with her seriously (or, alternatively, taking her seriously), however, he addresses her as Jane.
7. In fact, Theo looks steadily, sharply, etc. at Janey throughout.
8. Here, Theo's feelings are referred to as *ai* (*ai ni oboreta hyôjô*), but the reference to the feelings his facial expression reveals is from the perspective of Janey.
9. *Aogu* means both 'to turn one's face upward (skyward, heavenward)' and 'to look up to, respect revere'.
10. Albeit incorrect, or at least, incorrectly interpreted by Janey; see Kövecses model and its comments concerning love's interference with accurate perception.
11. *Niyaniya* stands in some respects between *nikoniko*, which refers to a smile of "pure" happiness, and *nitanita*, which is an unpleasant (lit., "slightly ghastly") smile. *Niyaniya* can have coarse or rude overtones (Asano 1978: 219).
12. Literally, 'with a puff, whiff [of air]'.
13. Another verb for falling in love, with overtones of loving to the point of trance-like ecstasy.

References

Asano, Tsuruko (ed). 1978. *Giongo~Gitaigo Jiten.* Tokyo: Kadokawa Shoten.

Coleman, Samuel. 1991. *Family Planning in Japanese Society.* Princeton NJ: Princeton University Press.

Hendry, Joy. 1981. *Marriage in Changing Japan.* Rutland VT/Tokyo: Charles E. Tuttle, Co.

Iwao, Sumiko. 1993. *The Japanese Woman: Traditional Image and Changing Reality.* Cambridge MA: Harvard University Press.

Katsumata, Senkichiro (ed). 1954. *Kenkyusha's New Japanese-English Dictionary.* Tokyo: Kenkyusha.

Kövecses, Zoltán. 1988. *The Language of Love: The Semantics of Passion in Conversational English.* Lewisburg: Bucknell University Press/London & Toronto: Associated University Presses.

Matsumoto, David. 1996. *Unmasking Japan: Myths and Realities about the Emotions of the Japanese.* Stanford: Stanford University Press.

Morohashi, Tetsuji, Kamada, Masashi, and Yoneyama Entarô (eds). 1982. *Kôkanwa Jiten: Chûkan.* Tokyo: Taishûkan Shoten.

Ôno, Tôru. 1981. *"Ai" "Aisu" ni tsuite. Kokugogaku* 126: 13–23.

Radway, Janice A. (1984) *Reading the Romance: Women, Patriarchy, and Popular Literature.* Chapel Hill/London: The University of North Carolina Press.

Wierzbicka, Anna. 1992. *Semantics, Culture, and Cognition: Universal Human Concepts in Culture-Specific Configurations*. New York/Oxford: Oxford University Press.

Sounds of the Heart and Mind

Mimetics of Emotional States in Japanese

Debra J. Occhi
University of California, Davis

Introduction

A second grader writes about Parent's Day at her elementary school in Sendai, Japan: *...Iyoiyo watasitati no ban. Watasi wa,* ***dokidoki*** *to issyo ni, asi ga* ***gaku-gaku*** *sinagara mae ni dete ikimasita...* 'At last it was our turn. I came forward, with my **heart pounding in excitement** (*doki doki*) while my legs **trembled nervously** (*gaku gaku*)' (Tagami 1998: 1). The terms *gaku gaku* and *doki doki* in her anecdote are vivid and economical means of communicating emotion in Japanese. Although such terms are common in discourse and popular media, their rules for usage are not clear-cut and have been little studied.[1]

Doki doki and *gaku gaku* belong to a general class of terms called *gitaigo* 'mimetics' which provide verbal resources for describing emotion and other physical states in Japanese. These vernacular lexemes are closely related to onomatopoeia and manner adverbs (respectively, *giongo* and *giseigo*). Specifically, these three classes of terms share morphophonological characteristics including sound symbolism (Hamano 1986), and in some cases, image-based metaphoric and metonymic links as well. Recent research has described the affecto-imagistic nature of *giseigo* and in many cases, the embodied nature of *gitaigo* (Harada 1998, Kita 1997, McVeigh 1996). *Gitaigo* show morphosyntactic flexibility as do the other modifiers, and as reduplicated forms, are distinguishable from them through pitch pattern, which also marks syntactic role.

This research examines usage norms of a subset of *gitaigo* which are called *kanzyoogo*, or *gitaigo* of emotion. Specifically, the reduplicated forms of *kanzyoogo* in their syntactic manifestation as compound verbs with *suru* 'do', whose usage is little studied, will be compared to emotional adjectives for which both English and Japanese literature is available. When emotional adjectives appear in discourse, evidential modification is necessary in sentences with non-first person sentential subject/experiencers. Data indicates that this is not always the case for *kanzyoogo*, even in describing similar emotions. Such difference in usage is due to the strong metonymic links that *kanzyoogo* terms exhibit to the social scenarios which evoke them. *Kanzyoogo* predicate not just emotions, but whole scenarios that evoke particular emotions and feeling states. The data on which these findings are based include sample sentences found in dictionaries and utterances appearing in popular audio/visual and print media (especially advertising and *manga* comics), the results of a questionnaire administered by the author, interviews conducted by the author, and example sentences found in a survey of the literature on Japanese mimetics.

Examining usage of these terms in regards to evidential marking draws our attention to the linguistically marked boundary of speaker's consciousness of emotional expression and description relative to sentential subject. These boundaries vary cross-linguistically. In Japanese one usually delineates information regarding persons as being directly related to the speaker's own thoughts or actions, or as indirectly perceived if pertaining to the thoughts or behavior of another person. This phenomenon is one among many by which one may ascertain who is the subject in this pro-drop language, and is especially clearly marked in the usage of non-mimetic emotional adjectives. Specifically, with non-first person subjects, evidentiality must be indicated by reference to indirect sensory perception through markers such as *-garu* 'show signs of', *rasii* 'seems', *soo da* 'looks as if', etc. (Shibatani 1990: 383–4). This linguistic phenomenon is embedded in Japanese cultural ideology, in which speakers are reluctant to characterize the motives of other individuals as independent actors. However, there is a contrasting ideological force encoded in the term *rasisa*, 'typicality', which is the notion that a person in a particular situation has indeed a specific role to play.

The issue taken up in this paper is whether *kanzyoogo* and adjectives of emotion behave similarly in expression of self's emotion *versus* description of another person's apparent emotional state. The data discussed here indicate that they do not. One criterion that appears to govern usage of emotional mimetics (but not adjectives) is how the state may be perceived, either internally through sensation or externally through observation. The nature of perception varies within the class of *kanzyoogo* depending on the meaning of the individual terms, and is, furthermore, dependent on the social scenario which is associated with a particular term. Data indicates that there are even *kanzyoogo* terms which can only be used in describing a third-person's behavior as perceived by the speaker, and not by the experiencer.

The Grammar of Mimetics

Mimetics in Japanese use the same set of phonemes as do Sino Japanese lexemes (*kango*). The basic phonological shape is $C_1V_1C_2V_2$–$C_1V_1C_2V_2$. Examples include *doki doki* 'excited pounding of the heart' and *waku waku* 'thrilled'. Some but not all of the reduplicated *gitaigo* have semantically related variants, e.g. *dokiN*, *dokiQ* (with N representing a nasal and Q a geminate stop). This morphologic flexibility allows for nuances of meaning: *doki doki* 'pounding heart', *dokiN* 'one loud thump of the heart', *dokiQ* 'heart skips a beat'. There are also $C_1V_1C_2V_2$–$C_1V_1C_2V_2$ non-mimetic reduplicated native Japanese morphemes (which undergo voicing, unlike *kanzyoogo*) which can be written in *kanzi* characters like *hitobito* 人々 'people' and *tokidoki* 時々 'sometimes' (Norimitu Tosu (1997: 225) argues, in fact, that reduplicated forms in Japanese are all similarly motivated, as elaborations expressing continuation). However, the majority of mimetic terms, including the ones examined here, are nearly always written in *kana* moraic writing. In teaching children, *giongo* onomatopoeia are written in *katakana*, and *gitaigo* in *hiragana*, but variation in script choice in media is common. Like non-reduplicated *kango* nominals such as *benkyoo* 'study', the *gitaigo* I focus on here take the verb *suru* 'to do', thus becoming compound verbs. Not all types of mimetics can participate in *suru* constructions.

Shibatani (1990: 153–157) breaks the mimetic word class into three groups: *giseigo* 'phonomimes' or onomatopoeia, representing natural sounds; *gitaigo* 'phenomimes' which represent "states, conditions, or matters of the external world", and *gizyoogo* 'psychomimes' which "symbolize mental conditions or sensations". Kindaichi (1978: 6–8) derives similar classes. The first distinction is between onomatopoeic *giseigo*, and three kinds of *gitaigo*, which symbolically assign noise to noiseless activity of animates and inanimates. *Gitaigo* subcategorizes into 'pure *gitaigo*', which describes inanimates, *giyoogo*, describing the condition of animates, and *gizyoogo*, which describes the condition of the human heart/mind (人間の心の状態を表わすようなもの). In my experience native speakers blur distinctions between internal and external conditions, as detailed later. In this paper I will describe the category of interest as *gitaigo*, with a particular focus on the subcategory of emotion, *gizyoogo*. There are marked syntactic differences within the category of mimetics. These differences will be discussed briefly here.

Syntax and Prosody of Gitaigo

Hamano (1986) presents both the formal (particularly, phonological) and sound symbolic characteristics of Japanese mimetics. Her point that "their formal characteristics cross over the boundary into the regular stratum of Japanese" is made with respect to reduplication. She outlines the grammar of mimetics but without reference to any person restriction in subject position. Like Shibatani (1990), Hamano relates the richness of the mimetic system to the relative paucity of verbs; in English one may gaze or glare, but in Japanese one uses the basic verb *miru* 'to see' or even *suru* 'to do' modified by mimetics (respectively, *sige sige* 'gaze' or *gyoro gyoro* 'glare') to get the desired effect. Sound symbolism plays such a large role in meaning that even authors who do not discuss the notion of sound-symbolism theoretically as part of linguistic phenomena state that *gitaigo* and *giongo* are "things which in our daily speech depict sound, voice, movement, condition, or psychological effect through **meaningless sound, aside from those things which have clear meaning or grammatical function**" (Asano 1978: 1, emphasis added).

Within the class of reduplicated bisyllabics are also pairs of otherwise phonologically identical terms whose syntax and semantics vary due to their pitch patterns.[2] For instance, with *kan kan* in (1) and (2) below, the pitch patterns are HLLL and LHHH respectively (Gomi 1989: 39). Therefore we see the onomatopoeic *giongo* form in (1):

(1) *kan kan to tataku* (HLLL, adverbial)
kan kan QUOT hit[3]
'to hit with the sound of *kan kan*' (a clanging sound)

In (1), *kan kan* is adverbial in that it takes *to* and a verb other than *suru*, but in (2) we see the (metaphorically related) mimetic *gizyoogo* nominal meaning 'extreme anger'.

(2) *kan kan ni naru* (LHHH, nominal)
kan kan DAT become
'to become angry' (Hamano 1986: 31–2, 48).

Kan kan as a mimetic (i.e. not onomatopoeic) *gitaigo* adverbial can also describe a burning hot sun or hot coals (Gomi 1989: 39). Relationships such as these, which cross sense modalities metonymically/metaphorically linking emotion and manner, are common among *giongo* and *gitaigo*. Furthermore, even within the group of emotional gitaigo, there are cases such as *ira ira* 'irritation' wherein pitch pattern variations align to differences in syntax while the core meaning remains constant. HLLL *ira ira* appears in (3) using *suru* "to do" as the main verb.

(3) *ore wa ira ira site iru* (HLLL, with *suru* verb)
I TOP ira ira do-CONT am
'I am irritated'

With the LHHH pitch pattern we have the nominal form:

(4) *ira ira ga tunoru* (LHHH, barenominal)
ira ira SUBJ increase
'The *ira ira* (irritated feeling) increases'

Gomi (1989: 11) explains that the *ira ira* in example (4) is a shortened form of *ira ira to sita kanzyoo* 'the feeling of irritation'. However, in that clause, *ira ira* would, preceding *suru*, be HLLL. From this we see that the strength of sound symbolism maintains the term's meaning while it allows variation in pitch pattern, which indicates grammatical role. The two variants of *ira ira* (i.e. with *suru* and as a bare nominal) are thus in complementary distribution. Not all mimetics can appear in both variants. The young writer of the anecdote at the beginning of this chapter was using *doki doki* as a bare nominal, although its appearance in that role is innovative. This type of variation, furthermore, supports the attribution of metaphor/metonymy rather than homonymy between *giongo* and *gitaigo*.

Interestingly, Kindaichi (1978) compares the difference in accentual patterns of mimetics to the difference between adverbs (said to be like HLLL) and adjectives (like LHHH), that is, the difference between non-mimetic modifiers ending in *-ku* (*ren'yookei*) and *-i* (*rentaikei*), respectively, e.g. *itosi-ku natta* 'became dear' versus *itosi-i desu* 'is dear'. In taking his argument further, however, in a frame similar to that of (4) above, the non-mimetic modifier must first undergo nominalization with *-sa*, to become *itosi-sa ga tunoru* 'dearness increases' i.e. 'speaker grows increasingly fond of someone'. Unfortunately, he does not discuss emotional *gizyoogo* whatsoever, and so we cannot be sure how they may be treated in this classification. Only reduplicative bisyllabic *gizyoogo* terms with HLLL pitch pattern that may take the verb *suru* "do" were used in this study in order to compare their usage to those of non-mimetic emotional adjectives.

The Embodied Nature of Gitaigo

We observe in the definitions of *kan kan* above (i.e. describing heat, noise, and anger) that mimetics and onomatopoeia may interact in a kind of linguistic synaesthesia. Moreover, meaning shifts from bodily sensation to mood. Interviews indicate that speakers intuit this relationship to varying degrees. In comparing my questionnaire data, which specifically asked for emotion terms, to reference works which categorize terms variously according to their physical or mental properties, similar discrepancies of judgement also arise. Depending on the author, dictionaries reveal different levels of metonomy; some of the terms used most often in the questionnaire responses detailed below were not defined as having emotional connotations in texts. In some cases, they did not appear as entries of any type. Attempts to strictly differentiate terms into physical versus mental or emotional quickly enter murky territory. For instance, *muka muka* is described in terms of nausea and anger, with varying emphasis on either interpretation (cf. Matsuki 1995 for more on anger in Japanese). The mind-body problem is moot here; the question is how permeable the sensation may be to outside observation, as inferred by evidentiality marking. Kindaichi (1974: 8, 18), who saw emotional *gizyoogo* as expressing *ningen no kokoro*, 'the human heart/mind', notes that Japanese people use these terms to describe the attitudes of **others**.

Sotaro Kita's (1997) work on mimetics, i.e. *gitaigo* of motion functioning as manner adverbials, analyzes their relationship to gesture. Emotional *gizyoogo* mimetics such as HLLL-pitch *doki doki* and *ira ira* which take the verb *suru* 'to do' as compound verbs were not part of Kita's study. Preliminary comparisons indicate that *gizyoogo* mimetics display different behavior relative to sentential subject than that of the non-emotional HLLL *gitaigo* terms that Kita discussed. Further research is needed, but for the time being I will call the reduplicative emotional mimetic terms discussed in this paper "HLLL type 2" to differentiate them from the terms Kita studied.

However, as a native speaker of Japanese, Kita (1997: 386) eloquently describes the embodied nature of *gitaigo* thus:

> Japanese mimetics have a unique psychological effect. They evoke vivid "images" of an experience, full of affect. This imagery is not only visual but can also be based on other perceptual modalities and physiological states. The meaning is felt, by native speakers, to be direct and real, as if one is at the scene.

Perhaps it is this evocative potential, accomplished in part by sound symbolism, which motivates writers such as Gomi (1989) and Asano (1978) to ascribe to *gitaigo* notions of naturalistic states and intranslatability. I realized the importance of bodily imagery and gesture to *gitaigo* the day I was invited to try wearing a kimono. I asked the hostess to define the sensation one gets in one's legs and feet after sitting for a while in formal *seiza* style, that is, sitting on the floor with one's knees pointing forward and lower legs tucked straight back underneath. I'd call the feeling 'pins and needles' or say that my legs 'went to sleep on me'. She held her hands at chest height, palms facing one another, and made small motions with her fingers as if tickling something as she thought, and then said, "*biri biri*", which means "vibration, as if electric."

Kita's "at the scene" feeling is echoed in the words of another native speaker and analyst, Soga Tetsuo (1991: 48):

「一般に擬音語・擬態語は、いろいろな音や要素を発言して、受け取る人に直観的にあるイメージお想起させる結果を持っている」

'In general, *giongo* and *gitaigo* express various sounds and feelings, with the effect to the hearer as causing **intuitive remembrance of an image**.' That image, and the remembrance of it, is a part of native-speaker intuition where language and culture intersect in the realm of emotion. *Gitaigo* and especially *gizyoogo* are, in Japanese, a very important part of the language of sentiment.

The ideologically conventionalized nature of *gitaigo* expression is expressed in Gomi Taro's illustrated work; he feels that *gitaigo* are too "raw" to be properly studied by linguists, and likens the terms to animals living indifferently to the zoologists who may try to study them: "Onomatopoeic expressions [inclusive of *gitaigo*] remind us of this **natural state of affairs**" (Taro 1989: 7–8, emphasis added). Asano (1978: 1–2) also invokes a nativistic and naturalistic argument when she says that "*giongo/gitaigo* are the hardest parts of the Japanese language for non-native speakers to grasp", and conversely, that "they cannot be explained satisfactorily to non-native speakers by native speakers". My data indicate that the naturalistic states include prototypical situations which evoke certain emotions, in the spirit of *rasisa* 'typicality'. Of course, none of these phenomena—including the ideological stance of incommensurability—are limited to Japanese.

Understanding how these terms are acquired is another project altogether, but some data on how they are taught will further underscore their scenario-specific nature. Yasui (1986) analyzes use of *giongo* and *gitaigo* by children in their first year of middle school (12 years old) in a writing exercise wherein the children chose terms and constructed sentences. Yasui found that, combining error rate scores for the terms whose sentences contained the most errors with overall rates of usage for each terms emotional *gizyoogo* fared the worst, particularly *doki doki* (80%). Interestingly, she states that the errors were semantic, although she does not describe in detail her criteria for correct usage. She concludes that "It can be said that children can't yet manage the use of words that express the warmth of the human heart" (1986: 50). These results are a bit startling in that *gitaigo* expressions of motion and manner (e.g. *hira hira* 'lightly fluttering, like falling flower petals'), as well as *giongo* (*kusyon* 'achoo', i.e. a sneezing sound) appear as early as the second grade in children's nationally-approved storybook readers currently in use in Sendai (i.e. Inoue 1989). We also saw *doki doki* used in a semantically correct manner in this chapter's opening passage, which was written by a second grader. In school texts mimetics including *kanzyoogo* are presented in the context of a storyline without other explicit definition. They appear later in semantic multiple-choice questions on exams. Sachiko Takeshita, a local elementary teacher, said that in teaching mimetics, the teacher helps the students construct appropriate sentences with the terms. It also seems to her that second graders use the term *doki doki* often in their own writing (personal communication). The anecdotal finding that *giongo/gitaigo* terms are not explicitly defined in children's textbooks (although other terms were) supports the judgements of the native-speaker linguists cited above that mimetics are considered naturalistic and intuitive aspects of Japanese language, taken in the educational setting as parts of the story scenarios in which they appear. Furthermore, the classroom emphasis on constructing sentences with *gitaigo* reinforces their scenario-dependent imagery.

The Epistemology of Gitaigo

This section presents data on *gitaigo* usage as displayed in linguistics literature, in interview data, and in the results of a questionnaire. I compare *gizyoogo* usage in this section to that of *keiyoosi* 'adjectives'. I rely on the analyses of adjectival use presented in Kuroda (1979), Teramura (1982), and Higashi (1992).

Kuroda notes the epistemological difference between adjectives which express sensations or emotions and those which do not, as in 'I am happy' versus 'I am tall', respectively. In Japanese grammar, this difference is quite clearly marked. Specifically, in attributing a sensation or emotion to a non-first person subject one must either transform the adjective into a verb, as in (6b),

(5) *watasi wa atui*
I TOP hot
'I am hot'

(6) a. **kare wa atui*
b. *kare wa atu-gat-te iru*[4]
he TOP hot-feel CONT
'he is hot'

or one must affix an evidential modifier (*atui mitai da* 'looks hot', *atu soo da* 'seems hot'). Conversely, to use the non-direct forms in the first person is odd, implying a disembodied state on the part of the speaker. The restrictions on non-first person subjects can be overcome by embedding the adjectival form into a relativized or nominalized constituent, or through the use of a question structure. There is also a stylistic option, however, which allows these restrictions to be overcome; namely, the use of an omniscient narrator voice, as in novels. However, these options are discussed using only third person subjects in sample sentences. Second person subject seems logically impossible in omniscient narration (barring perhaps, the voice of some god?). In the case of embedded subjects, second person subject is problematic, as in:

(7) ?*anata ga mottomo uresii syunkan wa itu desu ka*
you SUBJ most happy moment TOP when COP Q
"When is the moment when you are the most happy?"

However, in contrast, *gitaigo* will work in this slot:

(8) *anata ga mottomo doki doki suru syunkan wa itu desu ka*
you SUBJ most excited/heart pound do moment TOP when COP Q
"When is the moment when you are the most *doki doki*?"

None of the authors surveyed here discussed adjectival usage in second person subject sentences. Teramura (1982) discusses emotional adjectives as one of four types of emotional expressions. Two of these types are verbs, one is adjectives of judgement (e.g. *osorosii*, 'scary'), and the fourth is the adjectival class we are most interested in here, 「感情状態の直接発出」, 'direct expression of emotional state'.[5] The latter he classifies as both subjective and stative. He notes the restriction on third person subjects, and, similarly to Kuroda, states that it may be overcome by nominalization and by past tense verb forms. He neither cites Kuroda nor mentions stylistic issues of narrator voice; however, their analyses are similar in scope. Neither does he touch on second-person sentence forms in Japanese, but he does mention that adjectival behavior should be described in Japanese dictionaries (Teramura 1982: 140–150).

Higashi (1992) reworks the data on emotional adjectives and acceptability, noting that the person constraints appear even in verb use in conversation; one must also say that someone **seems to be**, rather than **is**, going somewhere. She concludes that conversation, but not narrative, requires mood, and that bare verbs and adjectives can only express the mood of the speaker.[6]

Adjectival behavior, therefore, seems to contradict what popular comparisons of English and Japanese describe as differences in psychic boundaries. According to the stereotypes of Western European, particularly English-speaking American, individualism (cf. Foley 1997: 265) versus Japanese groupism and intuitive communication (particularly in the work of Doi, Nakane, and other *nihonzinron* (Japanese essentialist) authors on culture, and in the recent linguistic work of Yamada (1997)), one might expect that Japanese could express or speak for one another's emotions. We see the reverse, however, in non-first person forms in adjectival sentences in the two languages. That is, we can say in everyday English discourse "she's happy." In Japanese, one must say the equivalent of "she looks/seems happy." How these phenomena interact with nonlinguistic behavior is an interesting problem, but the question here is whether the evidentiality restrictions on Japanese adjectives and verbs are equally present in *gizyoogo* usage. If they are, there may be an underlying cognitive schema governing multiple word classes.

Gitaigo and Imagery

Recall that *gitaigo* are mimetics which are sound-symbolically and metonymically related to onomotopoeia; that is, they share morphological and semantic characteristics. The syntax of *gitaigo* is a less well understood aspect; I will compare usage restrictions of *gizyoogo*, i.e. type 2 HLLL emotional mimetics, to emotional non-mimetic adjectives. Here I focus on reduplicative forms, the most common, and possibly the most productive, in describing emotional states. Some terms are obvious tropes based on the body. These often have lexical roots (in *giongo* or elsewhere) from which their meanings extend through metonomy, e.g. *atu atu*, the appearance of a couple who are head over heels in love, which originates from the adjective *atui*, 'hot' (Gomi 1989: 13). Some are strongly localized; of two lexemes which indicate excitement, consultants locate *doki doki* in the heart, while *waku waku* is more diffuse. For some speakers, *doki doki* connotes love as well as excitement.

Not only do these terms predicate sensory experience, they also evoke social scenarios. These emerge both in casual definitions and in sample sentences completed by native speakers. For instance, a woman who took some friends and me net fishing differentiated between *doki doki* and *waku waku* by saying, "if you're thinking about coming net fishing in Chigasaki you are *waku waku*, and if your sweetheart is going to be waiting there you are *doki doki* as well."

In Andrew Chang's (1990) *giongo/gitaigo* thesaurus, sample sentences with second person subjects are rare, and are only formed in the negative command frame, "don't do X". In these *gizyoogo* sentences framed as negative command constructions, social scenario effects include the notion of speaker-hearer hierarchy, and do not require evidential marking regarding knowledge of the hearer's emotional state:

(9) *sonna chiisa na koto de kuyo kuyo suru na yo*
that kind of small COP:ADN thing INST mope/brood do NEG EMPH
"don't let such a trivial matters (sic) get to you" (1990: 144).

As in English, second person markers are not necessary in command forms in Japanese. Note that such a frame, ending with the direct negative *na* and assertive sentence-final particle *yo*, implies social inequality, with the speaker of higher status than the hearer. For terms in Chang's 'strong emotion' category, such second person sentences appear in only 2% (1/62) of the sentences, with third person usage favored at 69% (43/62) and first person appearing 29% (18/62) of the time. Gomi (1989: 10) gives sentence (10) in the preface to his *gitaigo/giongo* dictionary. It is interesting that in both cases the addressee is being admonished for a seeming oversensitivity, or an apparent lack of toughness.

(10) *uzi uzi* (HLLL) *suru na*
weakness of spirit/hesitation do NEG
"Don't be bashful"

Asada (1996) compares *ira ira suru* to *iradatu* "to get irritated/exasperated", a related compound verb.[7] She specifically mentions that her data do not include the kind of *ira ira* as in (3) above (that is, nominal LHHH) but she does not detail the differences between the two terms, probably because her article is written in Japanese, for native speakers. In her sample sentences, *ira ira* only takes 1P and 3P subjects. A sample sentence with *iradatu*, however, employs the 2P negative command construction similarly to those above, meaning 'don't get irritated', an admonishment similar to those in (9) and (10) above. The extent to which *gitaigo* may be acceptable in negative command sentence constructions is not fully understood, although we see here that such sentences are not impossible.

Questionnaire Results

My data on usage and acceptability were gathered by means of a questionnaire submitted to 75 students in an introductory linguistics course at Tohoku University (m=61, f=14). Speakers were asked to list five *gizyoogo* (instead of that somewhat technical term, the phrase used was *kanzyoo o arawasu gitaigo*, 'mimetics that express emotion'), and then to choose one with which to complete frame sentences varying by tense and person.

The verb 'to do' *suru* was part of the sentential frame, thus limiting responses to HLLL type 2 mimetics. The questionnaire was intended to test the necessity for evidentiality marking in second person forms, as in the case of adjectives. Recall that in the literature cited above there has been no conclusive discussion of *gitaigo* as being restricted in the grammatical sense as to selection of person and verb tense in NPs.

The first section of the questionnaire yielded a list of 84 terms, whose frequencies are shown in Table 1. Note that *doki doki*, the top ranked term, was listed most often here as a *gizyoogo* term used to express feelings, although it is believed by some speakers to be strictly onomatopoiec. This finding underscores the fuzzy nature of these metonymically polysemous categories. Only 21 of those 84 terms were selected by the same respondents for use in completing frame sentences. In the frame sentences, which varied by person and tense, respondents were asked to fill in the *gizyoogo* word and to modify the sentence as needed to make it acceptable, or to indicate if acceptability was impossible.

Two interesting response patterns emerge from the data. The first pattern emerges when comparing *gizyoogo* usage to that of emotional adjectives. It is only in novels with an omniscient narrator that third person constructions without evidential modifications can be used. That is, only in a novel could one say the equivalent of "She is happy"; elsewhere one must say something more like "She seems happy". Although the available *gitaigo* literature does not specify restrictions as to selection of tense and person in NPs, second and/or third person constructions were deemed ungrammatical by some speakers, as shown in Table 2. That is, the speaker could not state flatly that the second or third person was experiencing or had experienced the sensation indexed by the *gizyoogo*. This usage restriction parallels that of emotional adjectives in normal contexts. The reason given by interview consultants for this usage is that the experiencer alone is privy to the sensation, and non-first persons may only guess in labelling the experiencer's state. However, overall rejection of acceptability of sentences lacking evidential marking was quite low.

Among the terms used in sentences, *doki doki* 'pounding heart due to excitement, perhaps romantic' and *muka muka* 'queasiness perhaps caused by anger' were most frequently rejected by speakers in second or third person sentential frames, a logical result given the nature of the sensations they describe, which refer to internal organs. Conversely, an exceptional case to this grammati-

Table 1. Kanzyoogo Usage Frequencies in Questionnaire Responses[10]

Most Common Responses

f	*Word*	*Gloss*
45	*doki doki*	a pounding heart
39	*muka muka*	sick, queasy, surge of anger
38	*ira ira*	irritation or anger because things are not going as desired
34	*waku waku*	thrilled; bursting with excitement in anticipation
19	*uki uki*	happy, excited, in a buoyant mood
18	*hara hara*	anxious; apprehensive about an outcome
14	*niko niko*	smiling happily
13	*pun pun*	very angry

Less Common Responses

f	*Word*	*Gloss*
9	*siku siku*	sobbing, or in pain from a tooth or stomachache
8	*kan kan*	extremely angry
8	*biku biku*	trembling, afraid or nervous, scared
7	*kari kari*	mental irritation, frustrated
7	*sowa sowa*	nervously excited
7	*meso meso*	uncontrolled weeping
7	*run run*	lighthearted
5	*piri piri*	extremely irritated, overly busy
4	*uzi uzi*	hesitant, irresolute
4	*hera hera*	laughing frivolously or ambiguously
3	*iya iya*	reluctant, with a heavy heart
3	*zoku zoku*	a chill down the spine from fear, anticipation, joy
3	*tun tun*	sullen unsociability, prim, morose
3	*fura fura*	strolling or loafing aimlessly
3	*mera mera*	creeping around
2	*kiri kiri*	in a whirl
2	*niya niya*	smiling faintly but meaningfully
2	*pin pin*	energetic and healthy
2	*muya muya*	can't say what one wants to
2	*ran ran*	glaring with glittering eyes

Least Common Responses (f=1): *atu atu, iso iso, itya itya, uzu uzu, uda uda, uto uto, odo odo, oro oro, ka ka, gaku gaku, gasa gasa, gami gami, kaya kaya, gaya gaya, gira gira, kusa kusa, kura kura, gura gura, guru guru, kuyo kuyo, kote kote, koro koro, goro goro, zaku zaku, sara sara, saba saba, zawa zawa, sibu sibu, jime jime, jin jin, seka seka, dara dara, tuwa tuwa, tobo tobo, neti neti, nori nori, noru noru, bata bata, pata pata, bari bari, piku piku, bisi bisi, hiya hiya, buru buru, puru puru, huwa huwa, hoku hoku, poku poku, muzu muzu, metya metya, moya moya, yosi yosi, raku raku, wai wai, waza waza*

cal pattern, *tobo tobo*, which describes 'walking wearily, trudging' could only be used in the third person construction. Other terms which did not appear in the

Table 2. Sentence Usage Frequency (f) and Unacceptability (UA) Judgements for second/third person subject sentences

Word	*f*	*UA*
ira ira	24	1
doki doki	18	6
muka muka	5	3
waku waku	5	2
hara hara	2	1
biku biku	2	1
run run	1	1
tobo tobo	1	1

frame sentences are said to exhibit this pattern. These express negative emotions such as *tun tun* 'sullen unsociability' and *syaa syaa*, 'brazen lack of apology where one should feel shame for one's behavior'. Whether they can take negative second person commands varies with the term; of these, only *tun tun* seems to work. Acceptability judgements vary among speakers, so the issue of how *gizyoogo* compares to adjectives is not clearly resolved. Furthermore, the extent to which these terms are considered embodied or external remains fuzzy. However, it is clear that we cannot assume that *gizyoogo* always describe sensations internal to the subject; it seems that the speaker applies a situational model linking the subject's circumstances or behavior to the *gizyoogo* term. This finding is verified by the second response pattern which emerged from the questionnaire data.

In a few cases, respondents modified the evidentiality of the sentence, similarly to adjectival evidentiality marking. However, in the majority of cases, where acceptability was not rejected for second or third person frames, speakers tended to add situational description or evidence for the emotional state to the sentence. For instance, under *ira ira* "irritation/anger" descriptions included *tabako ga nakute* "not having cigarettes" and *dare ka o matte* "waiting for someone". In the case of *doki doki* "a pounding heart" respondents expanded the sentence with scenario descriptions such as *zyoseitati no mae de* "in front of women" (by men) and *tesuto no mae ni* "before a test". Simpler embellishments included references to time and place. It is interesting that women tended to use simpler modifications. Unfortunately, the gender ratio here is too unbalanced to draw reliable conclusions about gendered differences in usage. Responses that situate feelings may indicate that respondents were using the novel's omniscient narrator framework in modifying the sentences.

In interviews, some speakers were willing to make direct statements about persons close to them with *gizyoogo*, as in (11) about father[8] to mother.

(11) *kare ga ira ira site iru*
he SUBJ irritation do CONT
"he's angry"

In this situation the speaker is warning her/his mother. Social distance may be a factor at play here. A similar instance of reporting the irritation of a relative appears in Harada's discussion of the cross-sensory nature of *gitaigo* (1998: 85, interlinear gloss added):

(12) *Ani wa kesa kari kari-kari site iru*
elder brother TOP this morning from worked-up do CONT
"My elder brother is *kari-kari* (worked up) from this morning."

Recall also the earlier discussion of social inequality allowing usage of second person subject in negative command forms as found in dictionaries. Usage of these vernacular *gizyoogo* terms in discourse may index various speaker-hearer relationships of closeness and empathy, or of social dominance, thus allowing speakers to provide information which would be improper to discuss in other contexts or with other lexical means. Further research using conversational data will be necessary to tease out these motivations and their relationship to genre, style, and speaker/hearer relationships.

Issues of Genre

In spoken Japanese, *gitaigo* are considered part of the vernacular; these terms are not often heard in news broadcasts or other formal speech settings. In written form they are used heavily in mass media such as *manga* 'comics' and in advertising. In Natsume Fusanosuke's (1993) *manga* cartoon adaptation of the Edo era sex manual *Danzyo no situkekata* 'Manners for Men and Women', we see *doki doki* accompanying the pictures in *Dai-ni, arabati no sikata* 'Part two, how to sleep together for the first time' (i.e. the woman's first time) in which the couple enters the marital bedroom.

In the *manga*, the characters are clearly undergoing description by an omniscient narrator as in novels. Hinata (1986: 60) has observed elsewhere that, "in *manga* the *gitaigo siin* which accompanies the lovers' dramatic reunion can be likened to the flow of background music." *Siin* is defined, however, as 'silence in a situation where one would usually expect some noise' (Sotaro Kita, p.c.).

The evocative power of imagery underlies the frequency of *gitaigo* use in advertising. Here, the use of *gitaigo* terms also seems to be an attempt to create or reinforce associations between the product and the sensation, as in *doki doki Tokyo* Japan Railways ads distributed throughout the more rural Tohoku region (Figure 4). They may also create a shared feeling with the product, as in the case of the *waku waku* 'excited' pizza dough of the Pizza California kitchen: *kyoo pizza ni naru. Waku waku* 'Today (I) become pizza. Wowee!'.

These associations are possible through reference to scenarios of shared meaning, such as the excitement of going to a big city, or the anticipation involved in contemplating a future meal. Taking the evocation of sensations to an extreme, we see commercials on Japanese television such as those of the summer of 1997, wherein the sole action was that of persons drinking the advertised products (beer or juice drink), accompanied only by the sounds of their loud gulping, there being no voice-over naming the product until the very end of the commercial message. Rather than presenting words describing the sensation, viewers were made to watch and listen to the actual situation in progress. This convention reappeared in the winter of 1998, with the actor slurping down *ochazuke* 'rice with hot green tea and seasonings', and is still prevalent as fall approaches. Gitaigo can be regarded as intermediate between this bold presentation of imagery and formal description.

Conclusions

From the survey of related literature on adjectives and *gitaigo*, we see that analysis of the former is not exhaustive, but is much more common. *Gitaigo* are considered vernacular, associated strongly with the natural and animal world. Like many other vernacular forms in other languages, *gitaigo* have been relatively ignored by linguistic scholars until fairly recently. Metonymic and metaphoric extensions among sense modalities (e.g. *kan kan*), as well as between semantically similar lexemes with different pitch patterns (e.g. *ira ira* LHHH and HLLL), result in fuzzy categorization. The class is, nonetheless, firmly grounded in sound symbolism embedded in a morphophonemic framework.

In data on *gizyoogo* terms, which refer to emotional states, distinctions are made as to whether a term denotes an inner, perceived state or one that is used to describe observed behavior. In this regard they form a parallel to the epistemological distinctions made for adjectives by Kuroda (1979), Teramura (1982) and others; however, with *gizyoogo*, data from questionnaires and interviews indicates that usage restrictions are not categorical. Inner states, like the pounding heart of *doki doki*, for some speakers, are constrained to first person subjects; conversely, 'outer' states like *tobo tobo* trudging, are restricted to third person subjects, although there is variation in usage. In either case, the terms show strong association to scenarios as evidenced by native speakers' preference for adding information regarding time, place, or manner. Strong links are displayed between bodily action, sensation, situation, and emotion. Social closeness or hierarchy may also influence usage. Advertising media co opt *gitaigo* because they come from vernacular speech and, with their strong imagistic potential, catch the attention of listeners and readers, but in doing so, they also reinforce vernacular usages. Ads also play on *rasisa* 'typicality' effects, naturally assigning an emotion to an experiencer of a given scenario.

These terms, as all other forms of meaning, are produced "against a background of taken-for-granted knowledge (knowledge about the social and physical world and forms of textuality, 'common sense', linguistic and generic conventions etc.)" (Hodge and Kress 1993: 210); that background will require close scrutiny in analyzing *gitaigo*. In this vein the comments of native speaker linguists have been especially valuable. Syntax of the type 2 HLLL *gizyoogo* terms deserves further study and comparison to that of other mimetics. Furthermore, the cultural implications of the usage phenomena described above for adjectives, that one cannot assert directly about another's emotional state, provide an interesting point for comparison to much of the literature on Japan, which often describes Japanese culture as empathic (Lebra 1976: 38) wherein intuitive communication is valued over speech (Yamada 1997).

Japanese emotional mimetics occupy a middle zone between more easily expressed onomatopoeia and manner adverbs, on the one hand, and emotional adjectives, which require evidentiality marking, on the other. The interwoven nature of physical and psychological states and social scenario effects in *gitaigo*, as well as issues of discourse versus written genres, render questionnaire-based and frame-sentence elicitation methods problematic, however. Now that the outlines of *gitaigo* grammar are understood, I am seeking natural data from everyday discourse. Data from other genres of discourse are needed to develop more nuanced interpretations of the epistemology and grammatical expression and predication of emotions, particularly their expression and predication by different word-classes.

As speakers of a language we may employ various grammatical and discursive means to express any given thought or emotion. What may be difficult to express through one manner of expression may be easily communicated through another. This flexibility of expression has interesting implications for the study of interaction between language and thought. If we consider notions of "thinking for speaking" (Slobin 1996), then it follows that different constructions— i.e. *gitaigo* or adjectival— may predicate different construals of the same scene. Thus, different grammatical constructions may reveal and evoke differing emotional consciousness. In this vein we may consider that while adjectives are one step removed in the analytic dimension of abstract thought, the embodied, naturalistic conventions expressed by *gizyoogo* allow speakers to appeal directly to the physically based, culturally shared experiential consciousness of the listener.

Acknowledgments

I'm grateful for insightful comments received from several people, including Tony Backhouse, Chidori Nakamura, my colleagues in Martha Macri's and Charles Fillmore's/Yoko Hasegawa's seminars, and especially, Sotaro Kita, Gary Palmer, and Janet S. Smith. An earlier version of this paper was presented to the 1996 American Anthropological Association meeting, where I received helpful comments from the audience. Also, I am indebted to Kaoru Horie, Kuniaki Ito, Hiromu Kato, Shigeru Sato, Kei Yoshimoto, as well as the introductory linguistics students who took the questionnaire, all of whom are from Tohoku University, and to my interview consultants in Sendai and elsewhere. Yale romanization is used except with proper names. Japanese works appearing herein are translated by me, with the original Japanese text included occasionally.

Notes

1. An adult native speaker said that she would not have used *doki doki* as a nominal, that "only children can write like this." We see later that this kind of nominalized form is said to be the result of deletion of other clausal elements. Perhaps this young author is keen to a change in progress.
2. Japanese, with the exception of a few dialects, is a pitch-accent language.
3. Abbreviations are as follows: C Consonant, V Vowel, H High pitch, L Low pitch, COP Copula, COP:ADN Copula Adnominal, COP:CONT Copula Continuative, DAT Dative, EMPH Emphatic, INST Instrumental, NEG Negative, Q Question, QUOT Quotative, SUBJ Subject, TOP Topic.
4. That the verb attached to non-first person emotional adjectives *garu* 'to feel' used here includes the meaning *furi o suru* 'to pretend' must be mentioned here. Understanding that link allows one to argue more strongly for 'territory of information' boundaries (cf. Kamio 1995) limiting epistemic access to another's emotional state, as portrayed in this adjectival usage phenomenon. I'm grateful to Janet S. Smith for emphasizing this point. It may be that the 'verbiness' of constructions with type 2 HLLL *gitaigo* ('verby' in that they take *suru* 'to do'), is partially responsible for their behavior, although this is another issue that cannot be completely analyzed here.
5. No mention of *gitaigo* is included.
6. Unfortunately for the present study, Higashi treats all modal sentence-final particles (SFP) alike;

in the sentences analyzed in this study, speakers used only a few SFPs to modify *gitaigo* sentences. Many thanks to Koji Nabeshima for discussing this article with me.

7. *Iradatu*, although commonly written in *kanzi* 苛立つ, employs an unconventional reading of the first *kanzi*, which means 'caustic' (and is sometimes reduplicated in writing *ira ira* as well, although syllabic *kana* writing is more common for the latter). The second *kanzi* is the verb, *tatu*, 'stand' and also appears in the idiom *hara ga tatu*, lit. "the belly stands" meaning 'to get angry.'
8. This example is taken from taped data. Other consultants, in reading this sentence, have questioned the use of *kare* 'he' to indicate one's father, since it generally implies a woman's love interest. Specifically why the seeming incongruity exists (in indexing one's mother's spouse with *kare*) is an issue under separate investigation.
9. Total N=75; males=61, females=14. Females ordered the top responses as follows: *waku waku* 12, *doki doki* 11, *ira ira* 8, *muka muka* 6, *uki uki* 6. Future research will further explore possible relationships of gender and other social differences to usage, with better gender balance among consultants. Only emotional connotations of the terms are provided here in the glosses, although most of them have other metonymically related meanings.
10. Total N=75; males=61, females=14. Females ordered the top responses as follows: *waku waku* 12, *doki doki* 11, *ira ira* 8, *muka muka* 6, *uki uki* 6. Future research will further explore possible relationships of gender and other social differences to usage, with better gender balance among consultants. Only emotional connotations of the terms are provided here in the glosses, although most of them have other metonymically related meanings.
11. In this example, as mentioned in the text, all but 3rd person were stated to be unacceptable.

References

Asada Hideko. 1996. "*Ira ira suru*, *iradatu*, and *zireru*". *Nihongogaku* 15, June, 40–46.

Asano, Tsuruko. 1978. *Giongo/Gitaigo Dictionary*. Tsunegawa Shoten: Tokyo.

Chang, Andrew C. 1990. *A Thesaurus of Japanese Mimetics and Onomatopoeia: Usage by Categories*. Taishukan: Tokyo.

Foley, William. 1997. *Anthropological Linguistics*. Basil Blackwell: London.

Gomi Taro. 1989. *An Illustrated Dictionary of Japanese Onomatopoeia*. Japan Times Press: Tokyo.

Hamano Shoko Saito. 1986. *The Sound-Symbolic System of Japanese*. PhD Dissertation: University of Florida.

Harada Rie. 1998. "Sound symbolic emotion words in Japanese". In Angeliki Athanasiadou & Elzbieta Tabakowska (eds), *Speaking of Emotions: Conceptualization and Expression*. Mouton: Berlin/New York, 83–98.

Higashi Hiroko. 1992. "Person Limitations in Sentences With Emotional Adjectives". In Tajima Gando & Niwa, Kazuya (eds), "*Japanese Theoretical Research 3*." Osaka: Izumi Shoin, 45–68.

Hinata Shikeo. 1986. "Onomatopoiea and mimetics in comics". *Nihongogaku* 5, July, 57–67.

Hodge, Robert and Gunter Kress. 1993. *Language as Ideology*. New York: Routledge.

Inoue Hisashi. 1989. *New Japanese, 2nd Grade Part II*. Tokyo Shokoo: Tokyo.

Kamio Akio. 1995. "Territory of information in English and Japanese and psychological utterances". *Journal of Pragmatics* 24: 235–264.

Kindaichi Haruo 1978 "An Outline of *Giongo & Gitaigo*". *Giongo/Gitaigo Dictionary*. Tsunegawa Shoten: Tokyo, 4–25.

Kita Sotaro. 1997. "Two-dimensional semantic analysis of Japanese mimetics". *Linguistics* 35: 379–415.

Kuroda S.-Y. 1979. "Where epistemology, style and grammar meet". In *The (W)hole of the Doughnut: Syntax and its Boundaries*. E. Story-Scientifica: Ghent, 185–203.

Lebra, Takie Sugiyama. 1976. *Japanese Patterns of Behavior*. University of Hawaii Press: Honolulu.

Matsuki, Keiko. 1995. "Metaphors of anger in Japanese". In J. R. Taylor and R. E. MacLaury (eds), *Language and the Cognitive Construal of the World*. Mouton de Gruyter: Berlin, 137–157.

McVeigh, Brian. 1996. "Standing stomachs, clamoring chests and cooling livers: Metaphors in the psychological lexicon of Japanese". *Journal of Pragmatics* 26:25–50.

Natsume Fusanosuke. 1993. *Manners for Men & Women: Edo and Meiji Era Romance Studies*. Chikuma Shobo: Tokyo.

Palmer, Gary 1996 *Towards a Theory of Cultural Linguistics*. University of Texas Press: Austin.

Shibatani Masayoshi. 1990. *The Languages of Japan*. Cambridge: Cambridge University Press.

Slobin, Dan I. 1996. "From 'thought and language' to 'thinking for speaking'". In J. J. Gumperz and S. Levinson (eds), *Rethinking Linguistic Relativity*. Cambridge: Cambridge University Press, 70–96.

Soga Tetsuo. 1991. *Giongo & Gitaigo Reader*. Kogaku Shoten: Tokyo.

Tagami Ayana. 1998. *"Doki doki sita zyuugyoo sankan* 'Heart-pounding Class Observance' in 'Monsters' Ballad". In Takahashi Izumi (ed), *Second Grade Room 1 Newsletter*. Sendai: Haranomati Shogakkoo.

Teramura Hideo. 1982. *Syntax and Meaning in Japanese, Volume One*. Kurosio: Tokyo.

Tosu Norimitsu. 1997. "Reduplicated Noun Phrases in Japanese". In K. Yamanaka and T. Ohori (eds), *The Locus of Meaning: Papers in Honor of Yoshihiko Ikegami*. Kurosio: Tokyo, 221–5.

Yasui Fusako. 1986. "Childrens onomatopoeia/mimetics". *Nihongogaku* 5, July, 47–56.

Yamada Haru. 1997. *Different Games, Different Rules: Why Americans and Japanese Misunderstand Each Other*. NY: Oxford University Press.

Bursting with Grief, Erupting with Shame

A Conceptual and Grammatical Analysis of Emotion-Tropes in Tagalog

Gary B. Palmer, Heather Bennett and Les Stacey
University of Nevada at Las Vegas

> Mameng leaned heavily against Linda Bie's breast and cried soundlessly. Her body shook in anguish and desperation, and in the pit of her stomach, because of her sudden loss, she felt a nausea rising up with a rending coldness, shattering her foothold on life. Now her heart seemed to be drying up, squeezing her lungs and throat with steely tightness. Then all at once she seemed to be bursting with an agony so great that she lost control of herself, at last and cried out, "My God!" — Bulosan (1997)

The emotion experienced by Mameng in Carlos Bulosan's *The Cry and the Dedication* followed on the killing of Dante, an intellectual and member of a small unit of post-war Filipino revolutionaries.[1] What caught our attention in this passage was the phrase "bursting with agony." Is this metaphor coherent in English and other languages, or does it reveal something peculiar to Tagalog? And what of the drying up of the heart and the tightness of the lungs? These seem more familiar, but perhaps not entirely conventional in English. We might be more inclined to speak of a shriveling of the heart and a tightness of the chest. Zoltán Kövecses (Personal communication) has suggested that the metaphor of bursting normally signals intense emotions in other languages, so grief must be intense in Tagalog. There seems to be much in the passage that is culturally specific, yet not incomprehensible to speakers of English. The passage raises the question of whether metaphors of emotion are universal or culturally determined, which is to say, socially constructed.

Most linguists, psychologists, and anthropologists today will agree that emotion and language are tightly intertwined. In recent years, the field of cognitive linguistics has abandoned the idea that metaphors are singular figures of speech which carry no meaningful cultural ideas. Instead, some scholars now hold that metaphors are cognitive processes which help to create and maintain people's view of culture and play a significant role in their capacity to conceive emotions (Gibbs 1992, Kövecses 1990, n.d., Lakoff & Turner 1980, Palmer 1996). George Lakoff and Mark Johnson (1980) showed that metaphor is "pervasive in everyday life, not just in language but in thought and action." Raymond Gibbs (1992: 572) summarized the view of cognitive linguists by claiming that "conceptual metaphors are independent of language but motivate the meanings of many verbal metaphors and provide coherence to linguistic expressions that are traditionally viewed as individual exceptions."

The analysis of emotion metaphors in the English language has become a well-developed field of study and continues to expand. However, claims of the universality of metaphorical concepts cannot be validated until further researches have been completed in other languages. Kövecses (n.d.), who attempts to discover cross-cultural regularities in metaphorical conceptualization, admits that we will never understand whether or not the way we think about our emotions is shared by non-English speakers without analyzing emotional metaphors in other cultures. Basic emotional concepts have been studied in Palau and Turkish and metaphors have been studied as well in Hungarian, Japanese, and Chinese (Kövecses n.d.), but thousands of other languages exist and must be investigated in order to establish the universality of metaphorical meanings. Palmer (1996: 227) is optimistic that "the stock of metaphorical imagery is very rich in any language," but adds that each culture will vary from others in the classification and prioritization of meaningful groups. This paper attempts to further cross-cultural studies in cognitive linguistics by examining and categorizing the use of certain emotion metaphors in the Austronesian language Tagalog, the national language of the Philippines. We categorize the expressions in terms of both semantics (Appendix I) and grammatical construction. We find considerable support for certain proposed universals of emotional expression as well as conceptualizations that are specifically Tagalog. Analysis of the grammar of emotional tropes reveals that emotional processes typically happen in body parts, with body-part terms functioning as actors or undergoers of static processes, but, grammatically speaking, emotional processes are not caused to happen by external agents.

Emotion Metaphors in Tagalog[2]

The emotion language of Tagalog reveals several metaphorical concepts which have been assumed to be at least near-universals. There are two central metaphors which have been most frequently encountered in completed studies: THE BODY IS A CONTAINER FOR THE EMOTIONS and EMOTION IS FORCE (Lakoff 1987, Kövecses n.d.). THE BODY AS CONTAINER metaphor category is present in Tagalog when referring to such emotions as pride, shame, fear, grief, and anger (to be discussed later in the paper). EMOTION IS FORCE, which Kövecses (n.d.) claimed to be a "universal way of understanding emotion," is also evident in Tagalog. This general-level metaphor can be expanded to specific-level metaphors such as EMOTION IS A NATURAL FORCE and EMOTION IS INTERNAL PRESSURE, both of which appear in Tagalog categorizations. Kövecses (n.d.) combined these classifications and arrived at the concept EMOTION IS INTERNAL PRESSURE INSIDE A CONTAINER, which is realized in the Tagalog emotion metaphors of anger, shame, and grief.

Numerous emotions are experienced in every culture, but our English emotion concepts may not always be transferable; that is, they may differ in important respects from the meanings of similar emotions in other cultures. Kövecses (n.d.) contended that there are five basic emotions that are felt by all people: anger, sadness, fear, joy, and love. If happiness be taken as equivalent to joy, the list includes all the basic emotions. The English emotion concepts which have been analyzed metaphorically form a "fairly representative sample": anger, fear, happiness, sadness, love, lust, pride, shame, and surprise. The emotion metaphors that we have found in Tagalog can be roughly classified in English as grief, sadness, pride, lust, happiness, love, fear, shame, anger, and calm. Since all the basic emotions can be found in this list, there is some basis for comparison to previous work in English. However, that is not to say that these emotions are essentially the same as their English counterparts. That is an issue that will require much more study to resolve.

Happiness and Sadness

Positive emotions such as happiness and love are metaphorically classified as being UP (except, perhaps, for love), LIGHT, WARM, or VALUABLE. Negative emotions, however, like hate and sadness have generally been viewed as DOWN, DARK, COLD, NON-VALUABLE, or ILLNESS (Kövecses n.d.). In Tagalog, the metaphors associated with happiness and sadness accommodate portions of this framework exactly. That is, happiness is up, sadness is down and dark.

HAPPINESS IS UP, BOUNDLESS
langit ng buhay 'heaven life'
ikapitong langit 'seventh heaven'
sa lupa man ay may langit din 'on earth there is also heaven'

HAPPINESS IS LIGHTNESS/WEIGHTLESSNESS
magaan ang katawan 'light body'
magaan ang pakiramdam 'the feeling of light weight; lightness of body'

SADNESS IS DARK
gabi ng buhay 'night life'

SADNESS IS DOWN
magbigat ang dibdib 'heavy chest'
pagkarapa 'prostrate (dejected, disappointment)'

It is clear that the positive emotion of happiness is consistent with the findings of Lakoff and Johnson (1980) and Kövecses (n.d.): that it is viewed as UP, BEING IN HEAVEN, and LIGHT. Kövecses (n.d.) reports that these metaphor categories are paralleled in the Chinese concept of happiness, as studied by Ning Yu (1994). The negative interpretation of sadness carries the opposite metaphorical concepts: DARK and DOWN. Also, the two emotions can be classified with regard to the master metaphor THE BODY AS A CONTAINER. Specifically, as with the closely related emotion of grief, THE CHEST (OR HEART) IS A CONTAINER. In Tagalog, this might be phrased more accurately as THE HEART IS A SOURCE. For happiness, Tagalog speak of *umaawit ang puso* 'singing the heart'. Sadness, however, is compared to pain or metonymically referred to an uncomfortable pressure in the chest.

SADNESS IS INJURY TO THE CHEST OR HEART
sugat sa puso 'pain/cut in the heart'
dumudugo ang puso 'bleeding the heart'

PRESSURE IN THE CHEST FOR SADNESS
magbigat ang dibdib 'heavy chest (heavy heart, depression, disappointment)'
naninikip ang dibdib 'tightness in chest, inability to breathe'

Sugat sa puso and *magbigat ang dibdib* might best be regarded as metonymies that have been metaphorized (Kövecses, personal communication). The last two examples suggest physical strain and bodily discomfort, metaphorized in the first instance as weight.

Another comparison between the Tagalog emotion concepts of happiness and sadness involves the mental processes experienced by the speakers as they perceive the emotion. Whereas happiness suggests attentiveness, sadness represents the inability to think and, to a greater degree, understand. The following metonymies exhibit these classifications:

ALERTNESS FOR HAPPINESS
matalas ang kaisipan 'increased alertness'

INABILITY TO THINK FOR SADNESS
wala ang isipan 'inability to think'
malayo ang isipan 'thought processes far away; thoughts focused elsewhere'

INSANITY FOR SADNESS
nabaliw sa lungkot 'crazy from sadness'

Tagalog speakers also talk of *magbulaklak na landas* 'a flower trail (leading to happy, prosperous life)' when experiencing happiness, perhaps suggesting that the emotion is a progressive, hopeful, and promising journey. For this reason, it has been classified under the specific metaphor category HAPPINESS IS A JOURNEY.

Sadness can lastly be grouped into the metonymical category PHYSICAL REACTION FOR SADNESS. In Tagalog, speakers experience *walang ganang kumain* 'decreased appetite' when feeling sad. Thus, the experience of sadness is embodied in the perception of physical needs.

Grief

Closely allied to sadness is grief. In Tagalog, GRIEF IS PRESSURE IN A CONTAINER. Filipinos relate the emotion to *parang puputok ang dibdib* 'like a bursting chest (extreme sorrow and sacrifice)'. Thus, the body is seen as a container for grief, more specifically, THE CHEST IS A CONTAINER FOR GRIEF. The expression 'like a bursting chest' gives the connotation of intense pressure on that container, causing it to erupt.

Another expression for grief is *lumuha ng bato* 'tears (eye) of stone (grieve intensively)'. Tagalog speakers use this expression to emphasize the hardness of the emotion. Thus, INTENSE GRIEF IS HARDNESS.

One of the expressions for grief has obviously come from Spanish Catholicism. *May koronong tinik* 'there is a crown of thorns', suggests the suffering of Christ on the cross. The phrase *luksang tutubi* 'black dragonfly (false mourning)' referring to "gaudy apparel of those who do not really mourn" may also derive from Christian traditions of wearing black in mourning.

Love

Phrases describing love and affection fall into four categories: (1) social metonymy (GRASPING FOR LOVE, TOGETHERNESS FOR AFFECTION), (2) TO LOVE IS TO BE SMITTEN, (3) LOVE IS DEATH and (4) the heart is the source or experiencer of love. At least the first three are concordant with the studies of Kövecses (n.d.) and Lakoff and Johnson (1980). The Tagalog term *kapit-tuko* 'grasp-gecko (hold tightly, deeply in love)' is deceptively complex in its figuration of love. It is obviously metaphor, in that the gecko stands for a lover, but it is also metonymy in that one may actually grasp the beloved and because it brings the loved one close, as is usual in scenes of love. Somewhat similar is the term *kapiling* 'together in heart, emotional togetherness', from *piling* 'side of'. The second love metaphor, TO LOVE IS TO BE SMITTEN, is expressed by the phrase *masama ang tama* 'direct hit (of Cupid's arrow) (fall in love)'. The final expression, *patay na patay* 'dead (intensive) (passionate fondness, not limited to persons)', is seemingly an intensification of the former, elaborated into the more specific LOVE IS DEATH metaphor.

Three expressions position the heart as the source or experiencer of love. These were taken from video melodramas, which draw much of their imagery from the American popular media. The expressions are somewhat unusual in preposing the body-part term.

puso ko'y sa 'yo lang 'my heart is only for you' (P)
pusong nagmamahal 'loving heart' (P)
puso ko'y nangungulila 'my heart feels abandoned' (P)

Fear and Shock

Fear is a multifaceted emotion metaphor in Tagalog, one which seems to support Kövecses' analysis of fear in English. Kövecses concluded that expressions for fear were representations of physiological and behavioral reactions, and that fear was also categorized as being a natural force and occurring in a container. All three of these findings are illustrated in Tagalog. There are four specific-level tropes that sub-categorize the emotion phrases: KNOWING FEAR FOR FEAR, FEAR IS A NATURAL FORCE, THE BODY IS A CONTAINER FOR FEAR, and FEAR IS A PHYSICAL REACTION.

The metonymy KNOWING FEAR FOR FEAR is realized in the Tagalog term *hindi nakakakilala ng takot* 'not familiar with fear (knows no fear)'. Kövecses (personal communication) regards this as an instance of the general metonomy PRECONDITION FOR STATE—-to know something stands for something — which exists in Hungarian and English as well. A closely related metonomy *malabo ang kaisipan* 'blurred thought process; inability to think', which can be classified as BLURRED THOUGHT FOR FEAR. Fear can also be categorized under the metaphor FEAR IS A NATURAL FORCE, as exemplified by the Tagalog phrase *parang nagulat sa kulog* 'like shock from thunder (sudden, strong fear)'. The metaphorical classification of NATURAL FORCE assumes that the emotion, fear, "affects us while we passively undergo its effects" (Kövecses 1990: 78). An identical categorical metaphor exists in the English language. We have only a single example to demonstrate the metaphor that THE BODY IS A CONTAINER FOR FEARLESSNESS/BRAVERY: *malakas ang loob* 'inside swells (fearless)', but no less than 15 instances of fear as a physical reaction. This suggests that the dominant mode of expression of fear in Tagalog is via metonymies based on physical reactions:

FEAR IS A PHYSICAL REACTION
tumatayo ang balahibo 'stand feathers (feathers stand, feel goose pimples)'
bahag ang buntot 'between legs the tail (cowed, abject fear)'
namuti ang talampakan 'white soles of feet (running in fear)'
nanlalambot ang mga tuhod 'weakness of knees'
nanginginig ang mga buto 'trembling of limbs/ bones'
nangangatog ang puwit 'trembling buttocks (great fear)'
maputla ang mukha 'pale the face; loss of blood from face'
huminto sa paghinga 'stop breathing; breath taken away'
nanlalamig ang boong katawan 'chillness in the body; decreased body temperature'
humahangos ang paghinga 'increased breathing rate'
pinapawisan ng malagkit 'stickiness of sweat'
inaalon ang dibdib 'rising and falling (like waves) of chest (rapid heart beat due to strong fear)'
nalalagas ang buhok 'loss of hair'
namumuti ang buhok 'graying of hair; hair turns white with fear'
namugto ang mata sa kakaiyak 'deepening the eyes of crying; sunken eyes'

It is assumed that universally, across both linguistic and cultural boundaries, people experience similar, if not identical, physiological and behavioral reactions to certain emotions. Kövecses (n.d.) recognized that the "physiological aspect of the [fear] concept is greatly elaborated in language." Kövecses (1990) listed some physical responses of fear including physical agitation, increased heart rate, blood leaving the face, inability to move or speak, and drop in body temperature. At least three of these conditions are exhibited in Tagalog expressions for fear, including *maputla ang mukha* 'pale the face; loss of blood from face,' *nanlalaming ang boong katawan* 'chillness in the body; decreased body temperature,' and *inaalon ang dibdib* 'rapid heart beat due to strong fear.' In addition, other Tagalog metonymies for physical reactions associated with fear have corresponding expressions in English. Of those, *tumatayo ang balahibo* 'stand feathers' connotes goose bumps or chills to Tagalog speakers. An English equivalent is *hair standing on end*. A second phrase, *bahag ang buntot* 'between legs the tail,' corresponds to the English *he put his tail between his legs and ran*. The metaphor of *nangangatog ang puwit* 'trembling buttocks,' we can only assume, could be compared to the English *shaking in one's boots*. Another metonymy, *namuti ang talampakan* 'whites soles of feet,' depicts the universal reaction of running away in fear. The remaining metonymies listed incorporate physical reactions of the eyes, hair, and respiration, all of which are physical reactions to fear.

Shock is hardly separable from fear. In Kövecses' description of fear metonymies in English, he claimed that the physiological effects that the emotion generated were the inability to move or speak and the loss of blood from the face. His description could also fit the physiological effects of shock in English and Tagalog. Fear and shock should probably be grouped into a single emotion category, but it is not clear whether either would serve as the superordinate, nor is it clear whether their relationship should be regarded as synchronic or diachronic with fear leading to shock or *vice versa*. We have three expressions:

LOSS OF MOVEMENT, SPEECH FOR SHOCK
patay na tuod 'dead stump of tree (shocked, unresponsive)'
napipi 'speechless (temporary loss of speech due to strong feelings)'

PALENESS FOR SHOCK
ibinabad sa suka 'soaked in vinegar (pale)'

The similarity of the English fear and the Tagalog shock metaphor categories can perhaps be explained by common elements in the two emotion concepts. For example, the expression *ibinabad sa suka* 'soaked in vinegar' is glossed as pale from 'shock *or* fear' [emphasis added], giving the impression that the same term might serve to convey either shade of emotion.

Shame and Sensitivity

It is clear from a discussion by Vincente L. Rafael (1988) that there is a master metaphor SHAME IS PRESSURE INSIDE A CONTAINER. Furthermore, there is a relationship between shame and inner feelings, specifically the *utang na loob* 'debt of gratitude or debt of the inside.' *Hiya* 'shame' can emerge as an 'outbreak' or an 'eruption':

> As a case in point, we take Rafael's [1988] ethnohistorical discussion of Tagalog *hiya* 'shame' and *utang na loob* 'debt of gratitude or debt of the inside.' According to Rafael, "to have no *hiya* is to have no *utang na loob*" (1988: 127). But gratitude is closely related to respect (*paggalang*): "One has an *utang na loob* to one's mother (and never the reverse) by virtue of having received from her the unexpected gift of life. It is assumed that one will never be able to repay this debt in full, but instead will make partial payments in the form of respect (*paggalang*)" [italics in original]. One way of making these payments to parents and elders is to use the honorific terms *ho* and *po*. Failure to return the gift by giving respect would lead to an "outbreak" or "eruption" of *hiya*, that would leave one speechless, "utterly unable to return even in words what one has received" (1988: 131). (Palmer and Brown 1998: 334).

Like shock, a conceptual metonomy for shame in Tagalog is LACK OF EXPRESSION FOR LACK OF SHAME OR SENSITIVITY, exemplified by the phrases *tabla ang mukha* 'board face (unresponsive, no shame)' and *makapal ang mukha* 'thick face (impenetrable, no shame)'. Similar expressions refer to the thickness of the skin: *balat-karabaw* 'skin-carabao (thick skinned, no shame)' and *balat-sibuyas* 'skin-onion (thin skinned, sensitive)'.

Anger

Anger is the most frequently studied emotion, and is presumed by most cognitive linguists to have similar core patterns cross-culturally (Kövecses 1990, n.d., Lakoff 1987). Palmer (1996: 231) speculated that "since anger is probably everywhere correlated with rising body temperature and blood pressure, it is quite possible that some core images and figurative descriptions of anger are universal." Many metaphors for anger can be subsumed under the notion that ANGER IS A FLUID IN A CONTAINER. The intensity of anger is measured in terms of increasing heat and pressure (Lakoff 1987: 385–6). This generalization is supported by studies in English, Japanese, Chinese, Zulu, and Hungarian. The majority of Tagalog anger concepts are most readily categorized under the more specific metaphors ANGER IS HEAT OR FIRE and ANGER IS PRESSURE IN A CONTAINER. Two of these expressions also conform to the metaphor of anger as fluid in a container. The concept of anger as heat or fire is found in both English and Zulu (Taylor and Mbense 1998). As in Zulu, and unlike English, anger as heat in Tagalog is most often construable as dry (smoking, roasting, burning, hot) or unspecified as to dryness versus wetness.

ANGER IS PRESSURE IN A CONTAINER
nagpuputok ang butse 'burst the gizzard (bursting with anger, neck swells with anger)'
nanlilisik ang mga mata 'pressure in the eyeballs; bulging eyes'
pumuputok ang butse 'bursting the ribs'
umalsa ang galit 'anger rises (refers to rising heat and blood pressure in state of anger)'

ANGER IS HEAT OR FIRE
gatungan ang galit 'add fuel to anger (provoke anger)'
kumukulo ang dugo 'blood boils (very angry, much annoyed)'
mainit ang ulo 'hot head ("like hot things, an angry person often hurts feelings")'
nagbabaga ang katawan sa galit 'roasted by anger'
nagpapanting ang tainga 'warming the ear, tingling sensation'
umalsa ang galit 'anger rises (refers to rising heat and blood pressure in state of anger)'.
umuusok ang tuktok 'top is smoking (very angry)'

The phrase *nagpapanting ang tainga* 'warming the ear, tingling sensation' is a metonomy which suggests that anger takes place in the head. In addition, the expression *mainit ang ulo* 'hot head ("like hot things, an angry person often hurts feelings")', not only recognizes the physiological effects of increasing heat, but also locates anger in the head. But the Tagalog concept of the "hot head" is quite different from English, in that it indexes the effects of the hot head on other persons, rather than the feeling state of the angry person. This idiom is consistent with the findings of Palmer and Brown (1998) that Tagalog speakers focus more readily on the causes and behavioral reactions to emotions than on their own feeling states.

The metaphor ANGER IS PRESSURE IN A CONTAINER may be realized as pressure in the body cavity (*pumuputok ang butse* 'bursting the ribs' and *nagpuputok ang butse* 'burst the gizzard (bursting with anger, neck swells with anger)' or in the head, giving the metaphor THE HEAD IS A CONTAINER: *nanlilisik ang mga mata* 'pressure in the eyeballs; bulging eyes'. The expression *magbara ang ilong* 'stuffy nose (quick tempered)' may be an example of the head as a container metaphor, but more likely it is a metonymy referring to the irritability that goes with a stuffy nose. Nevertheless, Tagalog metaphors support the idea that the pressurized container metaphor for anger is a cross-cultural universal, due, no doubt, to the fact that people universally experience similar physiological processes, which are realized as muscular tensions and internal pressures. Kövecses (n.d.) stated the notion as follows: "the embodiment of anger appears constrain…the kinds of metaphors that can emerge as viable conceptualizations of anger." The concept of anger rising in the body is also found in Japanese (Matsuki 1989). It is interesting that the heart does not appear in any of the Tagalog expressions as the locus of anger. This contrasts with Zulu, in which bad-tempered person is said to have a short heart.

Anger in Tagalog is also expressed in terms of aggressive behavior or hostile reactions, thus forming the metonomy AGGRESSION FOR ANGER:

gustong manampal ng mukha	'desire to slap face'
gusto mong pumatay	'you want to kill'
kayang pumatay ng tao	'able to kill a person; capable of murder'
matalim ang paningin	'sharp the sight, stabbing with eyes, aggressive visual behavior'

Taylor and Mbense (1998: 214) list no expressions of this kind for Zulu, though they do find that anger is a dangerous animal and a provocation ("You are a cockroach in my ear", "You are sticking your finger in my ear", "He looked at me with long (sharp) needles").

Finally, ANGER IS PLANTING: *mapagtanim* 'prone to planting (hold a grudge)'. Perhaps this metaphor suggests the maturation of the emotion from a small seed of anger, which will be repeated, grow, or intensify through time. Underlying all these tropes is the understanding that anger increases. There seems to be little lexicalization of hate in Tagalog (Nikolaus Himmelmann, personal communication). We have one metaphor, HATE IS A BAD TASTE, exemplified by the metonymical phrase *maasim ang mukha* 'sour face' which was sub-glossed as 'ill feeling, hatred'. It is interesting to note that Heider (1991) found that anger is less of a focal emotion in Indonesian than it is in English. Sadness and confusion, on the other hand, are more central emotions in Indonesian than in English.

Conceit and Pride

Of the emotion concepts studied by linguists, pride and surprise are the least metaphorically comprehended (Kövecses n.d.). We have two expressions that were glossed as 'pride' by Surian[3] (1982), but one of our consultants judged that 'conceit' is a better gloss for both. These are *lumalaki ang ulo* glossed as 'a big head (proud, boastful),' *lumaki ang loob* 'grow inside (pride; feeling or emotion is likened to "an elastic container")'. Another expression, *pakiramdam ay tumangkad* 'feeling of tallness; increase in body size,' was glossed as 'pride' by one of our consultants, but another judged 'conceit' to be the better gloss. The expression *maipagmamalaki* 'pride' from the root *laki* 'size, grow' was found in Ramos (1971) and explained to us as follows: *ang maipagmamalaki ay paraan ng sadya ng pagpapakita ng kahit na anong bagay na alam mong magugustuhan ng ibang tao 'maipagmamalaki* is a way of purposely showing anything you know others would like'. Our last example is *tumataba ang puso* 'heart increases in size,' glossed by one consultant as 'pride'. Another consultant judged that the meaning is very dependent upon context. It could mean 'pride,' but it could also indicate that one is sick, or even that one is overwhelmed with happiness and excitement, so that "the heart is getting out of the chest." The governing metaphor in all these cases is GROWTH OR EXPANSION IS CONCEIT OR PRIDE (or other emotion). The expressions *lumalaki ang ulo, lumaki ang loob*, and *tumataba ang puso* are also based on the metaphor THE BODY IS A CONTAINER FOR CONCEIT OR PRIDE (or other emotion).

Lust

Lakoff (1987) claims that the emotion of lust is often seen as relating to desire or love, but that lust metaphors in English have much more in common with anger than with love. However, in Tagalog, Kövecses' (n.d.) category of DESIRE IS HUNGER is more consistent with our findings. For in Tagalog, LUST IS HUNGER, as in the expressions: *makatulo-laway* 'makes saliva drip (attractive, said of woman by man)' and *parang gutom ng aso* 'like hunger of a dog (obsession with women)'. The metaphor of the latter example could be expanded to include A LUSTFUL PERSON IS AN ANIMAL, which is a specific metaphor for lust in English as well (Lakoff & Kövecses in Lakoff 1987: 410).

Calmness

We have only one figurative expression for calmness. It is *magpalamig ng ulo* 'have a cool head'. This was described to us as *ang pagpapalamig ng ulo ay ginagawa ng tao para maisan-tabi muna ang problema at kalmahin ang sarili* 'cooling the head is what a person does to put aside a problem for a while and calm him/herself'.

The Grammar of Tagalog Figurative Expressions for the Emotions

The purpose of this section is simply to provide a description and analysis of the grammatical constructions in the citation forms (Appendix II). It is likely to be inadequate as a grammatical description of Tagalog figurative expressions in general because examples taken from discourse will show a wider range of variation. To illustrate the problem, the English expression *swell with pride* may be heard in actual discourse as "she swelled with pride," or "he was (all) swollen (up) with pride," giving variations in tense, degree, and aspect. Nevertheless, it is interesting that similar constructions are given by both Surian ng Wikang Pambansa (1982) and native speakers. At the very least, this suggests that there are conventional vernacular citation forms for figurative expressions concerning the emotions.

Nikolaus Himmelmann (1991, n.d.) has characterized Tagalog as having an equational clause structure, which comprises a *predicate* and a *predication base* plus additional phrases containing arguments. The predicate may minimally be a word root with morphology indicating voice (actor oriented or undergoer oriented), mood (realis or irrealis) and control (active or stative) (Drossard 1994). Semantically, this root may be nominal or relational. The predication base is what the clause is about. It is normally a phrase introduced by the referential preposition *ang*. The expression *maasim ang mukha* 'sour face (ill feeling, hatred)' has this structure. The predicate is *maasim* (with the actor-oriented, irrealis, stative *ma-* prefixed to the root *asim* 'sour'). The predication base is *ang mukha* 'the/a face'. We will describe this construction as [PREDICATE *ang* ARGUMENT]. The relation of predicate to predication base appears to be a specific case of the more general relation of figure to ground or trajector to landmark (Langacker 1991). Lopez (1940: 11) regarded forms with the so-called "inverse" *ay* as normal (*ang saging ay halaman* 'the banana is a plant') and forms with initial predicate as indicating the "participation of emotion, of suspense, to emphasize a conception". Of the 78 tropes collected for this paper, 46 have the [PREDICATE *ang* ARGUMENT] structure. By contrast, only four have the *ay* structure, and two of those are possible calques from English (*puso ko'y sa 'yo lang* 'my heart is only for you', *puso ko'y nangungulila* 'my heart feels abandoned').[4]

Table 1. Tagalog Emotion Expressions by Predicate Type and Phrase Structure

	Active						Stative			other	
	-um-	*-in-*	*mag-*	*nag-*	*maN-*	*naN-*	*ma-*	*na-*	other	unoriented	Total
ang	11	1	2	3	-	4	11	7	-	5	44
ng	2	1	1	-	1	-	-	-	1	3	9
sa	1	1	-	-	-	-	-	2	-	1	5
exist.[a]	-	-	-	-	-	-	-	-	-	2[b]	2
na	-	-	1	-	-	-	-	-	-	2	3
other	3	-	-	1	-	1	2	-	2	6	15
Total	17	3	4	4	1	5	13	9	3	19	78

[a]Expression contains existential phrase.
[b]One existential phrase also contained a *sa*-phrase.

The preponderance of expressions in our corpus contain *ang*-phrases (44 out of 78; see also, Table 1). In these expressions, the argument in the predication base may be either an actor or an undergoer, depending upon the orientation of the predicate. If the predicate is actor-oriented (i.e. actor focus), as in 51 of the 78 expressions, the argument is an actor; if it is undergoer-oriented, the argument is an undergoer. Actor-oriented predicates take affixes *-um-*, *ma-*, or *mag-*. Undergoer-oriented predicates take affixes *i-*, *-in-*, *-in*, and *-an*. In one case the statistically modal structure is expanded with a locative *sa*-phrase (*nagbabaga ang katawan sa galit* 'roasted [the/a body] by anger').

In another nine expressions the predicate is followed by a noun-phrase introduced by the genitive preposition *ng* instead of the specific *ang*, giving the construction [PREDICATE *ng* ARGUMENT]. In two of these, the modal construction functions as the predication base for a higher predicate: *gustong* [*manampal ng mukha*] 'desire [to slap face]' and *hindi* [*nakakakilala ng takot*] 'not [familiar with fear]'. A similar expression with the actor-oriented predicate *pumatay* is *gusto mong* [*pumatay*] 'you want to kill'. In six expressions, the predicate is followed by a noun-phrase introduced by the locative preposition *sa*, giving the construction [PREDICATE *sa* ARGUMENT], as in *huminto sa paghinga* 'stop breathing'. The remaining structures include bare predicates (ex. *mapagtanim* 'prone to planting'), compound-word predicates (ex. *balat-karabaw* 'skin-carabao'), predicate-link-noun (ex. *ikapito-ng langit* 'seventh heaven'), existential phrase (*may koronong tinik* 'there is a crown of thorns'), and preposed argument (*pakiramdam ay tumangkad* 'feeling of tallness'). One of the *sa*-constructions is also existential and preposed: *sa lupa man ay may langit* 'on earth [wherever] there is also heaven'. Three expressions are introduced with *parang* 'like': 'like hunger of a dog,' 'like shock from thunder,' 'like a bursting chest.' Two expressions are introduced with *wala(ng)* 'without': 'without ability to think,' 'without desire to eat'.

In those prefixes that alternate between irrealis and realis forms (*ma-/na-*, *mag-/nag-*, *maN-*/naN-) the number of citations for each mood is nearly equal: 17/16. It may also be worthwhile noting that 31 expressions have active morphology and 23 have stative morphology. Finally, the two most common types of expressions have the active actor-oriented infix *-um-* in the predicate and an *ang*-phrase in the predication base (11) and the static prefixes *ma-* or *na-* in the predicate and an *ang*-phrase in the predication base (18), the latter showing a slight preference (11 versus 7) for the irrealis form. No reciprocal transfer, or "social" forms (*dahil sa, ipag-... + ang, mag-...-an + ang, magka-...-an + ang*) occur in these expressions. The body of this section will discuss the expressions as broken down by predicate morphology.

Expressions using active actor-oriented affixes (*-um-*, *mag-*, *nag-*, *nang-*)

–um-

Sixteen of the 78 expressions listed in Appendix II have the infix *-um-* in the predicate. The most common construction is [PREDICATE *ang* ARGUMENT]. All but one of the expressions with *-um-* are intransitive. In most instances with explicit actors, the actor appears in an *ang* phrase. Most commonly, the actor is a part of or location on the human body or an animal body: the heart (4 instances), the blood, the ribs, the head, the inner being, the crop (as of a chicken), feathers, or the top. In one phrase the actor is the gerund 'breathing' (*h-um-ahangos ang paghinga*). In one expression (*pakiramdam ay t-um-angkad* 'feeling of tallness'), the actor (*pakiramdam* 'feelings') is preposed, possibly suggesting that the term has high emotional salience. One expression (*kaya-ng p-um-atay ng tao*) is introduced with the conditional predicate *kaya*. The argument in this expression is an undergoer, that is, the person being killed. In three expressions, the actor is tacit: *h-um-into sa paghinga* 'stop breathing'; *l-um-uha ng bato* 'tears (eye) of stone (grieve intensively)'; and *walang ganang k-um-ain* 'decreased appetite'.

d-um-udugo ang puso 'bleeding the heart'
h-um-ahangos ang paghinga 'increased breathing rate'
h-um-into sa paghinga 'stop breathing; breath taken away'
kaya-ng p-um-atay ng tao 'able to kill a person; capable of murder'
k-um-ukulo ang dugo 'blood boils (very angry, much annoyed)'
l-um-aki ang loob
'grows inside (pride; feeling or emotion is likened to "an elastic container")'
l-um-alaki ang ulo 'big head (proud, boastful)'
l-um-uha ng bato 'tears (eye) of stone (grieve intensively)'
pakiramdam ay t-um-angkad 'feeling of tallness; increase in body size'
p-um-uputok ang butse 'bursting the ribs,' 'anger'
t-um-ataba ang puso
'heart increases in size,' pride, also sickness, extreme happiness, excitement
t-um-atayo ang balahibo 'stand feathers (feathers stand, feel goose pimples)'
um-aawit ang puso 'singing the heart'
um-alsa ang galit 'anger rises (refers to rising heat and blood pressure in state of anger)' 173)
um-uusok ang tuktok 'top is smoking (very angry)'
walang ganang k-um-ain 'decreased appetite'

mag- and *nag-*

Eight terms have predicates prefixed with *mag-* or *nag-*. Four terms use *mag-*, indicating actor orientation, irrealis mood, active control and characteristic, intensive, or repeated activity (Schacter 1987). The four *nag-* forms have realis mood. The constructions are very much like those with *-um-* predicates, in that most have *ang*-phrases in the predication base, and 6 of the 8 have arguments that are body parts (head, heart, nose, chest, ear, gizzard, the body itself). One of these makes explicit use of the emotion-term *galit* 'anger' as a secondary argument: *nag-babaga ang katawan sa galit* 'roasted [the/a body] by anger'. Another makes explicit use of the emotion term *nagmamahal* 'loving' in *pusong nagmamahal* 'loving heart'. The notion of a 'flower trail' in *mag-bulaklak na landas* does not refer to the emotion of happiness, *per se*, but to the circumstances that may bring it about.

mag-bara ang ilong 'stuffy nose (quick tempered)'
mag-bigat ang dibdib 'heavy chest (heavy heart, depression, disappointment)'
mag-bulaklak na landas 'a flower trail (leading to happy, prosperous life)'
nag-babaga ang katawan sa galit 'roasted by anger'

mag-palamig ng ulo 'have a cool head'
nag-papanting ang tainga 'warming the ear, tingling sensation'
nag-puputok ang butse 'burst the gizzard (bursting with anger; neck swells with anger)'
pusong nag-mamahal 'loving heart'

maN-, naN-

Our six forms include *mananpal*, from *maN-sampal*, *nang-ang-atog, nang-ungulila,* and three instances of *nan-*, from *naN*-l...). According to Schacter (1987), the related stem-forming prefix *paN-* can refer to characteristic activity, to harmful or destructive activity, or to activity directed toward multiple objects. In these expressions, the notion of harmful or destructive activity appears to fit. The prefix here is in the realis mood. All but two of the *maN-/naN-* expressions have *ang*-phrases in the predication base, and in all the actors are the body or body parts (buttocks, knees, eyeballs, heart). All but one have the incompletive aspect.

gustong manampal ng mukha 'desire to slap face'
nang-ang-atog ang puwit 'trembling buttocks (great fear)'
puso ko'y nang-ung-gulila 'my heart feels abandoned'
nan-lalumbot ang mga tuhod 'weakness of knees', 'fear'
nan-lalamig ang boong katawan
'chillness in the body; decreased body temperature', 'fear'
nan-lilisik ang mga mata 'pressure in the eyeballs; bulging eyes', 'anger'

Expressions with stative actor-oriented prefixes (*ma-*, *na-*, and *maka-*, *naka-kaki-*)

ma- and na-

Twenty-two of the 78 expressions have prefix *ma-* or *na-* in the predicate. Thirteen have *ma-*, which is actor-oriented, irrealis, and stative. Eleven of the *ma-* forms have the grammatical structure [PREDICATE *ang* ACTOR]. Six of arguments in the predication base refer to states of the body, parts of the body, location in body, or body products, including body, face (3), nose, chest, head, saliva, and inside. The face is thick, sour, or pale. The other parts are light, hot, or swelling. Four of the terms have thought processes (3 terms) or sight as the argument in the predication base. The thought processes are blurred, distant, or alert. The sight is sharp and stabbing. The term *ma-i-pag-mamalaki* 'pride' is complex in that it has an outer irrealis and stative *ma-* prefix, followed by an undergoer *-i-*, followed by the gerund-forming *pag-* and reduplication of the first-syllable of the base for incompletive aspect. It may have the sense of 'characteristically growing because of something'.

ma-asim ang mukha 'sour face (ill feeling, hatred)'
ma-gaan ang katawan 'light body (animated feeling)'
ma-init ang ulo
'hot head ("like hot things, an angry person often hurts feelings")'
ma-ipagmamalaki 'pride' < *laki* 'size, grow'
ma-kapal ang mukha 'thick face (impenetrable, no shame)'
ma-labo ang kaisipan 'blurred thought process; inability to think'
ma-lakas and loob 'inside swells (fearless)'
ma-layo ang isipan 'thought processes far away; thoughts focused elsewhere'
ma-pagtanim 'prone to planting (hold a grudge)'
ma-putla ang mukha 'pale the face; loss of blood from face'
ma-sama ang tama 'direct hit (of Cupid's arrow)(fall in love)'
ma-talas ang kaisipan 'increased alertness'
ma-talim ang paningin 'sharp the sight, stabbing with eyes, aggressive visual behavior'

Nine of the 78 expressions have the prefix *na-* (the realis form of the actor-oriented stative *ma-*) in the predicate. Seven of these conform to the construction [PREDICATE *ang* ACTOR (*sa* LOCATION)]. These 7 all have body-part arguments, including hair (2), eyes, soles of feet, buttocks, limbs/bones, and chest. The expression *na-mugto ang mata sa kakaiyak* 'deepening the eyes of crying; sunken eyes' appears to involve the metaphor ACTIVITY IS A LOCATION, as exemplified by the phrase *sa kakaiyak* 'in crying'. One of the two expressions with *sa*, as opposed to *ang*, has an explicit emotion-term, *lungkot*, for its argument, resembling in this respect the expression *nag-babaga ang katawan sa galit* 'roasted [the/a body] by anger'.

na-baliw sa lungkot 'crazy from sadness'
na-lalagas ang buhok 'loss of hair'
na-mugto ang mata sa kakaiyak 'deepening the eyes of crying; sunken eyes'
na-mumuti ang buhok 'graying of hair; hair turns white with fear'
na-muti ang talampakan 'white soles of feet (running in fear)'
na-nginginig ang mga buto 'trembling of limbs/bones'

na-ninikip ang dibdib 'tightness in chest, inability to breathe'
na-pipi 'speechless (temporary loss of speech due to strong feelings)'
parang na-gulat sa kulog 'like shock from thunder (sudden, strong fear)'

maka-

The prefix *maka-* is commonly glossed as aptative, because it often suggests the idea "be able to." (Schacter 1987, Ramos and Bautista 1986). It occurs in the expression *maka-tulo-laway* 'makes saliva drip (attractive, said of woman by man)'.

nakakaki-

Nakaki- is intense. It occurs in the expression *hindi nakakaki-lala ng takot* 'not familiar with fear (knows no fear)'.

Expressions using the orientational infix *-in-*

The infix *-in-* predicates undergoer orientation and realis mood. There are only three expressions with this prefix. In only one of these (*in-aalon ang dibdib*) is the undergoer explicit (*ang dibdib* 'chest'). In one expression (*i-b-in-abad sa suka* 'soaked in vinegar'), the predicate has an additional undergoer orientational prefix (*i-*). In the predication base the argument appears in a locative *sa*-phrase, so it is apparently a participant that is neither actor nor undergoer. One of these expressions has an argument in the genitive *ng*-phrase (*ng malagkit* 'stickiness') that cannot be the grammatical undergoer and is hard to construe as an actor for the predicate *p-in-apawisan* 'sweat on/from (someone)'. It seems to have the semantics of a possessor or an adjunct. Thus, it appears that predicates with undergoer orientation appear infrequently in these emotion figures. The number of instances is to low to discover a modal construction.

i-b-in-abad sa suka 'soaked in vinegar' (pale, shock or fear)
in-aalon ang dibdib
'rising and falling (like waves) of chest (rapid heart beat due to strong fear)'
p-in-apawisan ng malagkit 'stickiness of sweat'

Expressions with non-oriented predicates

Eighteen of the 78 expressions have predicates that lack explicit orientational affixes, suggesting that these are less grammaticized and more idiomatic expressions. Five of these have *ang*-phrases in the predication base. Three follow the predicate with a genitive *ng*-phrase. One complements the predicate with a locative *sa*-phrase. Two have existential predicates, one of these also having a preposed argument with a *sa*-phrase. Two have double predicates linked with *na*. Three are compound words. Two are simple noun-phrases.

Argument introduced with ang

bahag ang buntot 'between legs the tail (cowed, abject fear)'
gatungan ang galit 'add fuel to anger (provoke anger)'
parang puputok ang dibdib 'like a bursting chest (extreme grief or sorrow)'
tabla ang mukha 'board face (unresponsive, no shame)'
wala ang isipan 'inability to think'

Argument introduced with ng

gabi ng buhay 'night life (dark, tragic, or sad part of life)'
langit ng buhay 'heaven life (boundless happiness)'
parang gutom ng aso 'like hunger of a dog (obsession with women)'

Argument introduced with sa

sugat sa puso 'pain/cut in the heart'

Predicate followed by sa phrase

puso ko'y sa 'yo lang 'my heart is only for you'

Existential plus argument

***may** koronong tinik* 'there is a crown of thorns.'
*sa lupa man ay **may** langit* 'on earth there is also heaven (bliss of heaven; extreme joy)'

Double predicates linked with na

patay na patay 'dead (intensive)(passionate fondness, not limited to persons)'
patay na tuod 'dead stump of tree (shocked, unresponsive)'

Compound and simple noun-phrase predicates

balat-karabaw 'skin-carabao (thick skinned, no shame)'
balat-sibuyas 'skin-onion (thin skinned, sensitive)'
kapit-tuko 'grasp-gecko (hold tightly; deeply in love)'
luksang tutubi 'black dragonfly'
ikapitong langit 'seventh heaven'

Bare Stative Predicate

kapiling 'together in heart, emotional togetherness' < *piling* 'side of'

What do these grammatical constructions tell us of how speakers of Tagalog conceptualize the emotions? Much of the thinking about emotions clearly centers around the body, including locations within the body, and, most often, body-parts. The fact that body-part terms are found in *ang*-phrases of predication bases shows that they are core arguments. These constructions reveal that body-parts and other arguments are typically regarded either as actors or as undergoing stative processes, but they are seldom characterized as undergoers of transitive processes. Whether the citation forms take realis or irrealis mood is most likely governed by the discourse context.

Conclusions

In this paper we have presented and categorized a variety of emotion concepts in the Tagalog language, including metonymies, orientational metaphors and ontological metaphors. Kövecses (n.d.) generalized that "emotion is largely conceptualized in terms of a variety of metaphors," that certain conceptual metaphors were at least near universals, and that universal physiological reactions in emotional states were significant determinants of the language used to describe emotion. His theory holds true in Tagalog, as metaphors or physical metonymies exist for all the roughly equivalent English emotions of happiness, love, grief, sadness, fear, shame, anger, conceit, and lust. As expected, the general-level categories of THE BODY IS A CONTAINER and EMOTION IS FORCE OR INTERNAL PRESSURE were prevalent in Tagalog.

Specifically, we have found that the body, often the chest, is a container for certain unpleasant emotions such as fear, grief, shame, and anger, but only in anger is internal pressure attributed to heat and hot fluids. Anger is also commonly expressed as fire. Grief is closely allied to sadness in that it is expressed as pain, pressure in the chest region, and darkness. However our examples suggest that they are not identical. With grief (as with shame and anger), the pressure is from within 'like a bursting chest,' but sadness is realized as tightness of the chest, a heavy chest, or an injury to the heart. Notions of growth and increase are important in anger, pride, and bravery. Among the pleasant emotions, the notion of the body as a container is important only to pride. Orientational metaphors show up with frequency only in the polar emotions happiness (up and light of weight) and sadness (down). Sadness is also dark, but we have no instances of happiness as visual light. Cognitive states seem particularly salient in the expression of fear and sadness, both of which can be expressed as an inability to think. Increased alertness is associated with happiness.

Kövecses (1990) proposed a folk-wisdom hypothesis which he calls the "onion peel" theory. This idea recognizes the mind and body as containers, but defines the intensity of the emotion by depth. To paraphrase Kövecses (1990: 152), "a person is composed of several layers of emotions (feelings), thoughts, and actions," of which the outermost represent the conscious, public emotions and the innermost or deepest level feelings are private and true. Tagalog ethno-emotional theory bears some resemblance to this schema, but there are differences. Despite the *balat sebuyas* 'skin-onion' metaphor, the "onion peel" theory is applicable to the Tagalog emotion of shame only in its grossest outline. Kövecses' model is dependent on the assumption of depth in a container. Tagalog speakers, however, emphasize the thickness or thinness of the container's surface (onion skin, carabao skin, board), not the levels within, and when shame becomes intense, it "breaks out" as *hiya*. Thus, the emotion of shame itself appears to have only one or two levels, and nothing deep within. But Kövecses's schema of layered emotional depth does work for Tagalog when more emotions are taken into account. Shame is at the surface, but deeper levels harbor the inner feelings or *kalooban*, such as the *utang na loob* 'debt of the inner being.'

Metonymy is as important as metaphor in the construction of expressions for emotions. Many terms are based on both processes, as with the expression *tabla ang mukha* 'board face,' which metonymically suggests the behavior of one who lacks shame and metaphorically depicts the face as a board. Metonymy is particularly important in the language of fear, for which we have no less than 15 expressions depicting physical reactions that accompany the emotion.

A small group of expressions is based upon what might be called social ontology. That is, social experiences provide the source material for metaphor or metonymy. These expressions are not so much embodied, as they are socially grounded. These include expressions for love and affection (grasping for love, togetherness for affection) and anger as aggression ('desire to slap a face,' 'able to kill a person,' 'stabbing with the eyes').

This set of expressions shows no very obvious significant influence from foreign cultures. Only five expressions seem clearly European in origin: One is *masama ang tama* 'direct hit (of Cupid's arrow).' Another is *may koronong tinik* 'there is a crown of thorns.' The remaining three refer to *langit* 'heaven.' Only the term *luksang tutubi* 'black dragonfly (false mourning, referring to gaudy apparel of those who do not really mourn)' may show a native response to

European cultural elements. There may well be other expressions in these data whose origins are also foreign but less obviously so.

Analysis of the grammar of these expressions shows that core arguments, as defined by appearance in *ang*-phrases, are often body-part terms. Body-part terms and other types of core arguments are typically expressed either as grammatical actors or as undergoers of stative processes, but they seldom manifest as undergoers of transitive processes. The emotional processes of the body happen, but, grammatically, and therefore conceptually, they are seldom caused to happen. We can also make a more general observation. Most of the analyzed expressions, be they metaphor or metonym, have the dual structure [PREDICATE/PREDICATION BASE]. Furthermore, as metaphorical sources and metonyms, they exist in dual relationship to target (spoken about) concepts. It would appear that Tagalog emotion-metaphors link the dual conceptual structures of the figurative expressions to dual grammatical structure, where grammar is understood in the sense of cognitive linguistics as the symbolic linkage of phonology with semantics. Thus, to the extent that the expressions are consciously constructed, they provide two lines of evidence in favor of a heterogeneous dual-focus system of consciousness (Stamenov 1997).

In summary, our research has shown that Tagalog corresponds in many respects to proposed universals of emotional expression. Tagalog figurative expressions depict emotions as substances and pressures within containers, natural forces, orientations, physiological reactions, cognitive states, and social behaviors. Most Tagalog expressions have analogs in English. Yet there are hints that speakers of Tagalog have some unique concepts that derive from Tagalog discourse traditions, such as the notion that a hot head is so named because he or she endangers others in the immediate neighborhood, not just because he or she is experiencing heat or appears to be hot. Another notion that seems peculiarly Tagalog is the idea that shame may erupt, provided that one does not have a face like a board or the skin of a carabao. The equation of happiness to alertness seems at least slightly foreign to a speaker of English, as does the notion of bursting with grief with which we introduced this paper, though speakers of English sometimes say that one may have too much grief bottled up inside. More examples of Tagalog emotional expressions need to be examined and studies of emotion language in other Western Austronesian languages would be particularly useful for situating Tagalog among the world's traditions of emotional expression.

Notes

1. This paper was first presented at the Annual Meeting of the Southwestern Anthropological Association, Pasadena, April 1998. Nikolaus Himmelmann provided useful comments regarding the problematic status of 'hate' as a translation for any Tagalog emotion and the erroneous gloss of several expressions as 'pride'. Zoltán Kövecses provided useful guidance in our analysis of metaphors and metonyms. The authors thank Sara Stacey and Diana Shoup for serving as consultants to this project. Most of the Tagalog expressions discussed in this paper come from two sources: The first is Surian ng Wikang Pambansa (1982), a 300 page thesaurus of idiomatic expressions, with parallel explanations and definitions in Tagalog and English. The second is a questionnaire given to 10 Filipino women by co-author Les Stacey. The questionnaire simply requested Tagalog expressions for various emotions.
2. Conceptual metaphors and metonymies are presented in small caps. Conceptual metaphors have the structure TARGET IS SOURCE, as in EMOTION IS FORCE. Conceptual metonymies have the structure SOURCE FOR TARGET, as in ALERTNESS FOR HAPPINESS.
3. Surian ng Wikang Pambansa was previously the Institute of National Language (INL). It is now Linangan ng mga Wika sa Pilipinas. The INL was originally established to develop Filipino as the national language (Sibayan 1991).
4. *ko'y* < *ko* + *ay*

Appendix I: Semantic Categorizations of Tagalog Emotional Tropes

CONTAINER METAPHORS

THE BODY IS A CONTAINER FOR EMOTION

THE BODY IS A CONTAINER FOR CONCEIT AND PRIDE

lumaki ang loob 'grows inside (pride; feeling or emotion is likened to "an elastic container")'
lumalaki ang ulo 'big head (proud, boastful)'
tumataba ang puso 'heart increases in size,' pride, also sickness, extreme happiness, excitement

INSENSITIVITY IS HAVING THICK SKIN

balat-karabaw 'skin-carabao (thick skinned, no shame)'
balat-sibuyas 'skin-onion (thin skinned, sensitive)'
makapal ang mukha 'thick face (impenetrable, no shame)'

THE BODY IS A CONTAINER FOR FEARLESSNESS/BRAVERY

malakas and loob 'inside swells (fearless)'

THE BODY IS A CONTAINER FOR GRIEF

parang puputok ang dibdib 'like a bursting chest (extreme grief or sorrow)'

THE BODY IS A CONTAINER FOR ANGER

kumukulo ang dugo 'blood boils (very angry, much annoyed)'
mainit ang ulo 'hot head ("like hot things, an angry person often hurts feelings")'
umalsa ang galit 'anger rises (refers to rising heat and blood pressure in state of anger)'

THE HEART IS A SOURCE (WITHIN THE BODY AS CONTAINER)

umaawit ang puso 'singing the heart'
puso ko'y sa 'yo lang 'my heart is only for you'

THE HEART IS AN EXPERIENCER*
pusong nagmamahal 'loving heart'
puso ko'y nangungulila 'my heart feels abandoned'

EMOTION IS A MEASURE OF INTENSITY

EMOTION IS HEAT IN A CONTAINER

ANGER IS THE HEAT OF A FLUID IN A CONTAINER
kumukulo ang dugo 'blood boils (very angry, much annoyed)'

EMOTION IS POTENTIAL FOR GROWTH

ANGER IS GROWTH/PLANTING
mapagtanim 'prone to planting (hold a grudge)'

CONCEIT OR PRIDE IS GROWTH
pakiramdam ay tumangkad 'feeling of tallness; increase in body size'
maipagmamalaki 'pride' < *laki* 'size, grow'

FORCE METAPHORS

EMOTION IS A NATURAL FORCE

FEAR IS A NATURAL FORCE
parang nagulat sa kulog 'like shock from thunder (sudden, strong fear)'

EMOTION IS INTERNAL PRESSURE IN A CONTAINER

SHAME IS PRESSURE IN A CONTAINER
'outbreak' or 'eruption' of shame (*hiya*)–(Rafael 1988: 131)

GRIEF IS PRESSURE IN A CONTAINER
parang puputok ang dibdib 'like a bursting chest (extreme grief or sorrow)'

ANGER IS PRESSURE IN A CONTAINER
nanlilisik ang mga mata 'pressure in the eyeballs; buldging eyes'
nagpuputok ang butse 'burst the gizzard (bursting with anger; neck swells with anger)'
pumuputok ang butse 'bursting the ribs'

ORIENTATIONAL METAPHORS

HAPPINESS IS UP, BOUNDLESS
ikapitong langit 'seventh heaven'
langit ng buhay 'heaven life (boundless happiness)'
sa lupa man ay may langit 'on earth there is also heaven (bliss of heaven; extreme joy)'

HAPPINESS IS LIGHTNESS/WEIGHTLESSNESS
magaan ang katawan 'light body (animated feeling)'
magaan ang pakiramdam 'the feeling of light weight; lightness of body'

SADNESS IS DARK
gabi ng buhay 'night life (dark, tragic, or sad part of life)'

ONTOLOGICAL METAPHORS AND PHYSICAL METONYMIES

ANGER IS FIRE
gatungan ang galit 'add fuel to anger (provoke anger)'
nagbabaga ang katawan sa galit 'roasted by anger'
umuusok ang tuktok 'top is smoking (very angry)'

HEAT FOR ANGER
nagpapanting ang tainga 'warming the ear, tingling sensation'

COOL FOR CALMNESS
magpalamig ng ulo 'have a cool head'

GRIEF IS HARDNESS
lumuha ng bato 'tears (eye) of stone (grieve intensively)'

TO LOVE IS TO BE SMITTEN
masama ang tama 'direct hit (of Cupid's arrow) (fall in love)'

LOVE IS DEATH
patay na patay 'dead (intensive)(passionate fondness, not limited to persons)'

LUST IS HUNGER
makatulo-laway 'makes saliva drip (attractive, said of woman by man)'
parang gutom ng aso 'like hunger of a dog (obsession with women)'

ILL FEELING IS A BAD TASTE
maasim ang mukha 'sour face (ill feeling, hatred)'

HAPPINESS IS A JOURNEY
magbulaklak na landas 'a flower trail (leading to happy, prosperous life)'

AGGRESSION FOR ANGER
gustong manampal ng mukha 'desire to slap face'
gusto mong pumatay 'you want to kill'
kayang pumatay ng tao 'able to kill a person; capable of murder'
matalim ang paningin 'sharp the sight, stabbing with eyes, aggressive visual behavior'

SADNESS IS INJURY TO THE CHEST OR HEART
dumudugo ang puso 'bleeding the heart'
sugat sa puso 'pain/cut in the heart'

PRESSURE ON THE CHEST FOR SADNESS
magbigat ang dibdib 'heavy chest (heavy heart, depression, disappointment)'
naninikip ang dibdib 'tightness in chest, inability to breathe'

MENTAL STATE FOR EMOTION
ALERTNESS FOR HAPPINESS
matalas ang kaisipan 'increased alertness'

INABILITY TO THINK FOR SADNESS
malayo ang isipan 'thought processes far away; thoughts focused elsewhere'
wala ang isipan 'inability to think'

KNOWING FEAR FOR FEAR
hindi nakakakilala ng takot 'not familiar with fear (knows no fear)'

BLURRED THOUGHT FOR FEAR
malabo ang kaisipan 'blurred thought process; inability to think'

INSANITY FOR SADNESS
nabaliw sa lungkot 'crazy from sadness'

BEHAVIOR FOR EMOTION
GRASPING FOR LOVE
kapit-tuko 'grasp-gecko (hold tightly; deeply in love)'

TOGETHERNESS FOR AFFECTION
kapiling 'together in heart, emotional togetherness' < *piling* 'side of'

LACK OF EXPRESSION FOR LACK OF SHAME
tabla ang mukha 'board face (unresponsive, no shame)'

LOSS OF MOVEMENT/SPEECH FOR SHOCK
napipi 'speechless (temporary loss of speech due to strong feelings)'
patay na tuod 'dead stump of tree (shocked, unresponsive)'

PHYSICAL REACTION/APPEARANCE FOR EMOTION

PALENESS FOR SHOCK
ibinabad sa suka 'soaked in vinegar' (pale, shock or fear)

APPETITE FOR SADNESS
walang ganang kumain 'decreased appetite'

PHYSICAL REACTION FOR FEAR
bahag ang buntot 'between legs the tail (cowed, abject fear)'
humahangos ang paghinga 'increased breathing rate'
huminto sa paghinga 'stop breathing; breath taken away'
inaalon ang dibdib 'rising and falling (like waves) of chest (rapid heart beat due to strong fear)'
magbara ang ilong 'stuffy nose (quick tempered)'
maputla ang mukha 'pale the face; loss of blood from face'
nalalagas ang buhok 'loss of hair'
namugto ang mata sa kakaiyak 'deepening the eyes of crying; sunken eyes'
namumuti ang buhok 'graying of hair; hair turns white with fear'
namuti ang talampakan 'white soles of feet (running in fear)'
nangangatog ang puwit 'trembling buttocks (great fear)'
nanginginig ang mga buto 'trembling of limbs/bones'
nanlalambot ang mga tuhod 'weakness of knees'
nanlalamig ang boong katawan 'chillness in the body; decreased body temperature'
pinapawisan ng malagkit 'stickiness of sweat'
tumatayo ang balahibo 'stand feathers (feathers stand, feel goose pimples)'

EXPRESSIONS OF CHRISTIAN ORIGIN OR SHOWING CHRISTIAN INFLUENCE

luksang tutubi 'black dragonfly (false mourning, referring to gaudy apparel of those who do not really mourn)'
masama ang tama 'direct hit (of Cupid's arrow)'
may koronong tinik 'there is a crown of thorns'

EXPRESSIONS PERTAINING TO HEAVEN
langit ng buhay 'heaven life (boundless happiness)'
ikapitong langit 'seventh heaven'
sa lupa man ay may langit 'on earth there is also heaven (bliss of heaven; extreme joy)'

*EXPRESSIONS OF POSSIBLE ENGLISH INSPIRATION

puso ko'y sa 'yo lang 'my heart is only for you'
pusong nagmamahal 'loving heart'
puso ko'y nangungulila 'my heart feels abandoned'

Appendix II: Tagalog Emotional Tropes in Alphabetical Order

Numbers in parentheses not otherwise cited refer to page numbers in Surian ng Wikang Pambansa (1982). Citations with (LS) refer to information obtained from questions given to ten native speakers of Tagalog by co-author Les Stacey (1996). Citations with (P) refer to information from Palmer (n.d.)

bahag ang buntot 'between legs the tail (cowed, abject fear)' (99)
balat-karabaw 'skin-carabao (thick skinned, no shame)' (55)
balat-sibuyas 'skin-onion (thin skinned, sensitive)' (56)
dumudugo ang puso 'bleeding the heart' (LS)
gabi ng buhay 'night life (dark, tragic, or sad part of life)' (172)
gatungan ang galit 'add fuel to anger (provoke anger)' (173)
gustong manampal ng mukha 'desire to slap face' (LS)
gusto mong pumatay 'you want to kill' (P)
hindi nakakakilala ng takot 'not familiar with fear (knows no fear)' (266)
humahangos ang paghinga 'increased breathing rate' (LS)
huminto sa paghinga 'stop breathing; breath taken away' (LS)
ibinabad sa suka 'soaked in vinegar' (pale, shock or fear) (265)
ikapitong langit 'seventh heaven' (200)
inaalon ang dibdib 'rising and falling (like waves) of chest (rapid heart beat due to strong fear)' (160)
kapiling 'together in heart, emotional togetherness'; < *piling* 'side of' (P)
kapit-tuko 'grasp-gecko (hold tightly; deeply in love)' (127)
kayang pumatay ng tao 'able to kill a person; capable of murder' (LS)
kumukulo ang dugo 'blood boils (very angry, much annoyed)' (168)
langit ng buhay 'heaven life (boundless happiness)' (92)
luksang tutubi 'black dragonfly (false mourning, referring to … apparel …)' (139)
lumaki ang loob 'grows inside (pride; feeling or emotion is likened to "an elastic container")' (208)
lumalaki ang ulo 'big head (proud, boastful)' (295)
lumuha ng bato 'tears (eye) of stone (grieve intensively)' (69)
maasim ang mukha 'sour face (ill feeling, hatred)' (217)
magaan ang katawan 'light body (animated feeling)' (134)
magbara ang ilong 'stuffy nose (quick tempered)' (189)
magbigat ang dibdib 'heavy chest (heavy heart, depression, disappointment)' (161)
magbulaklak na landas 'a flower trail (leading to happy, prosperous life)' (196)
magpalamig ng ulo 'have a cool head' (P)
mainit ang ulo 'hot head ("like hot things, an angry person often hurts feelings")' (296)
maipagmamalaki 'pride' < *laki* 'size, grow' (Ramos)
makapal ang mukha 'thick face (impenetrable, no shame)' (218)
makatulo-laway 'makes saliva drip (attractive, said of woman by man)' (204)
malabo ang kaisipan 'blurred thought process; inability to think' (LS)
malakas ang loob 'inside swells (fearless)' (208)
malayo ang isipan 'thought processes far away; thoughts focused elsewhere' (LS)
mapagtanim 'prone to planting (hold a grudge)' (279)
maputla ang mukha 'pale the face; loss of blood from face' (LS)
masama ang tama 'direct hit (of Cupid's arrow)(fall in love)' (278)
matalas ang kaisipan 'increased alertness' (LS)
matalim ang paningin 'sharp the sight, stabbing with eyes, aggressive visual behavior' (LS)
may koronong tinik 'there is a crown of thorns.' (69)

nabaliw sa lungkot 'crazy from sadness' (LS)
nagbabaga ang katawan sa galit 'roasted by anger' (LS)
nagpapanting ang tainga 'warming the ear, tingling sensation' (LS)
nagpuputok ang butse 'burst the gizzard (bursting with anger; neck swells with anger)' (104)
nalalagas ang buhok 'loss of hair' (LS)
namugto ang mata sa kakaiyak 'deepening the eyes of crying; sunken eyes' (LS)
namumuti ang buhok 'graying of hair; hair turns white with fear' (LS)
namuti ang talampakan 'white soles of feet (running in fear)' (274)
nangangatog ang puwit 'trembling buttocks (great fear)' (256)
nanginginig ang mga buto 'trembling of limbs/bones' (LS)
naninikip ang dibdib 'tightness in chest, inability to breathe' (LS)
nanlalambot ang mga tuhod 'weakness of knees' (LS)
nanlalamig ang boong katawan 'chillness in the body; decreased body temperature' (LS)
nanlilisik ang mga mata 'pressure in the eyeballs; buldging eyes' (LS)
napipi 'speechless (temporary loss of speech due to strong feelings)' (245)
pakiramdam ay tumangkad 'feeling of tallness; increase in body size' (LS)
parang gutom ng aso 'like hunger of a dog (obsession with women)' (177)
parang nagulat sa kulog 'like shock from thunder (sudden, strong fear)' (145)
parang puputok ang dibdib 'like a bursting chest (extreme grief or sorrow)' (161)
patay na patay 'dead (intensive)(passionate fondness, not limited to persons)' (242)
patay na tuod 'dead stump of tree (shocked, unresponsive)' (242)
pinapawisan ng malagkit 'stickiness of sweat' (LS)
pumuputok ang butse 'bursting the ribs' (LS)
puso ko'y sa 'yo lang 'my heart is only for you' (P)
pusong nagmamahal 'loving heart' (P)
puso ko'y nangungulila 'my heart feels abandoned' (P)
sa lupa man ay may langit 'on earth there is also heaven (bliss of heaven; extreme joy)' (202)
sugat sa puso 'pain/cut in the heart' (LS)
tabla ang mukha 'board face (unresponsive, no shame)' (257)
tumataba ang puso 'heart increases in size,' pride (LS), also sickness, extreme happiness, excitement
tumatayo ang balahibo 'stand feathers (feathers stand, feel goose pimples)' (54)
umaawit ang puso 'singing the heart' (LS)
umalsa ang galit 'anger rises (refers to rising heat and blood pressure in state of anger)' (173)
umuusok ang tuktok 'top is smoking (very angry)' (287)
wala ang isipan 'inability to think' (LS)
walang ganang kumain 'decreased appetite' (LS)

References

Angeliki Athanasiadou and Elzbieta Tabakowska (eds). 1998. *Speaking of Emotions: Conceptualization and Expression*. Berlin/New York: Mouton de Gruyter.

Bulosan, Carlos. 1995. *The Cry and the Dedication*, Edited with an introduction by E. San Juan, Jr. Philadelphia: Temple University Press.

Drossard, Werner. 1994. "The Systematization of Tagalog Morphosyntax". *Arbeitspapier Nr. 19* (Neiue Folge). Institut für Sprachwissenschaft, Universität zu Köln.

Gibbs, Raymond W. 1992. "Categorization and Metaphor Understanding". *Psychological Review* 99(3): 572–577.

Himmelmann, Nikolaus P. 1991. "The Philippine challenge to universal grammar". *Arbeitspapier Nr. 15* (Neue Folge) Institute für Sprachwissenschaft, Universität zu Köln.

Kövecses, Zoltan. 1990. *Emotion Concepts.* New York, NY: Springer-Verlag.

———. In press. *Metaphor and Emotion. Language, Culture, and Body in Human Feeling.* New York: Cambridge University Press.

Lakoff, George. 1987. *Women, Fire, and Dangerous Things: What Categories Reveal about the Mind.* Chicago, IL: University of Chicago Press.

Lakoff, George and Mark Johnson. 1980. *Metaphors We Live By.* Chicago, IL: The University of Chicago Press.

Lakoff, George and Mark Turner. 1989. *More Than Cool Reason: A Field Guide to Poetic Metaphor.* Chicago: University of Chicago Pres.

Langacker, Ronald. 1987. *Foundations of Cognitive Grammar. Vol 1. Theoretical Prerequisites.* Stanford: Stanford University Press.

Lopez, Cecilio. 1940. "The Tagalog language (an outline of its psycho-morphological analysis)". *Publications of the Institute of National Language, Bulletin No. 5*, August 1940. Manila: Bureau of Printing.

Matsuki, Keiko. 1989. "Metaphors of Anger in Japanese". In *Language and Communication*, forthcoming.

Palmer, Gary B. 1996. *Toward a Theory of Cultural Linguistics.* Austin: University of Texas Press.

———. n.d. Tagalog Expressions Pertaining to Mental Experience: Cognition and Emotion in a Western Austronesian Language. Unpublished ms.

Palmer, Gary B. and Rick Brown. 1998. "The Ideology of Honor, Respect, and Emotion in Tagalog". In Angeliki Athanasiadou and Elzbieta Tabakowska (eds), 331–355.

Rafael, Vincente L. 1988. *Contracting Colonialism: Translation and Christian Conversion in Tagalog Society Under Early Spanish Rule.* Ithaca: Cornell University Press.

Ramos, Teresita V. 1971. *Tagalog Dictionary.* Honolulu: University of Hawaii Press.

Schachter, Paul. 1987. "Tagalog". In Bernard Comrie (ed), *The World's Major Languages.* New York: Oxford University Press, 936–958.

Sibayan, Bonifacio P. 1991. "The intellectualization of Filipino". *International Journal of the Sociology of Language 88*: 69–82.

Surian ng Wikang Pambansa. 1982. *Matalinghagang Mga Pananalita* (with English Equivalents). Maynila, Pilipinas.

Taylor, John R. and Thandi G. Mbense. 1998. "Rod dogs and rotten mealies: how Zulus talk about anger". In Angliki Athanasiadou and Elzbieta Tabakowska (eds), *Speaking of Emotions: Conceptualization and Expression.* Berlin/New York: Mouton de Gruyter, 191–226.

The Convergence of Sociocultural Theory and Cognitive Linguistics

Lexical Semantics and the L2 Acquisition of Love, Fear and Happiness

Howard Grabois
University of Alberta

Introduction

In the present study lexical semantics is explored in relation to second language acquisition, and how it is that we organize our lexicons. On a theoretical level, these issues are discussed in relation to both sociocultural theory and cognitive linguistics, in an effort to discover ways in which these two frameworks can be mutually informative. This study is part of a larger project, for which a methodology was developed based on the use of word association protocols. This methodology allowed for the creation of lexical networks for a series of domains which were considered to represent significant aspects of human experience. In the present study particular attention is paid to those domains associated with the emotions *love, happiness,* and *fear,* as well as *death,* given the centrality of emotions for this domain.

On an experimental level, the methodology elaborated in this study allows for qualitative as well as quantitative analyses of emotion concepts and lexical organization. It also allows for comparisons across experimental groups. In this study these are comprised of native speakers of different languages (English and Spanish), as well as different kinds of language learners, ranging from classroom learners to experts who have had years of experience in the culture of the target language.

Word Associations and Sociocultural Theory

The primary theoretical framework which informs this research is sociocultural theory, a theory of psychology and cognitive development which was first developed by L.S. Vygotsky and a small group of collaborators in the Soviet Union in the 1920's and 1930's. Within this framework A.R. Luria, one of Vygotsky's principal collaborators, showed a particular interest in word association experiments (see Michael Cole's introduction to Luria 1978). As early as the 1920s he used a word association methodology to illustrate the relationship between a child's social environment and cognitive and linguistic development. His experiments (Luria 1978) allowed for the comparison of rural children, urban children, and "street urchins". He was able to find interesting results based on reaction times, diversity of response, and the distribution of responses according to conceptual domains.

Despite Luria's early interest in word association experiments, they have been rarely used as a means of investigation within the sociocultural tradition. They have, as is well known, been used extensively within the western psychological tradition, where they have been taken to represent a window into the unconscious.[1] The present study represents an attempt to recast word association methodologies against a different theoretical background, one where the social construction of consciousness is central to an understanding of cognition. Thus, while the technique of eliciting associations to words may be familiar, the theoretical principles employed for analysis in many ways transform our understanding of the task itself.

Sense and Meaning

Of the Vygotskian ideas that inform this study, perhaps the most central one for the interpretation of word association data is the distinction between sense (*smysl*) and meaning (*znachenie*). Vygotsky, citing Poulhan, defines sense as "the sum of all the psychological events aroused in our *consciousness* by the word. It is a dynamic, fluid, complex whole… Meaning is only one of the zones of sense, the most stable and precise zone. A word acquires its sense from the context in which it appears; in different contexts, it changes its sense. Meaning remains stable throughout the changes of sense." (1986: 244, italics added.)

It is important to remember that in sociocultural theory all speech, and by extension all forms of higher thought are social in their origins. We can then think of cognition as distributed among the members of a community, and part of the process of acculturation as participation in that distribution.[2] Certainly this is true of all forms of higher cognition, and while lower forms of cognition (e.g. visual perception) undoubtedly exist prelinguistically, the argument can be made that the mediation of language serves to transform even these processes, so that they too become part of a socially and culturally constructed world.

Within the present study, just as sense and meaning form part of a continuum, we can also see that there is a continuum of commonality in word associations, ranging from those that are most common, to those that are highly idiosyncratic. It is then but a small jump to seeing those words which are common associations as forming part of meaning, and those which are less common as forming part of sense.

In discussing sense and meaning it is also important to consider contextualization. Sense is firmly rooted within specific discourses, while the stability of meaning allows it to become increasingly decontextualized, a process which then allows for recontextualization in different discourses. For the moment we will limit ourselves to Vygotsky's observation (1987) that decontextualization serves to both restrict a word, by stripping away sense, and to amplify that same word, by allowing for a re-synthesis in other discursive environments.

Construct Formation

Vygotsky's discussion of the different ways in which categories are formed during the process of development also informs this study. Very young children form syncretic heaps, and as they develop come to engage in complex thought, and finally conceptual thought. While this sequence is developmental, it is important to remember that the ability to engage in higher levels of thought does not preclude the use of previous levels. In fact, complex thought may be the most common form of thought, even for adults, as they engage in everyday activities.

The first phase is characterized by the creation of syncretic heaps, which Vygotsky, citing Blonsky, characterizes as "incoherent coherence" (Vygotsky 1986). There is no inner structure which binds these heaps together, rather they are determined by the material conditions of a particular instance. Accordingly, these heaps are completely context dependent and unstable. The connections between members of a heap are subjective, and even accidental.

In the second phase of development objects are grouped in complexes. The child no longer "mistakes connections between his own impressions for connections between things." (1986: 112) Still, the formation of complexes is derived directly from experience, and so remains highly dependent on context. Vygotsky describes a series of complexes that form a developmental sequence. Associative complexes are created based on the connections between a nuclear object and other objects, such that while each member of the category has something in common with the nucleus, they may have nothing in common with one another. Next are collections, where a category is based on one common attribute (e.g. color; red things, size; large things, or shape; round things). These in turn are followed by chain complexes; each object sharing an attribute with every other object to which it is directly connected, although they may or may not share attributes with those objects to which they are not directly connected. Chain complexes, in turn, are succeeded by diffuse complexes, where the more mechanistic chaining of objects is replaced by greater fluidity, and less determinate bonds. These complexes are less dependent on context. While they are still created out of concrete objects within the perceptual field, they are also open and potentially limitless categories, able to assimilate new objects from different contexts. Finally, pseudoconcepts are complexes which are so refined as to resemble concepts, while maintaining the structure of complex thought.

The final phase of development, conceptual thought, is characterized by the ability to generalize and engage in abstract thought on the one hand, and to connect and synthesize on the other. The ability to abstract alone is insufficient for the creation of true concepts, and can be better understood as preconceptual[3]. Thus concept formation requires two distinct processes, the ability to engage in abstract thought, and the ability to establish connections for specific contexts. Both require cognitive skills which are developed in the succession of stages of complex thought. Both of these processes are linguistically mediated through the word.[4]

Concept Formation

In discussing the differences between scientific and everyday (spontaneous) concepts Vygotsky emphasizes the difference between knowledge that is saturated with experience, and knowledge which is based on the ability to rise above the situational meaning of a word. We can once more see concern with a continuum that ranges from the experientially based and highly contextualized to the abstract and decontextualized.

Scientific concepts are also distinguished from spontaneous concepts in that they begin with conscious awareness, and that the use of scientific concepts implies the use of voluntary control. Scientific concepts thus begin with abstract thought, consciousness and volition, and work their way downward toward context and experience. Spontaneous concepts begin with context and experience and work their way upward. The ability to formulate scientific and everyday concepts do not remain independent however, as they follow the same path, either top down or bottom up.

Word Meaning In A Second Language

Of particular interest for this study is Vygotsky's (1987) claim that in learning a foreign language the system of meaning of the native language is maintained, and is simply transferred to the foreign language. This is reminiscent of Weinreich's model of bilingualism (Weinreich 1953), evoking either compound meaning (where the L2[5] lexeme is mapped onto the L1 concept) or subordinative meaning (where the L2 lexeme is mapped directly onto the L1 lexeme). What Vygotsky ignores, of course, is Weinreich's third type of model, where the L1 lexeme is mapped onto an L1 concept, and the L2 lexeme is mapped onto an L2 concept. Needless to say, the present study is predicated on the possibility of developing lexical organization in the L2, and this issue is explored at length throughout. In terms of sociocultural theory, the notion of inner speech provides a focal point for this exploration.

Inner Speech

For Vygotsky (1986) all speech is social in its origins, and once appropriated by the individual "goes underground" and becomes inner speech. In examining inner speech Vygotsky points to three semantic peculiarities. The first has to do with the distinction between sense and meaning. Vygotsky talks about sense as "a complex, mobile, protean phenomenon; it changes in different minds and situations and is almost unlimited." While in oral speech we move from meaning to sense, in inner speech sense takes precedence over meaning. The second peculiarity of inner speech is the way in which words are combined, or merge, a process that is analogous to agglutination. The third peculiarity is the unification of words in inner speech. "The senses of different words flow into one another- literally 'influence' one another- so that the earlier ones are contained in, and modify, the latter ones." (1986;246)

This description of inner speech is particularly relevant to the present study for two reasons. First, it provides a principled way of understanding what people do when they engage in word association activities. While the claim that word associations provide direct access to inner speech may be extreme, it is clear that word associations can provide a unique and even privileged tool for analysis[6] within the sociocultural framework. In fact, perhaps the biggest difference between inner speech and word association tasks is the structure and constraints imposed by the word association task itself. This might best simulate inner speech if subjects were instructed to give a large number of associations in a completely unconstrained fashion, beginning and ending new chains of association based solely on the flow of words into one another. Unfortunately, this sort of methodology would provide a body of data which would, practically speaking, be unanalyzable.

Given the sociocultural notion that inner speech is derived from social speech, it stands to reason that semantic organization is closely linked to the culture from which it is appropriated. Just as we can speak of cognition as socially distributed, and not simply taking place within an isolated psyche, we must also see the flux of sense which is characteristic of inner speech as having its origins in a particular culture, and as being mediated by the language of that culture. We may then state the central question of this study in terms of whether or not it is possible to establish inner speech in a non-native language, or if any second language learned as an adult will necessarily be regulated by the inner speech of the native language.

On the one hand one could argue that the nature of inner speech is so closely related to the ontogenetic development of mind that it has a high degree of stability, in which case we would expect L2 lexemes to be mapped onto the conceptual structure of L1 inner speech. This is consistent with Vygotsky's assertion (1987) that concepts learned in a foreign language classroom are essentially nothing more than a relexification of native language concepts. On the other hand one could argue that consciousness and cognition are situated; they are dynamic processes which are inseparable from the activities which the individual is involved in; not simply abstract abilities possessed by the individual and to be employed at her discretion. This line of thought would predict that the inner speech of L2 speakers could change when the L2 comes to serve as a linguistic tool for the negotiation of meaning.

To illustrate the dynamic between inner and social speech, and the Vygotskyan notions of sense and meaning, we might imagine a community, frozen in time, where everyone has exactly the same conceptual and lexical organization, and where sense and meaning are identically reproduced in each member of the group. In this community there would quite simply be no need to communicate.[7] At the other extreme, we might imagine a group who's member's share no conceptual or linguistically mediated organization, and where there is an utter lack of stability, such that there is only sense, and no meaning. In such a group communication becomes impossible, and the only conceivable state for the individual is one of autism.

The notion of legitimate peripheral participation (elaborated by Lave and

Wenger 1991), can then provide some clues as to how inner speech can come to be structured (or restructured) within the L2 system. Using the model of apprenticeship, Lave and Wenger show how novices within a community come to be experts. The novice's relationship to the community must first be legitimate (for example, he must be accepted into apprenticeship). Through participation in the activities of the community, the novice can then move from peripheral participation (the limited and controlled participation of the apprentice) toward participation at the center. Using this model to inform the present study, we can think about much classroom learning not as true participation in the activities of a speech community (in this case, comprised of those people that use the target language to structure and construct their reality), but rather as a preparatory phase which has the potential to legitimize participation in a speech community[8]. Once the language learner has become a legitimate participant he can then move from the periphery toward the center. It is this movement which will then allow a restructuring of inner speech, as the apprentice becomes more expert, and moves toward acceptance as a full-fledged member of the target speech community.[9]

Cognitive Linguistics

Another framework which informs this study is that of cognitive linguistics. This denomination does not refer to a specific and well delineated research program, but rather to the work of a series of researchers who share a set of assumptions and research interests (Fillmore 1976, 1978, 1992, Lakoff and Johnson 1980, Lakoff 1987, Johnson 1987, Langacker 1991, Taylor 1991, Clark 1993, Fauconnier 1994). However, much like the prototype category (see below) which is central for much of their thinking, there is no criterial set of principles or beliefs which is shared among the various researchers and theorists.

Part of what is shared among these researchers is a rejection of certain assumptions and belief systems which are associated with the Chomskyan paradigm. Chomsky (1980) proposes a narrow version of Cartesianism, whereby the abstract mathematical model of a system becomes the object of inquiry, rather than that which is immediately accessible in the ordinary world. One of the corollaries which can be derived from this is the notion of modularity.[10] This then allows for language to be studied autonomously of other aspects of cognition, and understood as an abstract system of rules and representations that operates at an intermediate level,[11] one which is not directly accessible to consciousness. Within this system meaning can be described through the use of formal logic and truth conditions, the formalism of which is generally realized in terms of criterial features.

Among those theorists under discussion there is a great deal of consensus as far as the rejection of Chomskyan assumptions is concerned. Language is understood holistically, in relation to general principles of cognition. This then leads to an emphasis on the idea that the mind is embodied[12] (Johnson 1987, Varela et al. 1991). Indeed, if one accepts the computational system as a model for the mind, issues of embodiment are simply not relevant. A computer, for example, can only be encased, never embodied. Emphasis on the embodied nature of mind, on the other hand, also explodes the belief that meaning can be constructed within an abstract system without reference to the individual's personal and corporal experience. Symbols can no longer be "semantically transparent",[13] and must be seen as cognitively complex, understood not only in relation to a semiotic system, but also in relation to one's experience of the world, which is inherently open and infinite.

Categories

Issues concerning the nature of categories have proven central to cognitive linguistics, and are based on discussions of classical and prototype categories. The notion of the classical category has its origins in Aristotle (Taylor 1995), who distinguished between the essence of a thing, and its accidents. In more modern terminology, the classical category is determined by the presence of necessary and sufficient conditions, which allow for clear category boundaries to be drawn. This in turn allows for all members of a category to have equal status. The use of the classical category has a robust tradition in twentieth century linguistics, particularly within the subfield of phonology, where binary features are often taken to be linguistic primitives. The classical category has also been employed extensively within structural frameworks as a means of formulating semantic theories.

Throughout the second half of the twentieth century a series of researchers from a variety of fields have pointed to the fact that the classical category is not adequate to describe what people do in everyday cognition. In Philosophy, Wittgenstein (1958) points to the difficulty of using criterial principles for categorization, and points to the possibility of creating categories based on family resemblance. In anthropology Berlin and Kay (1969) made discoveries about the ways different cultures categorize colors, and observed that there are specific colors which serve as focal points for color categories. In psychology Rosch (1973, 1975) found that for many categories people are able to make judgments about the "goodness" of membership (i.e. a chair is a better member of the category "furniture" than a telephone), demonstrating that not all category members are equal, as predicted by the classical category. In linguistics Bolinger (1965) railed against what he termed "the atomization of meaning", showing the logical impossibility of decomposing meaning into a set of abstract features. Labov (1973) engaged in a series of experiments where he looked at judgments about membership in the categories "bowl", "cup", and "vase" (based on drawings where the only difference was the relation of height to width, and the presence or absence of a handle), and found that category membership is not discrete, and that boundaries between categories are fuzzy rather than clear. All of this points to the idea that the classical category is insufficient for providing insight into how human cognition actually works, or into the origins of concept formation.

The notion of the prototype category can be understood as an alternative to the classical category. Accounts of prototype categories emphasize their realization at a basic level,[14] and point to two alternatives for their formation (Taylor 1995). The first sees a particular entity (or entities) at the core of the category such that there are specific exemplars of the prototype for any given category. The second posits the possibility that prototypes are formed, not around specific instantiations, but rather around the abstract core of the category.

While the prototype category provides a more experiential basis for word meaning, it is not without problems. These are made evident in Armstrong, Gleitman and Gleitman's (1983) now famous article, where they find that people can and do provide judgments concerning "goodness" of membership even for categories that are based strictly on abstract features, such as odd numbers. They argue that while prototype effects ("goodness" of membership) are taken as evidence for the existence of prototype categories, these effects can also be found in categories which are based on the presence of necessary and sufficient conditions. The fact that prototype effects are found is of interest, but has nothing to do with the core meaning of the word, which is based on the classical category. Prototype effects are illustrative of procedures that people use to identify categories, but do not constitute a principle for the organization of those categories.

There have been two ways of responding to the findings of Armstrong et al. Taylor proposes that it is not "illegitimate to speak of attributes, provided one does not intend by this term the atomic (or even molecular) semantic components of the classical theory." (1995: 63) Attributes are simply what allow people to perceive the commonality which exists between entities, a proposition which hardly seems controversial. Taylor goes on to say that "Armstrong *et al.* were surely correct to attribute the prototype effects of odd and even numbers to identification procedures. What is questionable is the proposition that there exists a core definition independent of recognition procedures." (1995: 71)

Lakoff (1987) takes a different approach. On the one hand he rejects the classical category as a woefully inadequate way of dealing with the complexity of human cognition. On the other hand he proposes that prototype effects do not necessarily imply a prototype structure, but only a structure which is able to generate prototype effects. It does not necessarily follow, therefore, that what causes prototype effects are prototype representations.

Aitchison (1994) sums up the situation nicely by observing that not all prototype categories have the same structure. A prototypical bird, for example, may best be understood in terms of a cluster of attributes which form a family resemblance. A prototypical color, on the other hand, can best be understood in terms of its centrality within a continuum. The prototype for vegetables may be domain dependent (i.e. farming or restaurants). "Prototypes are somewhat like *games*. They have a family resemblance, but no single definition covers them all". (1994: 67) The theoretical status of prototypes, then, is somewhat ambiguous. On the one hand they bring issues concerning categorization to the forefront of discussions of meaning, and research in prototype theory has successfully shown the inadequacy of the classical category. On the other hand, the task of establishing the prototype as a basis for human cognition has proved to be quite tricky, inspiring some researchers to concentrate on prototype effects only, and others to seriously question the validity of prototype theory (Kiel 1992).

Concepts Redux

Having briefly reviewed certain issues relating to prototype theory, we can return to the Vygotskian notion of concept formation, and the notion that this is dependent on two cognitive skills which become highly developed in the successive stages of complex thought, abstraction and synthesis. The notion that abstraction doesn't belong uniquely to the realm of concepts, but is developed as a cognitive skill in preconceptual stages, is in many ways counterintuitive to folk beliefs which equate conceptual thought with abstraction. In fact, the ability to abstract may be not only preconceptual, but prelinguistic as well.

The other skill that becomes increasingly developed as we pass through the stages of complex thought is the ability to synthesize. This implies that the connections and relationships between things are not purely coincidental, but are in fact crucial for the construction of meaning. In a very real sense, until things come to be understood in relation to other things, they don't even exist as entities per se, but are merely part of a protean flux. They are not only as yet unnamed, but are even unnamable. Once more, a review of the different stages of complex thought reveals that with each succeeding stage there in an enhanced ability to understand objects in terms of increasingly sophisticated relationships, ranging from the simplicity of two objects sharing one attribute, to the multiple relationships and connections that need to be comprehended for the formation of diffuse complexes. The cognitive skills inherent in synthesis are, just as with the ability to abstract, both preconceptual and essential for concept formation. Furthermore, just as folk beliefs about concepts obscure the fact that abstraction can be preconceptual, they also obscure the fact that synthesis, the ability to comprehend things in contexts, is just as crucial to concept formation as abstraction is.

Luria (1976) was particularly sensitive to how abstraction and contextualization are related to issues of categorization in his study of uneducated peasants in Uzbekistan in the early 1930's. His subjects were shown drawings of a variety of objects, and asked which ones belonged together in an effort to see how they created categories. Perhaps the most significant findings of this study were that they very often refused to create categories based on the abstraction of attributes, preferring to discuss their functional interrelatedness. Thus a hammer, a saw, a log, and a hatchet were cognitively inseparable, as they were all associated with the functional domain of working with wood. The typical educated western response, of course, would be to categorize the hammer, saw, and hatchet together as belonging to the abstract category of tools.

Ratner (1991) gives us a more modern take on the role of abstraction and concreteness, reminding us that they are part of a continuum that emerges from activity. "The comfortable, secure feel of invariant abstractions is only the external shell of a most unstable, variable lived struggle to produce concrete phenomena." (1991: 69) At the same time, he acknowledges the embodied, experiential origins of cognition. Where he differs from the cognitive linguists, however, is in positing that even embodied experience can be mediated by language, and that activity is not only embedded in but also creates social contexts. By discussing cognition as something we do rather than as something we have, and by situating activity within cultural and institutional fields, the inseparability of abstraction and context becomes increasingly clear.

Given this understanding of abstraction and synthesis, we can now return to issues concerning prototype and classical categories. It should be clear by now that prototype categories can be preconceptual (based on complex thought). In fact, Lakoff's description of Dyirbal morphological categories (1987) is a clear example of Vygotsky's chain complexes. Furthermore, the relationships that hold for prototype categories based on family resemblances match with uncanny precision the type of categories Vygotsky describes as comprising diffuse complexes.

Given these similarities between Vygotskian complexes and prototype categories, we can now return to issues concerning concept formation. One way in which scientific and everyday concepts differ is in their microgenesis; while scientific concepts are formed from the top down, everyday concepts are formed from the bottom up. Within the literature of cognitive linguistics it is clear that the primary interest is in everyday concepts. Langacker, for example, in describing networks discusses "how far 'upward' a speaker extends this network through the process of abstraction (schematization)", or "how far downward a speaker articulates the network into progressively more specialized notions." (1991: 267). If we are to recast this thinking in Vygotskian terms the parallels are striking. In fact, we can understand much of the research in cognitive linguistics as part of an attempt to analyze the formation of everyday concepts.

Scientific concepts, on the other hand, have been largely neglected by cognitive linguists for two reasons. First, researchers in cognitive linguistics tend to emphasize embodied experience as the basis for the construction of meaning, which points to a bottom up process. Second, the rejection of the classical category as a principle for human cognition has served to minimize the significance of abstraction for an understanding of human cognition.

The classical category, however, can prove useful for an understanding of scientific concepts. It is important to see the classical category, however, not as an organizing principle unto itself, but rather as one part of a cognitive process[15]. The danger is in equating the classical category to conceptual structure, rather than seeing it as associated with specific organizing principles (abstraction of attributes) which may help to structure some concepts. While scientific concepts may be influenced by these principles, they only reach the status of concepts in so far as they attain a degree of contextualization. These same principles can also serve for the restructuring of everyday concepts as scientific concepts. In this instance spontaneous concepts are initially formed based on contexts which emerge from embodied experience, and subsequently move toward abstraction. As their attributes become increasingly decontextualized, this can then serve as a starting point for recontextualization, and the re-interpretation of everyday concepts as scientific ones.

Applying Vygotskian notions of concept formation also provides an elegant account of prototype effects. It is hardly surprising that everyday concepts maintain a structure which is consistent with prototype theory, or even that scientific concepts will also show prototype effects to the extent that they are contextualized. This would then predict that virtually all concepts should show at least some prototype effects. It also predicts that the classical category, while not necessary for concept formation, does have privileged status for an understanding of human cognition, situated as it is at the juncture between everyday and scientific concepts.

From this perspective the data from the Armstrong et al. paper cease to be controversial, and in fact can be interpreted as following a predictable pattern. For example, one of the categories they explored was femaleness, where they found that "mother" was a better example of a female than "policewoman". If we are to understand femaleness purely as an abstraction of attributes, they are correct in assuming that "policewoman" should be as good an exemplar as "mother", given that both share the crucial criterial feature (+female). To understand femaleness as a concept, however, is to understand it as embedded in specific experientially and culturally determined contexts. Furthermore, to the extent that femaleness is an everyday rather than a scientific concept, we would expect the contexts in which different exemplars are embedded to play an increasingly important role. From this perspective, we would expect "mother" and "policewoman" to have very different standings in relation to femaleness, and for this difference to be reflected in judgments of category goodness. On the other hand, to the extent that a category such as "odd numbers" is a scientific concept (or has been reanalyzed as one), abstraction could play a more important role than contextualization for an understanding of the concept. The fact that in the Armstrong et al. study there is considerably more variation in judgments of goodness for femaleness than for odd numbers is entirely consistent with this analysis.

It is also important to consider that the extent to which a concept is everyday or scientific can vary significantly by the specific context in which it is used. If we look at some of the words used to elicit word associations in the present study, there can be little doubt that "death" and "poverty" can be considered examples of everyday concepts. A coroner, however, will have a specialist's criterial definition of death (i.e. lack of brain activity). Likewise, a government bureaucrat can have a specialist's definition of poverty (i.e. annual income below a set level). It is hard to imagine, however, that these scientific concepts have cognitive salience when the coroner is informed of the death of a loved one, or when the government bureaucrat sees images of the conditions in Rwandan refuge camps on the nightly news. The fact that words can variably evoke everyday or scientific concepts is reflected in the use of hedges (see Lakoff 1987). It is not difficult to see that utterances such as "technically speaking they're living in poverty" and "they're really living in poverty" not only emerge from different contexts, but also represent a shift in focus from the scientific concept to the everyday concept.

Networks

The notion that there is some sort of mental organization for the words people know is certainly not new. As Aitchison (1994) points out, the fact that we know so many words[16] and are able to access them quickly and easily suggests that they are not floating around haphazardly in our minds. She goes on to develop a model based on the notion that words are organized in a web according to semantic fields. Of course, this is highly reminiscent of connectionist models that consider networks to be much like the synaptic connections of the brain (Rummelhart and McCleland 1986).

Within cognitive linguistics the notion that the lexicon is organized within a network is also elaborated, although at a different level than in connectionism. Rather than a primary concern with implementation at the level of microcognition, there is greater interest in higher level cognitive functions. In addition, Lakoff's interest in metaphors as a means of structuring everyday cognition points to another kind of network relationship. Given the possibility of mapping from several source domains to a given target domain, or from one source domain to a variety of target domains, we can begin to understand metaphoric thought itself as forming a kind of network. In fact, the organization of metaphorical structure may be among the most useful ways of understanding cultural specificity for the construction of meaning.

The notion that lexical semantics can be understood in terms of a network model is explicitly elaborated by Langacker (1991), who presents the idea that any single cognitive structure (prototypes, schemas, etc.) is insufficient for an understanding of lexical meaning. He posits a network model which is inclusive of a variety of relationships. "Most lexical items have a considerable array of interrelated senses, which define the range of their conventionally sanctioned usage" (1991: 2). These senses can then be based on prototypes or schemas. This kind of network model can then include many of the generalizations which prototype categories and schemas allow for, while avoiding the pitfalls of a semantic model which is based on a single cognitive principle.

The kind of network model elaborated by Langacker has the added advantage of being able to deal with questions concerning polysemy and homonymy in a rather elegant fashion. For any particular lexical network, only a part may be relevant to its use in a particular situation.[17] Differences in sense and meaning for a particular word in different contexts have to do with what part of the network is appropriate, without necessarily implying that there are distinct networks. In the present study, for example, native English speakers were found to have the word “electricity” in their network for “power”, an effect that does not occur for native Spanish speakers. Instead of understanding “power” as having two separate networks, we can think of “electricity” as being part of the English speaker’s network for “power” through schematic or metaphoric extension. Polysemy and homonymy are then seen as part of a scale, and not as distinct phenomena. “Homonymy is better analyzed as the endpoint along the cline of relatedness— it is the limiting or degenerate case of polysemy, where the only relationship between the two senses consists in their common phonological realization.” (1991: 268)

Langacker talks about networks growing in two possible directions. Outward growth, through extension, is consistent with prototype categorization, where there is a similarity between members of a group, whether that is based on categorical perception, as with color terms, or on shared attributes, as with family resemblances. Upward growth is based on the use of schemas, which allows for the inclusion of category members which are unrelated by extension. Once again, this sort of conceptualizing of networks is entirely consistent with the ideas, outlined above, concerning prototype organization, complex thought, and the bottom up creation of everyday concepts.

Networks and Distributed Cognition

We have already seen in discussion of sociocultural theory how words have both sense and meaning, with meaning as the most stable part of sense. If we adopt a network approach much like Langacker’s, but which also takes into account the distributed nature of cognition, we can begin to see how the network model works on an interpsychological level as well as an intrapsychological one. We can begin to see meaning as that part of the network which is most stable among the individuals who comprise a speech community, and sense as that part of the network which is most individual.

In a sense, then, the most important network for the organization of the lexicon is the social network. Individuals, however, participate in a variety of social networks, and consequently, the discourses which both emerge from and hold these networks together. To the extent that Harré and Gillet (1994) are right, and the mind can be understood in terms of the discourses in which we participate, we can also understand the creation of meaning and sense in terms of the networks which a given individual is part of. Following this model, then, we can begin to consider expertise in a foreign language in terms of the extent to which the individual becomes well integrated into the speech community in which the target language is spoken.

The Experiment

Experimental Design

While word association experiments have a long tradition in the field of psychology, and a robust if less extensive tradition in studies relating to language and culture, there has been a dearth of methodological development. The primary exception to this has been the work of Szalay and his collaborators (Szalay and Brent 1967; Szalay and Maday 1973; Szalay and Bryson 1973; Szalay and Bryson 1974; Szalay and Deese 1978; Szalay and Maday 1983; Szalay 1984; Bovasso, Szalay, Biase, and Stanford 1993).

Szalay's most important methodological contribution was the development of a system which allows for the assignment of numerical values to associations based on their order of emission, such that the first word in a series of associations will have a greater weighted value than the last. Szalay accomplished this (Szalay and Brent 1967, Szalay and Deese 1978) through the use of a test/retest protocol with a three week interval between trials. He then compared each subject's initial responses to their subsequent responses, reasoning that the more stable responses would be repeated across protocols. Not surprisingly, he found that the first response given had the greatest probability of being repeated subsequently, with descending probabilities based on order of emission. The average probabilities were found to be the following: 1) 62%, 2) 48%, 3) 40%, 4) 34%, 5) 32%, 6) 30%, 7) 25%, 8) 21%, 9) 16%, 10) 10%, etc.

In the present research three lexical domains associated with emotions were explored: *love, happiness,* and *fear,* as well as one where emotions play a particularly important role: *death*. It should be noted that while word association experiments traditionally emphasize referential nouns, words were chosen for the present study which represent important aspects of human experience.

For each of the lexical domains individual subjects created lexical networks by providing continuous responses to the prime words, with the associations themselves subsequently becoming primes. Szalay's technique for providing numerical values to a list of continuous responses is then extended such that percentages of percentages are also taken. In this way the values of responses in subsequent levels can be determined in relation to the initial prime. The manner in which this was done can be seen in figure 1, where the number on the left side of each cell represents the value the word in that cell has in relation to the initial prime. The numbers in parentheses indicate the 14 cells with the highest relative values. The words in these cells are those used as subsequent primes, in order of descending value. Only cells with a minimum value of 9 are used, and only words which can have at least 3 such responses can serve as primes. As a result each subject, given one initial prime, has the potential to generate a network of up to 83 associations.

Pages with cell distributions as in figure 1 (p. 221) were used to collect the data, with each subject completing four such pages. The numbers on the left of each cell represent the absolute value of that cell, while the numbers in parentheses indicate words which will in turn become primes. After the initial prime for each page, columns are headed by a "p" and the number of the prime for that column. The protocols were administered verbally, with the subject uttering associations and the researcher writing down the responses. In order to attain a maximally complete network for each subject there was no set time limit for providing associations, but rather a fixed maximum pause between associations: 30 seconds if the pause was before a cell which would itself contain a prime, 15 seconds in all other cases.[18]

If a word recurred as a prime within a domain the subject was not asked to give associations to that word again, but rather the associations she had previously given were used. This was done because pilot testing showed that subjects would often get annoyed and impatient at having the same prime repeated. If, however, the same word surfaced as a prime within another domain it was repeated.

To illustrate the construction of networks, figure 1 contains the associations given by a native English speaker for the domain of *love*. The associations for *love* include *family, passion, emotion*. The first word given, *family* is used as the next prime (p1), soliciting responses such as *mom, dad, sisters*. The word with the next highest value, *passion*, is used as the next prime (p2), soliciting responses such as *love, intense, emotion*. After the word *belief* this subject paused for a period of longer than fifteen seconds, so the sequence was interrupted, and the next sequence, starting with *emotion* (p3) was initiated. The word with the fourth highest value, *mom*, serves as the next prime (p4), followed by *heart, letter, boyfriend, dad, love,* etc. The fourteenth prime follows a sequence which goes from *love* to *family* to *mom* to *caregiver*. The ninth prime, *love*, is a repetition of the initial prime, and so the responses which were given originally are repeated.

Subjects

Data was collected from five groups of subjects, each divided evenly by gender. While the Native English speakers performed the protocol in English, the Native Spanish speakers and the three groups of non-native speakers did so in Spanish. The experimental groups include:

- Native Spanish speakers (NS, n=32). These are divided equally by age: “students” and “adults”. The former come from a typical pool of university students, while the latter are people who are older, typically with a job, and often married or with children. This distinction is important because among the non-native speaker groups there are two groups of students (Second Language (L2) students and Foreign Language (FL) students) and one group of adults (Expert Spanish speakers).
- Expert Speakers of Spanish (ESS, n=32). These are native speakers of American English who had been living in Spain for at least three years. These subjects were administered a questionnaire based loosely on the questionnaire developed by Clahsen, Meisel and Pienemann for the *Zweitspracherwerb Italienischer und Spanischer* (ZISA) project as described in Hudson (1993).[19] All subjects received a minimum score of 29 out of 50, indicating a high degree of L2 participation in at least two of the major areas of focus within the questionnaire (education, work, social life, and family).
- L2 Spanish learners (L2, n=32). These are native speakers of American English who, having studied Spanish in an American university, were enrolled in a year abroad program in Spain. All were enrolled in programs that included “content” courses (literature, history, etc.) in the curriculum. Their average age was 21 (with a range of 19 to 22). All subjects had been in Spain for six to seven months at the time of their participation.
- Foreign Language Spanish learners (FL, n=32). These were native speakers of English, enrolled in Spanish courses at a major east coast university at a level beyond that needed to satisfy the university’s language proficiency requirement, equivalent to roughly two years of university language study. The average age of these subjects was 19.3 (range of 18 to 22).
- Native English speakers (NE, n=32). These were evenly divided between “students” and “adults”. None had any particular expertise in Spanish. The students had an average age of 19.6 (range of 16 to 22. The adults had an average age of 38.3 (range of 29 to 46). 14 of the adults currently had jobs (the other two being older graduate students), nine were married, and eight had children.

The words which would serve as initial primes were organized in a table which permitted their distribution among subjects in such a way as to control for any possible priming effects. In addition, the same 16-subject-sequence was repeated independently for each set of male and female subjects within each experimental group.

Method of Analysis

Correlations provided the primary means of quantitative analyze of the data. The following methods were implemented using SPSS 6.1 for Macintosh:

Following Szalay (Szalay and Deese 1978, Szalay and Brent 1967) only those words that were repeated within a group were analyzed. This is motivated by the idea that those tokens which are not repeated may be idiosyncratic to one individual's experience, and hence be minimally relevant to the intersubjective, socially constructed, sense and meaning of the word. This constraint was also implemented in such a way that any given subject could only account for up to half of the tokens of a word.

The data were "scrubbed" so that like words with some morphological variation were lumped together. This included plural/singular forms (*friend/friends*), masculine/feminine forms (*amigo/amiga* "friend m/f"), and some forms across word classes (*comprender/comprension* "to understand/understanding"). Once a decision was made it was applied consistently across domains, as well as across experimental groups of the same target language.

For data to be included in a correlation they had to meet one of the following criteria: 1) multiple (two or more) occurrences on both sides of the correlation 2) multiple (two or more) occurences with a corresponding singleton 3) multiples (three or more) with no corresponding singleton. Using these criteria, an average of 176 words were included in each correlation.

Quantitative Results

The correlations between groups provide the clearest evidence to the central question of this study: is it possible for non-native speakers to move toward native-like lexical organization? Figure 2 shows the correlations of each of the non-native Spanish speaking groups (ESS, L2, and FL) to native speakers. What is most striking about these correlations is that the ESS group achieves consistently higher correlations with the NS group than either of the other groups. Similar results were also found for other lexical domains that were part of the larger study. This can be taken as evidence that it is possible for non-native speakers to move toward native speaker lexical organization, although this may require a significant period of residence in the target culture, as well as a certain level of commitment to becoming integrated into that culture.

The data represented in figure 2 are also of interest in that they show little difference between the L2 learners and the FL learners relative to the NS group. This would appear to indicate that there is in fact little difference between these two groups, and that the experience of participating in an exchange program for several months has little effect on the students' lexical organization. This is somewhat misleading, however, as there are other detectable differences regarding the way that these two groups organize their lexicons. The fact that the L2 learners are not overtly moving closer to the native speakers does not mean that changes are not taking place, but simply that any changes that are taking place have yet to bring them significantly closer to native speaker lexical organization.

We can also see that, although the ESS group consistently achieves the highest correlations with the NS group, there are important differences by domain. For example, there is a relatively tight clustering of the r values for the three non-native groups for the domain of *love* while for *happiness* the difference between the expert speaker group and the other non-native groups is greater. We can also see that there are domains where the tendency is toward lower correlations, while other domains show a tendency toward higher correlations. These differences are hardly surprising, and reflect both relative differences between native and target language organization, and the ways in which these domains are used to mediate their activities. It is likely, for example, that exchange students will be called upon to engage in discourse concerning affective relationships and courtship. It seems relatively unlikely that they will need to directly confront the emotional implications and social circumstances of death in the target culture. Thus, there is likely to be a great deal of variability by domain in terms of initial distance from the target language, rate of movement toward the target language, as well as "ultimate attainment", or the degree of proximity to native speakers which non-natives are likely to reach.

Figure 1. Cell values and order of prime words

Pp Love	p1 family	p2 passion	p3 emotion
61 family (1)	37 mom (4)	29 love (9)	24 feeling (12)
48 passion (2)	29 dad (8)	23 intense (13)	19 happy
40 emotion (3)	24 sisters (11)	29 emotion	16 sad
34 heart (5)	21 brothers	16 desire	14 sensitive
32 letter (6)	20 house	15 belief	13 mind
30 boyfriend (7)	18 friends	14	12 heart
25 girlfriend (10)	15 home	12	10 cry
21 care	13 fun	10	p4 mom
16 red	10 safety	p5 heart	23 caregiver (14)
10 flowers	p6 letter	21 organ	18 friend
p7 boyfriend	20 alphabet	16 shape	15 cook
18 male	15 mail	14 red	13 work
14 friend	13 send	12 love	12 family
12 fun	11 stamp	11 beat	11 baby
10 companion	10 envelope	10 pump	9 talk
9 fight	9 symbol	p10 girlfriend	p11 sisters
p8 dad	p9 love (repeat)	15 female	15 siblings
18 parent	18 family	12 companion	12 friends
14 work	14 passion	10 love	10 talk
12 fun	12 emotion	p13 intense	p12 feeling
10 play	10 heart	14 hard	15 emotion
9 caregiver	9 letter	11 workload	12 happy
p14 caregiver	11 raise	9 tough	10 heart
14 infant	9 child		

•Shaded areas are for primes.
•Numbers in parentheses give the order of the prime according to value.
•Numbers at left of each cell give the value for that cell.

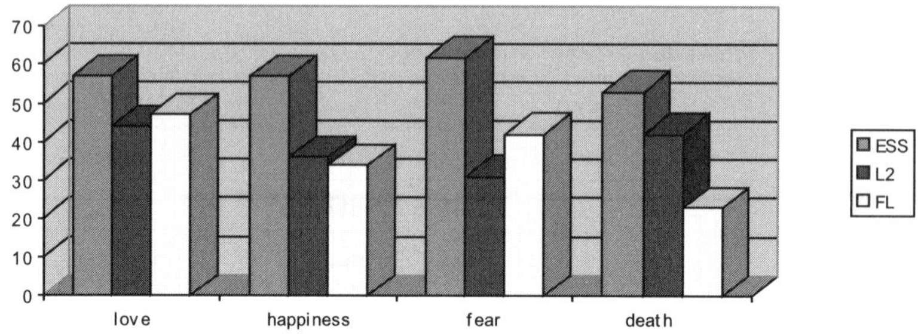

Figure 2. Pearson's correlations for group by domain

Table 1 includes not only the correlations seen in figure 1, but also those correlations comparing the non-native groups to each other. One can see that those groups which are adjacent to each other in terms of developmental stages (NS x ESS, ESS x L2, L2 x FL) tend to attain the highest correlations. Of these groups L2 X FL correlations show the highest average for the four domains under consideration, while in the larger study the NS X ESS correlations were slightly higher. The NS X ESS correlations also display the smallest range, showing not only the high degree to which expert speakers are approximating native speaker organization, but also that they are doing so fairly consistently across domains.

The L2 x FL correlations, on the other hand, while also showing a high average for correlations, display the greatest range (44–73), with a particularly low correlation for *fear*. As regards the low correlation for this domain, it is worth noticing that all of the correlations for *fear* are relatively low, with the exception of NS x ESS. Thus it may be, for the less expert groups, that the diversity of subjects' individual life experience tends to create a more diffuse

Table 1. Correlations of domains between experimental groups

	am	**fel**	**mi**	**mu**	**avg**	**rnge**
nat sp x exp sp	57	57	62	53	57	53–62
nat sp x L2	44	36	31	42	38	31–44
nat sp x FL	47	34	42	23	36	23–47
exp sp x L2	55	48	43	62	52	43–62
exp sp x FL	59	52	38	55	51	38–59
L2 x FL	71	56	44	73	61	44–73

am = amor/love, **fel** = felicidad/happiness, **mi** = miedo/fear, **mu** = muerte/death

range of responses, with a relatively limited role for linguistic mediation in the L2. If this is so, then what is extraordinary about this domain is the high correlation (r=.62) for NS x ESS.

The data in table 1 can also be used to make determinations about the relative distances between language groups. We can see, for example, that there is a large jump between the correlations for NS x ESS and those for NS x L2 and NS x FL. Among the non-native groups, however, there is no such marked distinction. One interpretation for this lack of dramatic difference is that the native language continues to be a mediating factor, even for the expert speakers.

Qualitative Results

Quantitative comparisons allow us to make relatively broad generalizations concerning similarity and difference between groups. Qualitative analysis, on the other hand, allows for a more detailed discussion of actual responses, as well as for comparisons between groups in different languages, a task for which quantitative analysis is inappropriate due to problems of translation. They can also provide examples of some of the psycholinguistic processes discussed above. Below are some observations based on a qualitative analysis of the results, organized by domain.

Love

For the NE group, words which are symbolic representations of love are of particular importance. This is most apparent for "heart" (NE: 2/632).[20] This word plays a much less central role for NS speakers ("corazon" 34/104). Other words which could be interpreted as symbolic of love, and which are important for the NE speakers, include "red" (NE: 7/273), "flowers" (NE: 15/172), and "roses" (NE: 26/116). In addition, the networks of the NE speakers also provides a series of words associated with the aforementioned "heart" that are not present in the NS group, such as "blood" (NE: 10/242), "pump" (NE: 21/132), "veins" (NE: 33/99), and even "aorta" (NE: 59/66). These differences between the two native groups illustrate two points. First, differences between language groups are determined not only by the words which enter a domain, but by the kind of word (i.e. symbolic, metaphoric, related to sensory cues, related to subjective response, etc.) as well. It would appear, for example, the NE group has a greater preference for indirect associations (metaphoric and symbolic) for the construction of the sense of "love" than the NS group, which shows a preference for sensory and referential associations. Second, symbols and metaphors can lead to chains where lexemes show no direct relationship to the initial prime of a domain (as in "aorta"). This is reminiscent of what Lakoff (1987) calls radial categories, and what Vygotsky calls chain complexes. Moreover, this type of association may also be responsible for the metaphoric or metonymic extension of the word's sense, as can be seen by the importance of "red" and "blood" for the NE speakers.

It is also noteworthy to observe that while associations which refer to people are important for both groups, there are differences in emphasis which are sometimes surprising. For example, folk wisdom emphasizes the importance and strength of the family as an institution in Spain, yet "family" (3/389) and "children" (6/279) both rank higher for the NE speakers than for the NS speakers ("familia" 10/254, and "hijos" 33/104 or "niños" 46/81). On the other hand, "friends" and "friendship" are of greater importance for the NS group ("amigos": 2/494, "amistad": 4/401) than for the NE group ("friends": 5/307). While these differences are of interest, it is important to not jump to conclusions about the absolute importance of family or friendship for each group, but rather, to understand that they are differences of sense for a particular domain.

Finally, there are a series of words like "ternura" (6/350), and "cariño" (8/297) which play an important role in the NS networks. While it is difficult to find precise translations for these words, similar words that are found in the NE group have much lower weighted values ("caring": 20/197, "affection": 32/102). This points, not only to a difference between the two groups, but also to methodological problems involved in making direct comparisons between lexical networks in different languages, as there is often no one to one correspondence between words.

Happiness

For all groups the prime "happiness"/"felicidad" inspires a particularly broad range of responses. Some of the salient differences between native speaker groups include the greater importance of "money"/"dinero" (NE: 16/170, NS: 52/72) for the NE group, and the greater importance of words like "peace"/"paz" (NE: 19/160, NS: 14/225) and "calm"/"tranquilidad" (NS: 7/329) for the NS speakers.

The kinds of images that are created also show differences between the two groups. The NS speakers seem to prefer imagery having to do with the beach/"playa" (NS: 29/110), ocean/"mar" (NS: 38/89) and nature/"naturaleza" (WS: 34/100). The NE speakers seem to prefer more domestic imagery, such as "children" (NE: 20/157, NS "niños" 28/114) and "puppy" (NE: 36/82).

Another interesting observation for this domain concerns the importance of the word "birthday"/"cumpleaños" for the non-native groups (FL: 5/486, L2: 6/394, ESS: 30/125). This word is peripheral for the NE group (65/56) and doesn't show up at all in the protocols of the NS group. This could be seen as an example of object control, particularly given the reduced importance of this word with the attainment of greater expertise. In other words, "cumpleaños" is a word which non-natives can access with ease, and which provides a focal point for certain aspects of "happiness" (domesticity, friends, family, parties, presents, etc.). It is also a word which can serve as a means of contextualizing certain aspects of "felicidad". In a more developed and sophisticated understanding of "happiness", however, this word loses its importance.

Fear

While all experimental groups have a large number of associations to this prime based on things that create fear (i.e. "pain", "darkness", "monsters", "danger" etc.) one of the differences between native speaking groups is that the NE speakers also give a large number of responses related to the effects of fear, and the responses it provokes (i.e. anxiety, nervous, stress, sweat, scream, shaking). This is hardly trivial, in a sense reflecting the difference between the material and objective conditions of fear, and personal and subjective responses to it. These are two very different ways of understanding a concept, and it would appear that the English "fear" has greater scope and complexity than the Spanish "miedo" through the inclusion of both of these aspects in its sense. For this domain the non-native speakers seem to occupy a kind of middle ground, given that they do provide some of the more "subjective" associations, yet far fewer than the NE speakers.

One of the associations which was given by the NS group to the prime "miedo", "soledad" (perhaps best translated as "aloneness") is particularly worth commenting on. This association is central for the NS group (5/394), yet for the NE group the closest word ("lonely") is rather peripheral (53/63). The FL and L2 speakers begin to approximate native performance with the word "solo" [alone] (FL: 7: 345, L2 6/214), and it is only the ESS group which finds the same word used by native speakers, "soledad" (ESS: 14/178) as well as "solo" (ESS: 46/78). What is of particular interest here is not only that the non-natives appear to be picking up on an aspect of "miedo" which is not particularly important for "fear", but also that they do so at early stages of learning by associating to a lexeme which is conceptually similar to an NS association, yet of a different word class (adjective as opposed to noun). It is only the more expert speakers who begin to assign the concept to the appropriate word class. This is hardly surprising, however, if we take into account Vygotsky's description of inner speech as asyntactic and infused with sense, rather than meaning. This leads to an interpretation whereby the notion of "soledad" becomes part of the sense of fear at an early stage for learners of Spanish, yet their lack of expertise leads them to provide a morphologically simple and relatively familiar form of the word. It is only the more expert speakers who begin to attain morphological precision.

Death

For the two native groups there are three principle groups of associations for this domain, one having to do with ceremonies and related objects (i.e. funeral, casket), another having to do with affective and emotional attitudes which may be adopted in relation to death (i.e. grief, sadness), and the third having to do with symbolic and metaphoric ways of understanding death (i.e. end, heaven). As often occurs, some associations are difficult to categorize, such as "black" (NE: 1/632) which can be interpreted both metaphorically (the darkness that begins after life) and as having to do with ceremony (the conventional color for mourners).

For the NE group, words which describe ceremonies stand out as being of primary importance ("funeral" 3/483, "coffin" 6/362, "cemetery" 8/275, "grave" 11/237, and "casket" 16/168). Metaphoric and symbolic associations have secondary importance (the aforementioned "black", "dark" 4/441, "end" 10/256, "final" 13/229, "night" 14/219, and "heaven" 19/159). Finally, affective responses to death also play a less central role ("mourning", 7/281, "sad" 12/234, "sadness" 14/227, "crying" 16/196, and "tears" 17/176).

While these three types of responses are also found in the NS protocols, there is a shift in emphasis. Affective responses for this group stand out as being particularly important ("dolor" [pain] 2/629, "tristeza" [sadness] 3/558, "soledad" [aloneness] 4/495, "pena" [sufferance] 6/386, and "angustia" [anguish] 7/367). In fact, words of this type represent five of the seven most important words in the network (along with "negro" [black] 5/441, and the reflexive "muerte" [death] 1/681). While words of this type are also present for the NE speakers, there is a rather dramatic shift in emphasis, such that the emotions experienced when faced with the death of someone close become a kind of focal point for an understanding of death. Words which describe the ceremony, on the other hand, are clearly of secondary importance ("ataud" [casket] 12/215, "tumba" [grave] 14/198, and "cementerio" [cemetery] 15/195). Finally, words which are metaphorical or symbolic are of decidedly lesser importance ("final" [final] 16/193, and "vacio" [empty/void] 19/150.

Conclusions

This study has addressed a set questions concerning the way concepts related to emotions are constructed, and has provided a series of results and analyses which shed considerable light on issues relating to lexical acquisition and organization.

In terms of methodology, this study has substantially refined and elaborated upon the use of word association protocols in a way which enhances this methodology as a means of investigation for issues relating to lexical semantics and intersubjective meaning. The methodology employed in this study represents an advance over previous techniques in several ways, primarily by using word associations for the construction of lexical networks, rather than simply for a series of associations to a single word.

The results of this study have considerable theoretical importance in relation to a series of issues relating to categorization, and inner speech. It has been shown that long term residents of a second language culture do reorganize their lexicons in the L2, in a way which progressively approximates the organization of native speakers. This can be taken as an indication that emotion concepts are not only embedded in specific cultural and discursive environments, but also that they can be approximated in an L2 through linguistic mediation and legitimate participation. Furthermore, this study addresses issues concerning inner speech, and the extent to which it may change through time, and through the mediation of language. This helps us to understand cognition, not as an individual possession, but as a dynamic process based on activity, and participation in a socially, culturally, and historically situated community.

The different lexical networks explored in this study lend themselves to a series of analyses, which, taken together, allow us to further our understanding of the relations between emotions and concept formation. Within the domain of *happiness* we are able to observe how different words and images may vary in importance across cultures. In the domain of *love* we are able to observe how, not only the discrete lexemes which go into a network may vary, but also how different emphasis may be placed on different kinds of words (metaphoric, referential, etc.). Within the domain of *fear* we can see how differences between ways of knowing emotion concepts can be as significant as the difference between emphasizing objective conditions and emphasizing the subjective responses to those conditions. Within the domain of *death* we can see how emotions can profoundly influence our knowledge of other concepts, and how this can be variable across cultures.

Finally, this study makes a contribution to our understanding of concepts in general, and the linguistic mediation of emotion concepts in particular, by integrating research on categorization developed within the framework of cognitive linguistics, with sociocultural theories of cognition. By focusing on ways in which these two theoretical frameworks are mutually informative, we are able to attain a more substantial understanding of the delicate relationship between cognition, concept formation, and lexical semantics.

Notes

1. See Searle (1994) for a discussion of how consciousness, rather than unconsciousness is central to an understanding of the human mind. He takes the position that models of the mind that posit an unconscious which is inaccessible to consciousness are essentially mistaken, driving a wedge between notions of intentionality and consciousness. As regards experiments which depend on word associations this shift in emphasis is of obvious importance; allowing an understanding of people's performance on this sort of task not as a window into some kind of murky and obscure unconscious, but rather as a kind of snapshot of the construction of consciousness. The "rediscovery" of the central issues of the human mind as having to do with consciousness are fully compatible with notions of the human mind as discursively elaborated (Harré and Gillett 1994), as well as with Vygotskian notions of inner speech (see below).
2. This idea finds reverberation in Bakhtin's (Holquist 1990) concept of ventriloquation. Wertsch (1991) talks about this process as the appropriation of voices which eventually become internalized.
3. The ability to isolate and abstract particular features is not only preconceptual, but may also be prelinguistic. Vygotsky makes this point clear in his discussion of Kohler's studies of tool use by chimpanzees. (Vygotsky 1987;158)
4. Linguistic mediation is, of course, not the only form of mediation possible. Examples of other semiotic systems which can serve to mediate higher cognitive processes include mathematics, art, and music.
5. Throughout this paper the terms "L1" and "L2" refer to the native language and second or target language respectively.
6. While for Vygotsky the basic unit of consciousness is the word, Wertsch (1985) argues that the word "is a unit of *semiotic mediation* of mental functioning, not a unit of mental functioning itself" (1985: 208). His rejection of the word as the basic unit of consiousness is based on i) its limitations in dealing with propositional and discourse referentiality ii) the inability of the word to account for all forms of higher mental functions (such as memory and attention), iii) the undo emphasis it places on social as opposed to natural forces of development. Following the thinking of activity theorists, Wertsch forwards Zinchenko's notion of "tool-mediated action" as a more appropriate candidate for a basic unit of analysis of consciousness. However, even if we accept the word only as a unit of semiotic mediation (and a potential tool itself), while denying it exclusivity as a unit of analysis, it still represents a significant unit for any

discussion of consciousness, with particular relevance for inner speech. Indeed, it is difficult to forward any discussion of sense, meaning, and concept formation without acknowledging the central (if non-exclusive) role of the word for semiotic mediation, and its ability to function on both the interpsychological and intrapsychological planes.

7. The stereotype of the old married couple that no longer talks might serve as a real life illustration of this extreme.

8. This may be somewhat of an oversimplification, as classroom learners themselves can become a community. The scope of activities of this community will certainly be more limited than that of a greater language community, although this will also vary, depending on the goals and attitudes which come to structure classroom activities, and the ways in which these activities are implemented.

9. The question of what it means for a non-native to become a full-fledged member of a speech community is one of great complexity. For the moment we will simply note that, just as there are no idealized speakers, so there is no idealized speech community for a given language. Instead we need to discuss speech communities which are formed by groups of people engaged in sets of activities, which in turn are mediated by the discourses of their members.

10. See Shore (1996) for a discussion of modularity as an organizing principle in contemporary American culture.

11. The use of the term "intermediate level of representation" comes from Searle (1994) where he discusses the mind as an emergent property of the brain. According to this point of view, then, there is only consciousness and gray matter for an understanding of human cognition. Intermediate levels of representation are those which operate at a psychological level between consciousness and the brain.

12. Schumann (1997) also places a great deal of emphasis on embodiment for an understanding of cognition. He proposes that the most basic "values" for motor activity and neural development are homeostasis and sociostasis which, while innate, are realized in relation to the infant's physical and social interactions with the world. Furthermore, the human brain, as it is not fully developed at birth, goes through its latter stages of development in conjunction with the infant's early experience.

13. Clark (1989) talks about symbols which are manipulated within a system of rules and representations as "semantically transparent", that is, defined exclusively in terms which can be determined system internally (for example, through the use of a feature matrix). "Meaning" in this sense in unequivocal, and not subject to interpretation. Clark's notion of semantic transparency is an excellent example of Reddy's (1978) conduit metaphor, whereby meaning is put into words by one person, and the same meaning is then taken out of those words by the interlocutor. Both Clark and Reddy reject the notion that human meaning and understanding can be understood in such mechanistic terms. Of course, both the conduit metaphor and the notion of semantic transparency can be applied to an understanding of encased systems (computer models) but fail to provide much insight into embodied cognition.

14. The notion of basic level categories is predicated to a large extent on Berlin's research concerning the creation of folk hierarchies (Berlin 1969, 1973). Lakoff (1987: 32) provides a succinct definition of basic level categories taken from Brown (1965: 321):

   - It is the level of distinctive actions.
   - It is the level which is learned earliest and at which things are first named.
   - It is the level at which names are shortest and used most frequently.
   - It is a natural level of categorization, as opposed to a level created by 'achievements of the imagination.'

A typical example of a basic level category is "dog", while "animal" is a superordinate category and "retriever" is a subordinate level category.

15. In discussing Vygotskyan theory Newman and Holtzman (1993) emphasize the inseparability of tool and result for human cognition: "The inner cognitive, attitudinal, creative, linguistic tools.... are inseparable from results in that their essential character (their defining feature) is the activity of their development rather than their function" (1993: 38). Following this idea it would be inappropriate to consider the classical category simply as a tool (which structures concepts) or simply as a result (the effect of more complex cognitive processes). Rather, it must be understood in terms of human activity (tool use) within specific social, institutional and historical contexts.

16. The number of words in an adult vocabulary is difficult to determine with accuracy. This is particularly so if we take into consideration issues of morphological variation which create difficulties for determining what in fact constitutes a word. Nonetheless, based on a variety of studies, Aitchison estimates the number of words in an adult vocabulary to be in the tens of thousands.

17. A well known example presented by Rommetveit (1991) can also be understood in these terms. The example has to do with whether a man who is mowing the lawn is working. His wife says he is working in the yard when faced with the accusation that he is lazy, but says he isn't working, but is puttering about in the yard, when asked if he is at the office. In the first case, the part of the network for "work" which is relevant for the context is highlighted (i.e. exertion, productivity, etc.). In the second case the part of the network which is not relevant for the context is highlighted (employment and earning money). Thus, depending on which part of the network she emphasizes in relation to the situation, she can say that he is working or not. This does not imply, however, a static network, as in both cases the part of the network which is relevant for "work" is created on line, and is not simply the activation of certain preset nodes.

18. In fact, the maximum pause length constraint was only relevant for a small number of subjects, mostly in the Foreign and Second Language learner categories. For the most part subjects provided associations quickly and in rapid succession.

19. Actual practice showed this questionnaire to be problematic, above all as certain types of questions which may have been relevant in the Muysken et al. study proved not to be pertinent to the present study. In the Muysken study subjects were guest workers with blue collar jobs, whose primary motivation for immigration was economic. In the present study subjects are mostly college educated, and their motives for living in a foreign country most often have to do with cultural interest, and quite often, affective concerns. Despite these problems the act of administering the questionnaire allowed the researcher to engage in a more subjective evaluation of the subjects' linguistic and cultural integration.

20. The ranking and cumulative weighted value of each word is given in parenthesis. The designation "NE: 2/650" for example, indicates that for native English speakers the word in question had the second highest ranking within the domain, with an absolute cumulative value of 650.

References

Aitchison, J. 1994. *Words in the Mind.* Cambridge MA: Blackwell.

Armstrong, S, L. Gleitman and H. Gleitman. 1983. "What some concepts might not be". *Cognition: International Journal of Cognitive Science 13(3):* 263–308.

Berlin, B. & P. Kay. 1969. *Basic Color Terms: Their Universality and Evolution.* Berkely CA: University of California Press.

Berlin, B. 1972. "Speculation on the growth of ethnobotanical nomenclature". *Language in Society 1:* 73–84.

Bolinger, D. 1965. "The atomization of meaning". *Language 41:* 555–573.

Bovasso, G., Szalay, L., Biase V. & M. Stanford. 1993. "A graph theory model of the semantic structure of attitudes". *Journal of Psycholinguistic Research 22:* 411–425.

Brown, Roger. 1965. *Social Psychology.* New York: Free Press.

Chomsky, N. 1980. *Rules and Representaions.* New York: Columbia University Press.

Clark, A. 1989. *Microcognition: Philosophy: cognitive science, and parallel distributed processing.* Cambridge, MA: MIT press.

Clark, E. 1993. *The Lexicon in Acquisition.* Cambridge and New York: Cambridge University Press.

Fauconnier, G. 1994. *Mental Spaces.* Cambridge and New York: Cambridge University Press.

Fillmore, C. 1976. "Frame semantics and the nature of language". In Steven Harnad et al. (eds), *Origins and Evolution of Language and Speech.* New York: New York Academy of Sciences, 20–32.

Fillmore, C. 1978. "On the organization of semantic information in the lexicon". *CLS 5, Proceedings of the Parasession on the Lexicon,* 140–173.

Harré, R. & Gillett, G. 1994. *The Discursive Mind.* Thousand Oaks CA: Sage Publications.

Holquist, M. 1990. *Dialogism: Bakhtin and his World.* London and New York: Routledge.

Johnson, M. 1987. *The Body In The Mind.* Chicago and London: The University of Chicago Press.

Kiel, F. 1989. *Concepts, Kinds, and Cognitive Development.* Cambridge MA: MIT Press.

Labov, W. 1973. "The boundaries of words and their meaning". In Roger Bailey and Charles-James Shuy (eds), *New Ways of Analyzing Variation In English.* Washington, D.C.: Georgtown University Press, 340–373.

Lakoff, G. 1987. *Women, Fire, and Dangerous Things.* Chicago and London: University of Chicago Press.

Lakoff, G. & M. Johnson. 1980. *Metaphors We Live By.* Chicago and London: University of Chicago Press.

Langacker, R. 1991. *Concept, Image, and Symbol; The Cognitive Basis of Grammar.* Berlin and New York: Mouton de Gruyter.

Lave, J. & E. Wenger 1991. *Situated Learning; Legitimate Peripheral Participation.* Cambridge UK: Cambridge University Press.

Luria, A. 1976. *Cognitive Development; Its Cultural and Social Foundations.* Cambridge MA: Harvard University Press.

Luria, A. 1978. "A child's speech response and the social environment." In Michael Cole (ed), *The Selected Writings of A.R. Luria.* White Plains, NY: M. E. Sharp Inc., 47–77.

Newman, F. and L. Holtzman. 1993. *Lev Vygotsky: Revolutionary Scientist.* London and New York. Routledge.

Ratner, C. 1991. *Sociohistorical Psychology and its Contemporary Applications.* New York: Plenum Press.

Reddy, M. 1978. "The conduit metaphor". In A. Ortony (ed), *Metaphor and Thought.* Cambridge and New York: Cambridge University Press, 284–324.

Rommetveit, R. 1991. "Psycholinguistics, hermeneutics, and cognitive science". *A Case for Psycholinguistic Cases* edited by Gabriela Appel and Hans W. Dechert. Amsterdam and Philadelphia: John Benjamins Publishing Company, 1–15.

Rosch, E. 1975. "Cognitive representations of semantic categories". *Journal of Experimental Psychology: General* 104: 192–233.

Rosch, E. 1978. "Principles of categorization". In E. Rosch and B.B. Lloyd (eds), *Cognition and Categorization.* Hillsdale: Lawrence Earlbaum, 27–48.

Rumelhart D. & J. McClelland. 1986. "PDP models and general issues in cognitive science". *Parallel Destributed Pocessing; Explorations in the Microstructure of Cognition 1*: Cambridge MA: MIT Press, 111–146.

Schumann, J. 1997. *The Neurobiology of Affect and Language.* Oxford: Blackwell Press.

Searle, J. 1992. *The Rediscovery of the Mind.* Cambridge MA: MIT Press.

Szalay, L. 1984. "An indepth analysis of cultural/ideological belief systems". *Mankind Quarterly:* 71–100.

Szalay, L. & J. Brent. 1967. "The analysis of cultural meanings through free verbal associations". *The Journal of Social Psychology 72:* 247–258.

Szalay, L. & J. Bryson. 1973. "Measurement of psychocultural distance: A comparison of American Blacks and Whites". *Journal of Personality and Social Psychology 26:* 166–177.

Szalay, L. & J. Bryson. 1974. "Psychological meaning": Comparative Analysis and Theoretical Implication. *Journal of Personality and Social Psychology vol 30:* 860–870.

Szalay, L. & Deese, J. 1978. *Subjective Meaning and Culture: An Assessment Through Word Associations.* Hillsdale: Lawrence Earlbaum Associates.

Szalay, L. & B. Maday. 1973. "Verbal associations in the analysis of subjective culture". *Current Anthropology 14:* 33–50.

Szalay, L. & B. Maday. 1983. "Implicit culture and psychocultural distance". *American Anthropologist 85:* 110–118.

Taylor, J. 1995. *Linguistic Categorization; Prototypes In Linguistic Theory.* New York: Oxford University Press.

Ushakova, T. 1994. "Inner speech and second language acquisition: An Experimental-Theoretical Approach". In J.P. Lantolf and G. Appel (eds), *Vygotskian Approaches to Second Language Research*. Norwood NJ: Ablex Publishing, 135–156.

Varela F., Thompson E., & E.. Rosch. 1991. *The Embodied Mind: Cognitive Science and Human Experience*. Cambridge MA: MIT Press.

Vygotsky, L. 1978. In Michael Cole, Vera John-Stiener, Sylvia Scribner, and Ellen Souberman (eds), *Mind In Society*. Cambridge MA: Harvard University Press.

Vygotsky, L. 1986. *Thought and Language*. edited by Alex Kozulin. Cambridge MA: MIT Press.

Vygotsky, L. 1987. *The Collected Works of L.S. Vygotsky; Volume 1, Problems of General Psychology*; edited by Robert W. Rieber and Aaron S. Carton. New York and London: Plenum Press.

Weinreich, U. 1953. *Languages in Contact*. Mouton Publishers.

Wertsch, J. 1985. *Vygotsky And The Social Formation Of Mind*. Cambridge MA: Harvard University Press.

Wertsch, J. 1991. *Voices of the Mind*. Cambridge MA: Harvard University Press.

Wittgenstein, L. 1958. *Philosophical Investigations*. Translated by G.E.M. Anscombe. Oxford: Blackwell.

Theory

Language And Emotion Concepts

What Experientialists and Social Constructionists Have in Common

Zoltán Kövecses
Eötvös Loránd University

Gary B. Palmer
University of Nevada at Las Vegas

Introduction[1]

In the Biblical *Genesis*, Eve eats the forbidden fruit, which we interpret as a metaphor for consciousness. It is a striking feature of the story that the first experience to accompany consciousness is an emotion — the emotion of shame. Thus, the narrators of the Old Testament must have regarded consciousness as a precondition for the emotions, or perhaps just for those with moral consequences. Language places further structure on emotional consciousness, and this is the structure that we are trying to discover and explicate. In this paper we discuss kinds of expressions and terms in the domain of emotion and theories of how these are constituted. We then offer a synthesis of experiential and social constructionist approaches. Finally, we discuss the implications of our findings and conclusions for the study of the consciousness of emotions.

In the history of the anthropological study of emotions and emotion language, it is particularly interesting to read Radcliffe Brown's ethnography, *The Andaman Islanders*, published in 1922. In this book, Radcliffe-Brown defined a *sentiment* as "an organized system of emotional tendencies centred about some object" (Radcliffe-Brown 1922: 234). He asserted that "a society depends for its existence on the presence in the minds of its members of a certain system of sentiments by which the conduct of the individual is regulated in conformity with the needs of the society" (Radcliffe-Brown 1922: 233–234). In his view, these emotional dispositions permeated the social system, which transmitted them from one generation to the next by means of collective expressions in ceremonials. Significantly, he asserted that "in human society the sentiments in question are not innate but are developed in the individual by the action of the society upon him" (Radcliffe-Brown 1922: 234).

The validity of Radcliffe-Brown's theory will not be at issue in this paper, but it does provide an useful historical point of reference as we examine contemporary theories of emotion and language. We find in Radcliffe-Brown significant points in common with the contemporary and popular social constructionist approach to emotion language. Catherine Lutz (1988), for example, argued that it is wrong to "essentialize" human emotions by holding that there are a few basic innate or universal emotions that are primarily psychological in origin.[2] Nevertheless, a growing body of new research on emotions and emotion-language in different cultures suggests that a position denying the universality of a few basic emotions cannot be sustained. D'Andrade (1995: 220) reviewed several studies and found a consensus that the number of unique basic emotions must be limited, but disagreement concerning exactly how many there are or which ones are basic.

As we seek a theory of the language of emotions, we will consider these opposing approaches and others and propose a synthesis that merges social constructionist and experientialist approaches. Essentially, this synthesis involves acknowledging that some emotion language is universal and clearly related to experience of the physiological functioning of the body. Once the universal emotion language is isolated, the numerous and important remaining differences in emotional linguistic expression can be explained by differences in cultural knowledge and pragmatic discourse functions that work according to divergent culturally defined rules or scenarios. This approach also allows us to see points of tension where cultural interests might contradict, suppress, or distort innate tendencies of expression. Thus, we need not be forever aligned in opposing camps pitting innatists against social constructionists. The two approaches should be regarded as complementary. Emotion concepts must frequently blend universal experiences of physiological functions with culturally specific models and interpretations, and emotion language must reflect this blend.

This survey of theories of emotion language is divided into three sections: (1) words and emotion, (2) meaning and emotion, and (3) some issues that inevitably arise in the study of everyday conceptions of emotion.

Words and Emotion

In this section, we will briefly discuss the most general functions and organization of emotion-related vocabulary, and then focus attention on a large but neglected group of emotion terms.

Expression and Description

We distinguish between expressive and descriptive emotion terms, which may be words or longer expressions. Some emotion words can express emotions.[3] That is, they predicate speaker's emotional experience at the time of speaking. Examples include *shit!* when angry, *wow!* when enthusiastic or impressed, *yuk!* when disgusted, and many more. It is an open question whether all emotions can be expressed in this way, and which are the ones that cannot and why.

Other emotion words describe (or name) the emotions that they signify: nouns and adjectives like *anger* and *angry*, *joy* and *happy*, *sadness* and *depressed*. With terms such as these, the question of whether speaker is conscious of the emotion depends on how the terms are used, whether as desriptive of speaker's emotional state or some other state of affairs. Under certain circumstances descriptive emotion terms can also "express" particular emotions. An example is *I love you!* where the descriptive emotion word love is used both to describe and express the emotion of love.

Our categories of descriptive and expressive emotion terms are analogous to Searle's categories of assertive and expressive speech acts (Searle 1990) in that descriptive terms have an assertive function and expressive emotion terms often constitute expressive speech acts. It is a peculiar feature of emotion-terms that they may accomplish both speech acts with a single utterance, both describing and expressing an emotion.

Basic Emotion Terms

Within the category of descriptive emotion words, the terms can be seen as "more or less basic." Speakers of a given language appear to feel that some of the emotion words are more basic than others. More basic ones include in English anger, sadness, fear, joy and love. Less basic ones include annoyance, wrath, rage, indignation, fright, and horror.

Basicness can mean two things (at least, loosely speaking). One is that these words (the concepts corresponding to them) occupy a middle-level in a vertical hierarchy of concepts. In this sense, say, anger is more basic than, for example, annoyance or emotion. Anger is a "basic-level" emotion category because it lies between the superordinate level category emotion and the subordinate-level category of annoyance. The other sense of "basicness" is that a particular emotion category can be judged to be a better example of an emotion than another at the same level. For example, anger is more basic in this sense than, say, hope or pride, which are on the same horizontal basic level.

These organizations of emotion terms have been extensively studied in the past decade for English (e.g. Fehr and Russell 1984; Shaver, et al, 1987). Cross-cultural research along these lines is just beginning. Using a methodology borrowed from Fehr and Russell (1984), Frijda (1995) arrived at five general and possibly universal categories of emotion in eleven languages. These basic emotion categories include happiness, sadness, anger, fear, and love. Smith and Tkel-Sbal (1995) investigated the possibility that emotion terms are organized prototypically in the Micronesian language of Palau, and Smith and Smith (1995) attempt to do the same for Turkish.

Metaphor and Metonymy

There is another kind of emotion-related expression: the figurative. The group of figurative expressions may be larger than the other two combined. Here the terms do not "name" particular emotions, and the issue is not how basic or prototypical the word or expression is. The words and expressions that belong in this group denote various aspects of emotion concepts, such as intensity, cause, and control. They are metaphorical and metonymical. The metaphorical expressions are manifestations of conceptual metaphors (see Lakoff and Johnson 1980). For example, boiling with anger is a linguistic example of the very productive conceptual metaphor ANGER IS A HOT FLUID (cf. Lakoff and Kövecses 1987; Lakoff 1987; Kövecses 1986, 1990), burning with love is an example of LOVE IS FIRE (cf. Kövecses 1988), and to be on cloud nine is an example of HAPPINESS IS UP (cf. Kövecses 1991b). All three examples indicate the intensity aspect of the emotions concerned.

Linguistic expressions that belong in this large group can also be metonymical, that is, based on pragmatic functions from term to target (Fauconnier 1997). Examples include *upset* for anger and *have cold feet* for fear. The first is an instance of the conceptual metonymy PHYSICAL AGITATION STANDS FOR ANGER, while the second is an example of the conceptual metonymy DROP IN BODY TEMPERATURE STANDS FOR FEAR (Kövecses 1990). A special case of emotion metonymies involves a situation in which an emotion concept is part of another emotion concept (see, for example, Kövecses 1986, 1990, 1991 a, b). This can explain why, for instance the word *girlfriend* can be used of one's partner in a love relationship. Since love, at least ideally, involves or assumes friendship between the two lovers, the word friend can be used in place of the basic emotion term.

Of the three groups identified above, the group of figurative expressions is by far the largest, and yet it has received the least attention in the study of emotion language. Figurative expressions are deemed completely uninteresting and irrelevant by most researchers, who tend to see them as epiphenomena fancier ways of saying some things that could be said in literal, simple ways. Further, the expressive and descriptive expressions in group one are usually considered to be literal. Given this bias in perception, we can better understand why the figurative expressions receive scant attention. If one holds the view that only literal expressions can be the bearers of truth and that figurative expressions have nothing to do with how our (emotional) reality is constituted, there is no need to study "mere" figurative language. But, if one holds the view that emotion language is relative to cognitive models, including conceptual metaphors and metonymies, then figurative language becomes important, if not central, to the semantic study of emotion language. This may explain much of the growing interest in the figurative language of emotions (see, for example, Baxter 1992; Duck 1994; Holland and Kipner 1995; Kövecses 1990).

Meaning and Emotion

Scholars have offered several distinct views in an attempt to characterize emotional meaning.

The "Label" View

The label view of emotional meaning maintains that the meaning of emotion terms is simply an association between a label, like the words anger and fear, plus some real emotional phenomenon, like physiological processes and behavior. This view is the simplest lay view of emotional meaning. It is based on the folk theory that meaning is merely an association between sounds (forms) and things. This understanding of meaning in general also forms the basis of a scientific theory of emotion. Schachter and Singer (1962) proposed that emotion involves three things: a label, plus something (emotionally) real, plus a situation. This view is an improvement on the simplest lay view, but both views exclude the possibility that emotion terms can have much conceptual content and organization. However, studies by Wierzbicka (1995), Shaver, et al, (1987), Kövecses (1990), and others, have discovered a great deal of conceptual content and structure in emotion terms.

The "Core Meaning" View

It is customary in semantics to distinguish between core (denotative, conceptual, cognitive, etc.) and peripheral (connotative, residual, etc.) meaning (see, for instance, Lyons 1977). What characterizes core meaning is a small number of properties, or components that are taken to define a category in an adequate manner. Core meanings should be capable of minimally distinguishing any two words, that is, by virtue of the smallest possible number of components. Since, in this view, the major function of definitions is systematic differentiation of meanings, core meaning is promoted to a central position as the only kind that really matters. Other kinds of meaning are viewed as peripheral and therefore less important.[4] Peripheral meaning or connotation is usually seen as consisting of various social, situational, or affective properties whose contributions to the cognitive content of words are taken as insignificant. Connotations are assumed to vary from person to person and from culture to culture. However, according to some researchers, like Osgood, (1964), certain connotations are universal — namely, the general meaning dimensions of evaluation (good vs. bad), activity (fast vs. slow), and potency (strong vs. weak).

The core meaning view of emotion categories typically assumes the idea that emotional meaning is composed of universal semantic primitives. A leading proponent of this view is Wierzbicka (see, for instance, Wierzbicka 1972 and 1995). For example, she defines the English emotion word anger in the following way: "X feels as one does when one thinks that someone has done something bad and when one wants to cause this person to do something he doesn't want to do." (1972: 62). This definition makes use of a small number of universal semantic primitives, such as THINK, DESIRE, WANT, BAD, GOOD, CAUSE, DO, etc. Wierzbicka regards it as a mistake to think of emotion words in particular languages, such as English, are universal in the sense that they have close correspondents in every language (e.g. Wierzbicka 1986, 1992a, and 1995). Thus, for example, the English word *emotion* is anything but universal; it does not seem to exist even in closely related languages. Instead, what are universal, Wierzbicka maintains, are the semantic primitives that make up the conceptual content of particular emotion words in particular languages.

However, in one respect Wierzbicka's approach is not very representative of the core meaning view. In defining an emotion, one uses the universals to make a clause that describes a scene or scenario: "X feels as one does when...." In a typical core meaning theory, the mere presence or absence of the primitives is defining and there is no syntax that governs their construction as concepts. But in Wierzbicka, syntax matters, because the semantic universals are combined in contingent clauses to construct scenes or scenarios ("X feels as one does when one thinks that..."). Wierzbicka's views will be discussed further in a later section.

To take another example of the core meaning view, Davitz (1969) characterizes the meaning of the English emotion word anger as being composed of HYPERACTIVATION, MOVING AGAINST, TENSION, and INADEQUACY. These components of meaning are derived from linguistic data produced by speakers of English. The clusters are taken to be capable of successfully distinguishing each emotion word in English. Furthermore, it is suggested that the same clusters can be applied to the study of emotion concepts in other cultures, such as Ugandan.

The "Dimensional" View

The dimensional view is sometimes difficult to distinguish from the core meaning view. In the dimensional view meaning is constituted by values on a fixed set of dimensions of meaning rather than by a selection from a fixed set of properties or features. Solomon (1976), for example, postulated thirteen dimensions that are sufficient to describe any emotion. These include DIRECTION, SCOPE/FOCUS, OBJECT, CRITERIA, STATUS, EVALUATIONS, RESPONSIBILITY, INTERSUBJECTIVITY, DISTANCE, MYTHOLOGY, DESIRE, POWER, and STRATEGY. The definitions of emotion concepts make use of all or some of these dimensions. Thus, according to Frijda the dimensions that apply to a given emotion provide a "component profile" that uniquely characterizes an emotion (Frijda 1986: 217–219). Researchers working in the dimensional approach attempt to eliminate a major alleged pitfall of the "core meaning" view in general: the large gap between emotional meaning and emotional experience. For example, de Rivera (1977: 121) states:

> ...there is bound to be a tension between these two poles—the one insisting that the investigator be faithful to experience, the other requiring the sparse elegance of precise relations between a few abstract constructs.

Clearly, de Rivera was aware of a gap between emotional meaning as defined in terms of "a few abstract constructs" (i.e. semantic components and dimensions) and the totality of emotional experience, that is, the complex experiences of people who are in particular emotional states. Another well known advocate of the dimensional approach is Frijda (1986), who distinguished even more dimensions, twenty-six altogether. Obviously, the aim is to reduce the meaning-experience gap, but at some point it seems likely that the more straightforward way to do this would be to simply describe the conceptualization of emotional experiences using the methods of linguistic ethnography.

The "Implicational" View

While the "core meaning" and "dimensional" views are both based on core meaning, the implicational view takes connotative meaning as its main point of departure. According to Shweder (1991: 244), "To study what something means is to study what it entails, implies, or suggests to those who understand it." For example, the sentence *One of my grandparents was a surgeon* suggests that my grand*father* was a surgeon and the sentence *She is your mother* implies that she is under obligation to care about your health (1991: 244–45). As these examples suggest, for Shweder, meaning is connotative, not denotative. It is the periphery, rather than the core, that counts in this view of meaning.

Shweder relativizes this approach to emotional meaning. One of his examples is anger. Shweder writes: "Anger suggests explosion, destruction, and revenge" (1991: 245). As we will see in the discussion of yet another view of emotional meaning, these properties of anger, together with others, show up in folk or emic representations of the meaning of anger.

The particular version of the connotative view of meaning that Shweder endorses is the nonuniversalist one, the cultural relativist view. Unlike Osgood (1964), Shweder believes, with anthropologists in general, that connotative meaning, and in particular emotional meaning, varies considerably from culture to culture. Making reference to work by several anthropologists, Shweder (1991: 245) writes:

> Emotions have meanings, and those meanings play a part in how we feel. What it means to feel angry … is not quite the same for the Ilongot, who believe that anger is so dangerous it can destroy society; for the Eskimo, who view anger as something that only children experience; and for working-class Americans, who believe that anger helps us overcome fear and attain independence.

Thus, in Shweder's view the connotative meaning of anger varies cross-culturally. This is a tack that contrasts to the one taken by Osgood (1964), whose interest lies in what is universal about connotative meaning.

Heider (1991) took a connotative approach in his study of Minangkabau (Sumatra) and Indonesian terms for emotions. Heider discovered clusters of synonyms for emotion terms. We are here regarding synonyms as a kind of verbal connotation. He constructed lists of over 200 emotion terms for each language and obtained synonyms from 50 Minangkabau, 50 Minangkabau Indonesian, and 50 Indonesian subjects for each term in the list. By drawing lines from each term to all its synonyms for each language, he was able to draw extensive maps of the lexical domain of emotion. Heider (1991: 27) suggested that each of the clusters of similar words "correspond best to what we mean by 'an emotion'." Those who think in terms of a small number of basic emotions might be surprised by Heider's discovery of "some forty clusters" with each having ties to "only one or two other clusters" (1991: 28). Heider also studied emotion prototypes, as discussed in the following section.

The "Prototype" View

In the section on "Words and Emotion," we have mentioned that some emotion words are more basic or prototypical than others. There, the question was: What are the best examples of the category of emotion? As we saw, the best examples of the category in English include anger, fear, sadness, joy, and love. We can also ask: What are the best examples, or cases, of anger, fear, and love, respectively? Obviously, there are many different kinds of each. When we try to specify the structure and content of the best example of any of these lower-level categories, we are working within the "prototype" view of emotional meaning as it relates to basic-level categories. This view has produced some intriguing results. Heider (1991) for example, found that anger is less of a focal emotion in Indonesian than it is in English. Sadness and confusion, on the other hand, are more central emotions in Indonesian than in English.

The structure of emotion concepts is seen by many researchers as a script, scenario, or model (e.g. Fehr and Russell 1984; Shaver, et al, 1987; Rimé et al, 1990; Wierzbicka 1990, 1992b; Heider 1991; Lakoff and Kövecses 1987; Kövecses 1986, 1988, 1990; etc.; Rosaldo 1984; Lutz 1988; Ortony, Clore and Collins 1988; Palmer and Brown 1998). For example, Lakoff and Kövecses (1987), described anger as a sequence of stages of events: (1) cause of anger, (2) anger exists, (3) attempt at controlling anger, (4) loss of control over anger, (5) retribution. That is, anger is conceptualized by speakers of English as a five-stage scenario. Similarly, Fehr and Russell (1984: 482) characterized fear in the following manner:

> A dangerous situation occurs suddenly. You are startled, and you scream. You try to focus all your attention on the danger, try to figure a way out, but you feel your heart pounding and your limbs trembling. Thoughts race through your mind. Your palms feel cold and wet. there are butterflies in your stomach. You turn and flee.

In other words, we have the unfolding of a variety of events that are temporally and causally related in certain specifiable ways. The sequence of events makes up the structure of the prototypical concept of any given emotion, like fear, while the particular events that participate in the sequence make up the content of the concepts.

One particularly interesting example of the scenario approach is that of Ortony, Clore and Collins (1988), who defined 22 emotion types. The types are defined in terms of their eliciting conditions and independently of language. Examples of such types are *displeased about the prospect of an undesirable event*, *pleased about the disconfirmation of the prospect of an undesirable event*, and *displeased about the confirmation of the prospect of an undesirable event* (p. 173). Their theory involves an element of appraisal: Events may be desirable or undesirable; actions may be praiseworthy or blameworthy; and objects may be appealing or unappealing.

Ortony, Clore and Collins (1988) argued that they have the best of two worlds: a theory that is culture free and applies universally, but nevertheless allows for culturally defined variation in emotional experience:

> at least at the meta-level, we feel comfortable that we have a theory based on culturally universal principles. These principles are that the particular classes of emotions that will exist in a culture depend on the ways in which members of a culture carve up their world. (Ortony, Clore and Collins 1988: 175)

But this position is not as relativistic as it may at first appear, because all cultures must carve along the same joints as defined by the researchers: The particular classes of emotions allowed to any culture are presumably limited to the 22 types in their theory.

Ortony, Clore and Collins (1988) believe it is wrong to start with language in the investigation of emotions. They regard it as a separate enterprise to investigate "the way in which emotion words in any particular language map onto the hypothesized emotion types" (1988: 173). If we compare their approach to the characterization of anger offered by Lakoff and Kövecses (1987), we can see that the eliciting conditions would have to be subsumed entirely within stage one, "cause of anger." The emotion language pertaining to the subsequent four stages would not map directly onto the emotion types proposed in the psychological approach of Ortony, Clore and Collins. Thus, the psychological approach would ignore much of the conceptual content that can be discovered by the inspection of emotion language. On the other hand, their approach might provide leads for a more fine-grained linguistic analysis of stage one.

Sometimes the prototype approach is combined with some other view of emotional meaning. For example, Wierzbicka (1990: 361) stated:

> … the definition of an emotion concept takes the form of a prototypical scenario describing not so much an external situation as a highly abstract cognitive structure: roughly, to feel emotion E means to feel as a person does who has certain (specifiable) thoughts, characteristic of that particular situation.

This definition actually combines the prototype approach with the "core meaning" approach, because the "(specifiable) thoughts" are constituted by the semantic primitives WANT, BAD, DO, SOMEONE, and others.

In the "prototype" approach, two kinds of views can be distinguished: the literal and the nonliteral conceptions of emotion. For example, Shaver, et al. (1987) and Wierzbicka (1990) apparently do not think that metaphorical and metonymical understanding plays a role in the way emotion concepts are understood and constituted. Others, however, believe that metaphorical and metonymical understanding does play a role. Although some of these researchers disagree about the exact nature of this role (see, for example, Holland 1982, Quinn 1991, and Geeraerts and Grondelaers 1995), many nevertheless believe that metaphors are important. Authors, from a variety of disciplines, such as Averill (1974, 1990), Averill and Kövecses (1990), Baxter (1992), Duck (1994), Holland (1982), Holland and Kipner, (1995), Quinn (1987, 1991), Wellman (in press), Lakoff and Kövecses (1987), Lakoff (1987), Kövecses (1986, 1988, 1990, 1991 a, b, 1993 a, b, 1994, 1995a, b) discuss the role and possible contribution of conceptual metaphors and metonymies to the conceptualization of emotional experience.

Finally, in a variety of publications Kövecses (1986, 1988, 1990, 1991 a, b) suggested that many emotions, such as love, fear, and happiness, have not just one, but multiple prototypes. That is, the proposal is that several members (or cases) can acquire the status of "best example" within an emotion category. This is because, given a category with several members, one member can be typical, another can be salient, a third can be ideal, and so on.[5]

The "Social Constructionist" View

Several scholars take emotion concepts to be social constructions. For example, Lutz (1988) gives the following account of *song* (roughly corresponding to anger) in Ifaluk:

(1) There is a rule or value violation.
(2) It is pointed out by someone.
(3) This person simultaneously condemns the act.
(4) The perpetrator reacts in fear to that anger.
(5) The perpetrator amends his or her ways.

This model differs considerably from the one associated with the English word *anger*. For example, while the view linked with the English word *anger* emphasizes properties of anger that relate to individuals, the view linked with *song* highlights the essentially social nature of this emotion concept. To account for the difference, Lutz claimed that this model of Ifaluk *song* is a socio-cultural construction whose properties depend on particular aspects of Ifaluk society and culture. Giving us more than a faint echo of Radcliffe-Brown, Lutz subtitled her book on emotions in Ifaluk *Everyday Sentiments on a Micronesian Atoll....* However, where Radcliffe-Brown emphasized the function of ceremonial in the social construction of emotions, Lutz followed the contemporary pragmatic emphasis in linguistic anthropology by characterizing discourse as pragmatic action that constitutes social sentiments and the meaning of emotion terms.[6]

The social-constructionist view of emotion concepts is also based, at least in the work of its leading proponents like Lutz and Averill, on the notion of prototype. The structure of most emotion concepts is seen as a highly conventionalized script from which deviations are recognized and linguistically marked in any given culture. Where the explicitly social-constructionist views differ from other prototype-based but nonconstructionist approaches is in their account of the content of emotion concepts.

Lutz's account of Ifaluk *song* can be seen as diametrically opposed to that of anger as discussed by Lakoff and Kövecses (1987). Taking the ANGER IS A HOT FLUID metaphor as an example, Lakoff and Kövecses claimed that, to the degree that the metaphors (especially the ANGER IS A HOT FLUID metaphor) that constitute anger are motivated by physiological functioning (e.g. increased body heat), the concept is motivated by the human body, rather than being a completely arbitrary social-cultural product. Since human bodies have obvious universal properties and functions, the approach of Lakoff and Kövecses predicts universalities in emotion concepts and emotion language. Lutz seems more concerned with denying universalities. Her disparaging view of "essentialism" seems to imply that the search for universalities is an error of Western psychology.

It is necessary to transcend this opposition between the view that the concept of anger is simply motivated by human physiology and the view that it is simply a social construction. We suggest that it is both motivated by the human body *and* produced by a particular social and cultural environment. Emotion concepts represent a blend of experiences originating in both these spheres. If we attempt to reconcile the two apparently contradictory views, social constructions must acquire bodily substance, that is, they must have some basis in universal bodily experiences, and bodily motivations must acquire specific social-cultural content and interpretation.

Some Issues

Several important issues emerge from the foregoing discussion. These include the "validity" issue, the universality of emotion prototypes and cognitive representations, the role of metaphor and metonymy, and the relation between lay concepts and scientific theories.

The "Validity" Issue

Which one of the views described above best represents our everyday conceptions of emotion? Is it the "label" view, the "core meaning" view, the "dimensional" or some other view, or a combination of any one of these? This is a tough question, and it seems that at the present time we have no reliable criteria to decide which of the views listed above is the one that can be considered a psychologically valid representation of emotion concepts. Although we have no direct evidence on the basis of which to favor any of the ways of representing emotional meaning, work in cognitive science in general suggests that prototypical cognitive models are our best candidates. "Prototype" views seem to offer the greatest explanatory power for many aspects of emotional meaning. These views, it will be remembered, come in at least two major versions: social constructionist and experientialist (i.e. bodily-based, in the sense of Lakoff 1987 and Johnson 1987). In our view, the two complement each other, and we will suggest a certain "marriage" between these rival theories.

The Universality of Emotion Prototypes: Are There Focal Emotions?

As several anthropologists and psychologists have argued (especially Berlin and Kay 1969 and Rosch 1975), focal colors appear to be universal. Is this also the case for the emotions? That is, is the prototype (the central member) for emotion X in language L a prototype (a central member) in other languages as well? Currently available evidence seems to indicate that it is not. The constructionists (like Harré and Lutz) argue that the absence of focal emotions correlate to focal colors is only natural, while others (like Russell 1991) argue that prototypical scripts, or at least large portions of them, are the same across languages and cultures. Wierzbicka (1995) maintains, with the constructionists, that emotion prototypes vary cross-culturally, but the semantic primitives that constitute culturally specific emotions are universal.

It has also been suggested that what is universal are some general structures within the emotion domain, corresponding, as Frijda (1995) puts it, to an "unspecified positive emotion" (the happiness/joy range), an "unspecified negative emotion" (the sadness range), "an emotion of strong affection" (the love range), "an emotion of threat" (the fear range), and an anger-like range. However, the prototypical or focal members of the basic emotion categories (or ranges) in different languages tend to be different to varying degrees (compare Ifaluk *song* with English anger). This situation seems to be unlike the situation for color. In color, the focal members of particular colors are exactly the same across languages and they correspond to measurable points on the spectrum of visible light. In emotion, despite the fact that the same general basic emotion categories may exist in all languages and cultures, there is still no physiological substrate on which each emotion can be precisely located (Heider 1991), there is no universal cluster of features for any emotion, and there is no invariant conceptual content for any emotion. Thus, there are no universal prototypes of basic emotions. In the final chapter, we will make some suggestions concerning some of the details of cross-cultural similarities and differences.

The Universality of Cognitive Representations

Studies discussed in this paper have utilized a variety of conceptual tools in their attempts to provide a cognitive representation of emotional meaning. These include semantic primitives, connotative properties, dimensions of meaning, scripts or scenarios, and conceptual metaphors and metonymies. The question arises: Which of these conceptual elements are universal? Again, authors disagree. Lakoff (1987) and Johnson (1987) suggested that none of these are. They argued instead that the only universals are basic image schemas arising from certain fundamental bodily experiences. In this work, we take this general direction.

The Role of Metaphor And Metonymy

Lakoff and Johnson (1980) argued that many everyday metaphors are not just linguistic, but conceptual in nature and can actually create social, cultural, and psychological realities for us. What is the role of conceptual metaphor in emotion concepts in a given culture? The more specific issue is this: Do conceptual metaphors constitute the cultural models associated with emotions, or do they simply reflect them, as proposed by Quinn (1991)? Here again, we will take the opposite tack and argue, on the basis of the prevalent "container" metaphor for anger, that conceptual metaphors, together with other factors, can contribute to how an emotion concept, like anger, is constituted. However, as Holland (personal communication) suggests, this "either/or" view of the role of metaphor might not be the best way of looking at the issue.[7] Moreover, it seems closer to the truth to believe that some metaphors have the capacity to create reality, in the sense of affording a cognitive model that governs thinking about an issue or situation, while others do not. Which ones do and which don't can only be decided on the basis of detailed future research.

Lay Conceptions Vs. Scientific Theories

What is the relationship between everyday emotion concepts as revealed in conventional language use and scientific conceptions of emotion? That is, how are lay and scientific theories of emotion related? This is an issue that Parrot (1995) addresses explicitly in relation to the lay "heart-head" distinction and the corresponding expert one of "emotion-cognition."

More generally, assuming that there is a relationship and that the relationship can be either strong or weak, somewhat on the analogy of distinct interpretations of the Sapir-Whorf hypothesis, we can imagine four theoretical possibilities, with several additional in-between-cases not specified here:

a. folk conception determines expert theory
b. folk conception influences expert theory
c. expert theory determines folk theory
d. expert theory influences folk theory

In the strong version, "determines" is intended in the sense of "leads to" or "produces." In the weak version, "influences" covers such disparate cases as "constrains," "builds on," or "makes it natural and popular."

Given this admittedly ad hoc classification, we can look at specific instances in emotion research and try to identify the specific relation that might obtain between a given lay view and a given expert theory. Averill and Kövecses have made some preliminary observations (e.g. Averill and Kövecses 1990; Kövecses 1991a; Kövecses, in press). For instance, Kövecses (1991a) showed how a number of expert theories of love focus and build on various aspects of the language-based folk model of love. The nature of the relationship between lay and expert theories in psychological domains, such as emotion, is a hotly debated topic today, as indicated by several recent collections of articles that bear on this question, such as those by Siegfried (1994) and Russel, et al. (1995).

Synthesizing Experientialist And Social Constructionist Accounts

To some degree the difference between experientialist and social constructionist approaches may be simply a matter of emphasis. The experientialist approach describes its target phenomena at a more basic level, closer to the level of psychobiological constraints while the social constructionist approach describes its target phenomena at a more socially embedded and specific level. The experientialist approach tends to include more feeling states in its definitions of emotions, but it often includes social description as well. For example, Kövecses's (1988: 58–59) prototype scenario of love includes such explicitly social content as "I view myself and the other as forming a unity," "I experience the relationship as a state of perfect harmony," "I see love as something that guarantees the stability of the relationship," and "Love is mutual."

The social constructionist approach, on the other hand, tends to include only social scenarios in its definitions and disregard feeling states. It also retains the notion that emotion concepts may occur as prototypes and variants, but these are regarded as primarily social in content and origin. But here, again, the boundaries between the two approaches are fuzzy. Lutz (1988: 84) recognized the importance of studying emotion metaphors, regarding them as "important entrées into an understanding of ethnopsychological conceptualizations." Although Lutz cited Lakoff and Johnson (1986) to justify this position, she did not seem to realize the universalist implications of their experientialist approach. Nevertheless, she recorded the Ifaluk expression "'My insides are bad' (*Ye ngaw niferai*)," which suggests the universal metaphor of the body as a container for the emotions (Lutz 1988: 92). She observed that "'Thoughts/emotions' (*nunuwan*) are often spoken of as 'coming out' or 'coming up' from 'our insides'" (Lutz 1988: 92) and that thoughts or emotions may be said to be "followed by others," implying that thoughts/emotions follow paths (Lutz 1988: 95). Using metonymy, when an Ifaluk is upset she may say "food does not taste sweet"; when grieving, she may say "my gut is ripping" (Lutz 1988: 99).

Kövecses (1990: 23) has pointed out that both the experientialist and social constructionist approaches view emotions as having similar elements:

> both approaches view emotions as having a causal aspect (the "social events" in the terminology above and "causes" in the terminology I will use); as having a purposive aspect ("goals" vs. "desire," or "purposive aspect"); and as having an actional aspect ("intended reactions" vs. "behavioral reactions").

But these three elements still do not include feeling states that are saliently physical in origin. In the experientialist account, emotions are emergent from physical experience. Nevertheless, for the most part, they are evoked by social events rather than physical ones. Since they arise out of social experiences, their experiencers must associate feeling states with conventional social events. To deny this is to ask the experiencer to forget or compartmentalize the social content of emotional experience. People who did that consistently would be unlikely to function adaptively in societies because they would be unable to reliably avoid damaging experiences or to repeat efficacious ones. People who experienced no reliable physical responses to emotionally evocative events would be unable to prepare their bodies and minds to respond adaptively to physical and social challenges. Therefore, emergent emotion concepts must blend and integrate psychobiological and socio-cultural experience.

It is not necessary that we brand either approach as entirely right or wrong. Both have strengths and weaknesses. The strength of the universalist approach is that it enables us to discover what is universal, thereby seeing more clearly what is relative and culturally determined. The strengh of the social-constructionist approach is that it is capable of showing how emotional meaning emerges in particular cultural contexts and pragmatic discourses and it attempts to capture the entire sociocultural system of emotional meaning, in contrast to the meaning of particular emotion words and expressions (Kövecses 1990: 24).

To be complete, as one would write a complete grammar, it is necessary, where emotional complexes exist as stable socio-cultural/psychobiological entities, to describe them in all their specificity, insofar as practical constraints permit. Otherwise, one's theory may predict emotional states and language that never actually occur in real cultures. The complete description of culturally specific social scenarios in emotion concepts does not preclude one from seeking cross-cultural commonalities or universals in either the psychobiological or the social content of emotion concepts.

Let us now state this synthesis point by point:

1. Emotions are experienced as feeling states evoked by social and/or physical events, but perhaps most typically by social events.

2. An emotion concept typically integrates content pertaining to all spheres of experience: social, cognitive, and physical. It also invokes imagery pertaining to language and discourse. This complex content is organized as a more or less stable configuration. The richness of content makes it difficult to accumulate comparable data on diverse languages and cultures because different researchers tend to select different kinds of data as representative. The scenario of ideal love described by Kövecses (1988) includes information pertaining to social action, cognition, and physiology. The account of *song* in Ifaluk, presented above,

pertains entirely to social events in phases 1–3, and 5 (Lutz 1988: 157). Only phase 4 mentions the emotion "fear," hinting at the the possible inclusion of cognitive and physiological information in the Ifaluk conceptualization of *song*.

3. The content of emotion concepts can best be described as scenarios. These vary widely on the dimensions of abstraction and complexity of phasing. The scenario of ideal love described by Kövecses (1988) is relatively abstract. It covers the whole process of falling and being in love, but it has only three phases. The account of *song* in Ifaluk, cited above, lies at the middle level of abstraction and deals with what appears to be a relatively short-term process with five phases.

4. The social action content of emotion language can best be described as culturally specific social scenarios that include imagery of language-use. In folk knowledge, these scenarios are probably represented simultaneously at several levels of abstraction and layers of metaphor. Choosing the right descriptive level may depend upon one's intended audience or readership.

5. Feeling states have an irreducible and probably universal psychobiological basis that accounts for many similarities in the conceptualization of emotions. Taking anger, for example, both English and Zulu figurative language characterizes anger as pressure in a container, as heat, as contained in the heart, and as bile (Taylor and Mbense 1998). Chinese shares with English all the basic metaphors of happiness: it is up, it is light, and it is fluid in a container (Ning Yu 1955).

6. Feeling states are also, in part, culturally determined. This is because events that evoke parallel emotions in different cultures are unlikely to induce them in precisely the same way. Perhaps it is only Zulus who experience the onset of anger as a "squashing in the heart" (Taylor and Mbense 1998). Perhaps it is only the Japanese who experience extreme anger as coming to the head (*atama*) with a "click" (Matsuki 1995). Perhaps it is only the Chinese who conceptually distribute their anger to various parts of the body rather than directing it towards offenders (Kövecses In press). Perhaps it is only Hungarians who conceptualize the angry body as a pipe containing a burning substance.

7. The content of well-formed emotion concepts often, or perhaps always, includes some recognition of experiencer's cognitive state, including ability to remember, to hold thoughts, to prioritize actions according to cultural conventions, and to think and speak rationally (to progress according to a conventional sequence of thoughts). This cognitive content is part of the configuration of an emotion concept.

8. Emotion concepts occur as prototypes with variants, providing a basis for polysemy in emotion language.

9. Languages vary in respect to whether their emotional discourses and vocabularies of emotion terms are more elaborate and focused in one sphere or another, that is, in the spheres of physiological experience, cognition, or social action. Thus, Tahitians apparently lack a general term for sadness and they lack the concept that it has external, social causes. In Tahiti, sadness may be *hypocognized* (Levy 1984, cited in D'Andrade 1995). In the Philippines, as perhaps in Ifaluk, the use of emotion language is typically pragmatic rather than expressive (Rosaldo 1990). In Tagalog, emotions are typically described in terms of their causes and consequences rather than in terms of the feeling states that they evoke (Palmer and Brown 1998).

10. All concepts are emotion concepts in that nothing can be thought without some direct or indirect connection to feeling states. Similarly, all language is emotion language in this sense. The terms that we normally think of as emotion terms in English are those that evoke imagery of the most intense physical and cognitive changes in feeling states.

11. Figurative language, including metaphor and metonymy, may express any aspects of emotion concepts. Some metaphors reflect universal notions, such as the idea that anger is conceptualized as heat and pressure in a container. Metonyms may also express universal aspects of emotions, such as the idea that anger is loss of muscular control, redness, a rise in body temperature, and loss of rationality. Other metaphors and metonyms may be specific to a culture, perhaps in part because their particular physical experience of anger is not shared by all cultures. For example, Zulus become wet with anger, but Americans do not (Taylor and Mbense 1998). Different social and physical environments provide different conceptual source materials.

Implications for Consciousness Studies

For Radcliffe-Brown, emotions were central to social systems, but he was not concerned with the conscious experiences of individuals. For him, the question was how do collective expressions of emotion serve social needs. In the introductory essay to this volume, it was shown that configurationists and psychological anthropologists improved our cross-cultural understanding of cultural constraints on emotions, but they also avoided or failed to see the problem of emotional consciousness. Recent studies have added little to the sum of our knowledge.

Sometimes it is possible to delineate what must be conscious experience underlying emotion-language, but more often the question is begged by contemporary theories in linguistics and linguistic-anthropology.

The discourse history seems crucial in determining the relation between emotion-language and conscious emotional experience. Expressive terms (*yuk*! *gosh*!) seem to provide evidence that speaker is aware of emotion, at least in those discourse situations where the actual expression of emotion is what is intended, but not necessarily in situations where speaker intends only to amuse, inform, or mislead. It is probably necessary to distinguish between awareness of experiencing an emotion and a meta-level awareness of a memory or conceptualization of that same emotion. A verbal expression might be meant to evoke either sort of emotional consciousness.

Lists of basic emotions (happiness, sadness, anger, fear, love, disgust, etc.) proposed by researchers vary in length and content. It does not appear that the basicness of emotions has any particular consequences for whether or not they are experienced consciously, in that one may be conscious or unconcious of an experience of happiness, sadness, etc. However, learning to experience less basic emotions, like hope, pride, and respect, may require conscious verbal instruction. These more intellectualized emotions may be both more consciousness-dependent and more language-dependent. To the extent that such emotions are important in organizing human relations and interdependencies, they would confer significant survival values. Thus, the emerging ability to conceptualize socially structured emotions beyond the basic ones may have provided a springboard for the co-evolution of consciousness and language in relations of mutual feedback.

Emotion metaphors allow for verbalization of different levels of emotional intensity, but it is not clear that the use of metaphor requires speakers to be consciously aware of making such discriminations. Metaphors are often highly conventionalized, suggesting an automatic production that may occur subconsciously. Metonymies may remove speakers one step from awareness of motivating experiences and even invoke emotions appropriate to more prototypical usages. For example, the term girlfriend, used for lover, may evoke the affection of friendship rather than the passion of romantic love. Emotion-metonymies must often be placed in the service of discretion and euphemism. Of course, verbalizing levels of emotional intensity is not the only function of emotion-metaphors. They do a lot more; they address all aspects of emotions, including cause, control, lack of control, responsibility, desire, and physiology, but all of these topics are also subject to a degree of conventionalization.

Much research has shown that emotions are more than registers of physiological experience; they also have conceptual structure. Thus, to the extent that consciousness of emotions accompanies verbal expression, it must include awareness of conceptual structure as well as feeling states. From the standpoint of cognitive linguistics, language is conceptual in both semantic and phonological structure. Thus, emotion-language itself should probably be regarded as integrated with and partially constitutive of the conceptual structure of emotions. Conversely, emotions include emotion-language as part of their conceptual structure.

The view of emotions as conceptual structures centered on prototypes provides us with a link back to Radcliffe-Brown's construal of sentiments as the instruments of a collective emotional consciousness. It is the shared conceptual structure in the aggregate collective consciousness that "contains" our prototypes of emotion, structured as scenarios, scripts, or, to use Lakoff's (1987) term, Idealized Cognitive Models. Language is both a reflection and an instrument of this collective consciousness. When we learn the culturally defined conceptual structures of emotions, we learn them in very large part through language. Of course, each individual must craft a working fit between culturally mediated knowledge of emotions and his or her personal experiences. With the interactional and cultural materials at hand, each fashions personal emotion constructs, which in part elaborate the collective emotional consciousness in the aggregate while also partly preserving what is shared. This is one reason why "implicit patterns behind various cultural activities tend to be both reaffirmed and remade" (Borofsky 1994: 346). It may also explain why for many persons the "ideal view" of love, for example, does not exist, though it may be readily discernable as recurrent themes in the public consciousness as set down in popular media and expressed in discourse. We can think of the public emotional consciousness as including what is shared by some members of a community (consciously held sentiments) together with the aggregate disparate conscious emotions of individuals and groups with all their possibilities for social interaction. The primary medium of the collective emotional consciousness is language.

The implications of the core-meaning view of emotion-language for our understanding of the consciousness of emotion are not encouraging. It is doubtful that the term anger evokes conscious experiences of such components as Davitz's (1969) HYPERACTIVATION, MOVING AGAINST, TENSION, AND INADEQUACY. These features seem too general to be likely objects of conscious attention. The same may be said for the dimensional view of Solomon (1976) who posited direction, scope/focus, object, criteria, status, evaluations, responsibility, intersubjectivity, etc. If there is conscious awareness, it must pertain to particular values taken by the dimensions.

The connotative approach leads us to a relativistic view of emotional consciousness, a search for the cultural constraints on emotion-language and awareness. This approach is discussed in the introductory essay by Palmer and Occhi. The implications of the social constructionist view are similar to those of the connotative and prototype views. They all imply cultural models of emotions that structure emotional consciousness, but all seem to allow for varying levels of awareness on the part of speakers, ranging from acutely aware to the peripheral awareness that might accompany highly conventional usages. Since all concepts are emotion concepts to some degree, however slight, by virtue of emergence within a neural network, it follows that all consciousness accompanying language use involves some awareness of emotional experience.

Researchers differ in the kinds of experience that they select as definitive for various emotions. Experientialists emphasize physical experience and resultant feeling states, while social constructionists emphasize culturally defined social scenarios.[8] These biases affect our understanding of emotional awareness that accompanies the usage of emotion-language. An aspect of emotional experience that receives insufficient attention in this research is the cognitive state of experiencer, including, but not limited to, ability to remember, to hold thoughts, to prioritize actions, and to think and speak rationally. Further research on this topic will produce findings pertinent to the problem of how emotion-language relates to consciousness of emotions.

Notes

1. This paper was originally presented in the Session on Languages of Sentiment at the Annual Meeting of the American Anthropological Association, November 20–24, 1996, San Francisco.
2. See especially, Lutz (1988: 4–5,9, 65–66).
3. The term *express* is used here as a synonym for *predicate*. We realize that the metaphor of *expression* is a bit misleading in that it connotes a folk model of language in which words and meaning are driven under force from the inside to the outside of a container and thence make their way via a conduit to the listener, but we think that many readers will accept it more readily than the alternative. In this paper, nothing hinges on the choice of terms.
4. For a more detailed discussion, see Kövecses (1990) and (1993).
5. On metonymic models such as these, see Lakoff (1987).
6. The pragmatic approach in linguistic anthropology is most clearly stated in Duranti (1997).
7. For a discussion of this issue, see Palmer (1996: 106–107).
8. It is not that experientialists think of physical experience as in any way more important than other kinds of experience. They have emphasized physical experience in order to make it clear that emotion concepts are motivated, or that they have an experiential basis. But in doing this, they have not claimed that physical experiences associated with the emotions are more important than other experiences. The primary motive was to call attention to a gap in thinking about emotion concepts. — Zoltan Kövecses

References

Averill, J.R. 1974. "An analysis of psychophysiological symbolism and its influence on theories of emotion". *J. Theory of Social Behavior* 4: 147–190.

Averill, J.R. 1990. "Inner feelings, works of the flesh, the beast within, diseases of the mind, driving force, and putting on a show: Six metaphors of emotion and their theoretical extensions". In D. Leary (ed), *Metaphor in the History of Psychology*. Cambridge: Cambridge University Press.

Averill, J.R. and Z. Kövecses. 1990. "The concept of emotion: further metaphors". In Z. Kövecses, *Emotion Concepts*. New York: Springer-Verlag, 160–181.

Baxter, L.A. 1992. "Root metaphors in accounts of developing romantic relationships". *J. Social and Personal Relationships* 9: 253–275.

Berlin, B. and P. Kay. 1969. *Basic Color Terms: Their Universality and Evolution*. Berkeley: University of California Press.

Besnier, N. 1990. "Language and affect". *Annual Review of Anthropology* 19: 419–451.

Borofsky, Robert. 1994. "On the knowledge and knowing of cultural activities". In robert Borofsky (ed) *Assessing Cultural Anthropology*. New York: McGraw-Hill, Inc., 331–347.

D'Andrade, Roy. 1995. *The Development of Cognitive Anthropology*. Cambridge: Cambridge University Press.

Davitz, J. 1969. *The Language of Emotion*. New York: Academic Press.

De Rivera, J. 1977. *A Structural Theory of the Emotions*. New York: International Universities Press.

Duck, S. 1994. *Meaningful Relationships*. Newbury Park, CA: Sage.

Fauconnier, Giles. 1997. *Mappings in Thought and Language*. Cambridge: Cambridge University Press.

Duranti, Alessandro. 1997. *Linguistic Anthropology*. Cambridge: Cambridge University Press.

Fehr, B. and Russell, J.A. 1984 "Concept of emotion viewed from a prototype perspective". *J. Experimental Psychology: General* 113: 464–486.

Frijda, N. 1986. *The Emotions*. Cambridge: Cambridge University Press.

Frijda, N., Markam, S., Sato, K. and Wiers, R. 1995. "Emotions and emotion words". In James A. Russell, et al., 121–143.

Geeraerts, D. and Grondealers, S. 1991. "Looking back at anger: Cultural traditions and metaphorical patterns". Preprints of the Katholieke Universiteit, Leuven, Belgium, no. 133.

Harré, Rom. 1986. "An outline of the social constructionist viewpoint". In Rom Harré, (ed), *The Social Construction of Emotion*. Oxford: Basil Blackwell, 2–14.

Heider, Karl. 1991. *Landscapes of Emotion: Mapping Three Cultures of Emotion in Indonesia*. Cambridge: Cambridge University Press.

Holland, D. 1982. "All is metaphor: Conventional metaphors in human thought and language". *Reviews in Anthropology* 9(3): 287–297.

Holland, D. and A. Kipnis. 1995. "American cultural models of embarrassment: The not-so egocentric self laid bare". In J. Russell, et al. (eds) *Everyday Conceptions of Emotion*. Dordrecht/Boston/London: Kluwer Academic Publishers, 181–202.

Johnson, M. 1987. *The Body in the Mind. The Bodily Basis of Meaning, Imagination, and Reason*. Chicago: The University of Chicago Press.

Kövecses, Z. 1986. *Metaphors of Anger, Pride, and Love: A Lexical Approach to the Structure of Concepts*. Amsterdam: John Benjamins.

———. 1988. *The Language of Love. The Semantics of Passion in Conversational English*. Lewisburg, PA: Bucknell University Press.

———. 1990. *Emotion Concepts*. New York: Springer-Verlag.

———. 1991a. "A linguist's quest for love". *J. Social and Personal Relationships* 8: 77–97.

———. 1991b. "Happiness: A definitional effort". *Metaphor and Symbolic Activity* 6: 29–46.

———. 1993a. "Minimal and full definitions of meaning". In R.A. Geiger and B. Rudzka-Ostyn (eds), *Conceptualizations and Mental Processing in Language*. Berlin: Mouton de Gruyter, 247–266.

———. 1993b. "Friendship." In Z. Kövecses (ed), *Voices of Friendship. Linguistic Essays in Honor of László T. András*. Budapest: Eötvös Loránd University Press, Budapest, pp. 131–176.

———. 1994. "Ordinary language, common sense, and expert theories in the domain of emotion". In J. Siegfried (ed), 77–97.

———. 1994. "Tocqueville's passionate 'beast': A linguistic analysis of the concept of American democracy". *Metaphor and Symbolic Activity* 9(2): 113–133.

———. In press. *Metaphor and Emotion. Language, Culture, and Body in Human Feeling*. New York: Cambridge University Press.

Lakoff, G. 1987. *Women, Fire, and Dangerous Things. What Categories Reveal About The Mind*. Chicago: The University of Chicago Press.

Lakoff, G. and M. Johnson. 1980. *Metaphors We Live By*. Chicago: The University of Chicago Press.

Lakoff, G. and Z. Kövecses. 1987. "The cognitive model of anger inherent in American English" In D. Holland and N. Quinn (eds), *Cultural Models in Language and Thought*. New York: Cambridge University Press, 195–221.

Lutz, Catherine A. 1988. *Unnatural Emotions: Everyday Sentiments on a Micronesian Atoll & Their Challenge to Western Theory*. Chicago: The University of Chicago Press.

Lyons, J. 1977. *Semantics*. 2 volumes, Cambridge: Cambridge University Press.

Matsuki, Keiko. 1995. Metaphors of anger in Japanese. In John R. Taylor, Robert E. MacLaury (eds), *Language and the Cognitive Construal of the World*. Berlin; New York: Mouton de Gruyter.

Ortony, Andrew, Gerald L. Clore, and Alan Collins. 1988. *The Cognitive Structure of Emotions*. Cambridge: Cambridge University Press.

Osgood, C.E. 1964. "Semantic differential technique in the comparative study of cultures". *American Anthropologist* 66: 171–200.

Palmer, Gary. 1996. *Toward a Theory of Cultural Linguistics*. Austin: University of Texas Press.

Palmer, Gary and Rick Brown. 1998. "The Ideology of Honor, Respect, and Emotion in Tagalog". In Angeliki Athanasiadou and Elzbieta Tabakowska (eds), *Speaking of Emotions: Conceptualization and Expression*. Berlin/New York: Mouton de Gruyter, 331–355.

Parrott, W. G. 1995. "The heart and the head. Everyday conceptions of being emotional". In J. Russell, et al. (eds), 73–84.

Quinn, N. 1987. "Convergent evidence for a cultural model of American marriage". In D. Holland and N. Quinn (eds), *Cultural Models in Language and Thought*. Cambridge University Press, New York, pp. 173–192.

———. 1991. "The cultural basis of metaphor". In J.W. Fernandez (ed), *Beyond Metaphor. The Theory of Tropes in Anthropology*. Stanford: Stanford University Press, 56–93.

Radcliffe-Brown, A. R. 1922. *The Andaman Islanders*. New York: The Free Press.

Rimé, B., Philippot, P., and Cisalomo, D. 1990. "Social schemata of peripheral changes in emotion". *J. Personality and Social Psychology* 59: 38–49.

Rosaldo, Michelle. 1984. "Toward an anthropology of self and feeling". In Richard A. Shweder and Robert A. LeVine (eds) *Culture Theory: Essays on Mind, Self, and Emotion*. Cambridge: Cambridge University Press, 137–157.

———. 1990. "The things we do with words: Ilongot speech acts and speech act theory in philosophy". In Donal Carbaugh, (ed), *Cultural Communication and Intercultural Contact*. Hillsdale, NJ: Lawrence Erlbaum Associates, Publishers, 373–408.

Rosch, E. 1975. "The nature of mental codes for color categories". *J. Experimental Psychology: Human Perception and Performance* 1: 303–322.

Russell, J.A. 1991. "Culture and the Categorization of Emotions". *Psychological Bulletin* 110(3): 426–450.

Russell, J. A., J-M. Fernandez-Dols, A. S. Manstead, and J.C. Wellenkamp (eds). 1995. *Everyday Conceptions of Emotion. An Introduction to the Psychology, Anthropology and Linguistics of Emotion*. Series D: Behavioural and Social Sciences — Vol. 81. Dordrecht/Boston/London: Kluwer Academic Publishers.

Schachter, S. and Singer, J. 1962. "Cognitive, social and physiological determinants of emotional states". *Psychological Review* 69: 379–399.

Searle, John R. 1990. "Epilogue to the taxonomy of illocutionary acts". In Donal Carbaugh (ed), *Cultural Communication and Intercultural Contact*. Hillsdale, N.J.: Lawrence Erlbaum Associates, Publishers, 259–428.

Shaver, P., Schwartz, J., Kirson, D., and O'Connor, C. 1987. "Emotion knowledge: Further exploration of a prototype approach". *J. Personality and Social Psychology* 52: 1061–1086.

Shweder, R.A. 1991. *Thinking Through Cultures: Expeditions in Cultural Psychology*. Harvard University Press, Cambridge, MA.

Siegfried, J. (ed). 1994. *The Status of Common Sense in Psychology*. Norwood, NJ: Ablex.

Smith, K. D. and Tkel-Sbal, D. 1995. "Prototype analyses of emotion terms in Palau, Micronesia". In J. Russell, et al. (eds), 85–102.

Smith, S. T. and K. D. Smith. 1995. "Turkish emotion concepts: A prototype analysis". In J. Russell, et al. (eds), 103–119.

Solomon, R. 1976. *The Passions*. New York: Doubleday Anchor.

Taylor, John R. and Thandi M. Mbense. 1998. "Red dogs and rotten mealies: how Zulus talk about anger". In Angeliki Athanasiadou and Elzbieta Tabakowska (eds), *Speaking of Emotions: Conceptualization and Expression*. Berlin/New York: Mouton de Gruyter, 191–226.

Wellman, H.M. In press. "The mind's 'I': Children's conception of the mind as an active agent." *Child Development*.

Wierzbicka, Anna. 1972. *Semantic Primitives*. Frankfurt: Atheneum Verlag.

———. 1986. "Human emotions: Universal or culture-specific?" *American Anthropologist* 88(3): 584–594.

———. 1990. "The semantics of emotions: Fear and its relatives in English". *Australian Journal of Linguistics* 10(2): 359–375.

———. 1992a. "Talking about emotions: Semantics, Culture, and Cognition". *Cognition and Emotion* 6(3/4): 285–319.

———. 1992b. "Defining emotion concepts". *Cognitive Science* 16: 539–581.

———. 1995. "Everyday conceptions of emotion: a semantic perspective". In J. Russell, et al. (eds.), 17–45.

Name Index

Aitchison, J. 210, 214
Armstrong, S.L. 213
Asada Hideko 161
Bakhtin 45
Bakhtin, reported speech 79
Benedict, Ruth 3
Besnier, Nico 3
Bodor, Peter 10
Briggs, Jean 13
Bulosan, Carlos 171
Chang, Andrew 160–1
Chomsky, Noam 207–208
Clark, A. 229
Das, Veena 44
Davitz 243, 256
Desjarlais, Robert 40, 55
Durkheim 56
Duranti, Alessandro 2–3
Foucault 40
Gal and Irvine 57, 60
Grima, Benedicte 55, 56
Heider 244
Geertz, Clifford 26
Gibbs, Raymond 172
Gleitman and Gleitman 209
Gomi Taro 157, 160
Hamano, Shoko Saito 154
Higashi Hiroko 158, 159
Himmelmann, Nikolaus 183
Hinata Shikeo 165
Holst-Warhaft 39, 44
Lutz 67, 247, 248
Holtzman, L. 230
Johnson, Mark 172
Kindaichi Haruo 153, 155
Kita Sotaro 156, 165
Kövecses, Zoltán 133, 134, 140, 143, 171
  "onion peel" theory 192
Kuroda, S.-Y. 158–9, 166
Lakoff, George 172, 210, 214, 229
Langacker, Ronald 212, 214
Lave, J. 207
Levy, Robert 12–13
Luria, A.R. 10, 202, 211
Matsumoto 135, 146
Natsume Fusanosuke 165
Needham 27
Newmann, F. 230
Ortony 246
Radcliffe-Brown, A.R. 237, 248, 255, 256
Radway 133
Rafael, Vincente L. 179
Ratner, C. 211
Reddy, M. 229
Rommetveit, R. 230
Rosaldo, Michele 2
Rosaldo, Renato 4
Salomon, Carol 58, 60
Sapir, Edward 40
Sawyer, Keith 46
Schweder 244
Searle, John 228

Shibatani Masayoshi 153, 154
Silverstein, Michael 40
Solomon 24, 32, 56
Stamenov, Maxim 17
Szalay, L. 216
Taylor, J. 209
Teramura Hideo 158–9, 166
Tetsuo Soga 157
Urban, Greg 57
Vygotsky, L. S. 10, 202, 203, 205, 206, 210
Weber, M. 39, 40, 41, 48, 50, 56
Wenger, E. 207
Wertsch, J. 228
Wierzbicka, A. 132, 242, 246, 247, 249

Subject Index

abstraction 210, 211
acquisition, language 201
adaptation 27
affect intensifiers 108
agency 81, 98
ai (Jpn.) 9, 10, 131, 132, 133, 137, 139, 140, 147
alienation 56
allo-repetition 81
alus (Jav.) 65, 99
amae (Jpn.) 132
Andaman Islanders 237
apprenticeship 207
Arabic 29
Aristotle 208
audience 42, 43, 53
authenticity 30
authority, voice of 79
Bangla 4, 5, 7
Bangladesh: See Wilce chapter, 40
belief system 26, 31
bias 27
Bible 237
Bihar, India 47, 51
blasphemy 50, 51
calques in Tagalog 184
canalization 54
categories 208–210
  associative complexes 204
  basic level 209, 229
  chain complexes 204
  classical 212
  collections 204
  diffuse complexes 204, 210
  exemplars 213
  family resemblances 212
  femaleness 213
  prototype 214–215
  pseudoconcepts 204
  schemas 214
categorization 227
Catholicism 175
Chinese 172, 174, 179, 254
Christianity 175
classical category 208–212
clause structure in Tagalog 183
code-switching 99
coerciveness 28
cognitive linguistics 172, 201, 207–208, 212
coherence in narrative 74
colonialism 40, 50
concept formation 204
concepts, scientific 204, 212
conceptual thought 204
conduit metaphor 229
congruities 28
connectionist models 214
consciousness 12–17, 40, 41, 54, 55, 57, 152, 207, 228, 229, 255
  as precondition for emotions 18, 237
  construction of 202
  dual-focus system 193

metaphor for 237
constraints 28
construal 168
contextualization 203, 211
control 92, 93
conventionalized linguistic expressions 134
corazon (Span.), word association 223
crying 188
cultural determinism 28
cultural models 238
cultural relativism 244
death 11, 16, 39, 49, 52, 54, 55, 57, 201, 226, 227
decontextualization 203
determinants 28
development, ontogenetic 206
developmental sequence 203
devotion 29
dinodai (Jav.) 94
direct forms 110, 113, 118
directives 113, 115, 117, 118
discipline 40
discourse events 5
discourses 18
of state 71
emotional *vrs.* on emotion 70
discursive environments 227
disempowerment 79
disenchantment 39, 48, 50
distal forms 110–113, 118, 119, 123
distributed cognition 215
Dyirbal 211
elements,
first-order 25
fundamental 25
native 30
non-native 30
original 25
elite classes 69
embodied 155, 156, 164, 168
mind 208
embodiment 229
emotion 151, 152, 153, 154, 157, 158, 160, 161, 167
concepts 227
basic 172
metaphors 8, 9, 10, 255
body part 172, 186, 191, 193
container 173, 177, 180, 181, 191
English 172
force 173, 177
heart 174, 176, 181, 182, 186, 191
pressure 173
universal 171
metonomy 8, 9, 252, 255
model 245
prototypes 248, 249, 254, 256, 258
scenarios 17, 68, 245, 254
schemas 67, 75, 81, 82, 97, 100
script 245, 248
terms 238
basic 239
descriptive 1
descriptive 239
expressive 1, 239
words 80, 238
agony 171, 173, 179, 181, 187, 188, 190, 191, 192
and cognitive state 2, 3–4, 6, 8–11, 254, 258
and evaluation 99
anger 12, 65, 244, 245
as basic 239, 240
conceptual metaphor for 240
container metaphor for 250
Davitz's theory 243
in Chinese 254
in Hungarian 254
in Japanese 8, 154, 156, 254
in Zulu 254, 255
metaphor for 248
song (Ifaluk) 247, 248
anguish 226
angustia (Span.) 226

annoyance 239
anxiety 225
as discursive event 68
as sociocultural institution 68
calm 65, 173, 183, 224
conceit 182
conceptual structure 256
confusion 67, 181, 245
connotative meaning 242, 257, 258
control of 65
core meanings 242, 256
denotative meaning 242
desire 182
dimensions of 243
disappointment 65
disgrace 94
disgust 5
dolor (Span.) 226
early research on 2–3
English word 242
equanimity 65, 75, 98
evaluation in 68
fear 5, 10, 14, 173, 176–178, 187–192, 201, 216, 225, 226, 227
  as basic 239, 240
  metaphor for 240
  metonymy for 240
felicidad (Span.) 224, 225
figurative expressions for 240
fright 239
grief 7, 8, 13, 48, 50, 52, 53, 55, 56, 60, 173, 175, 190, 191, 193
happiness 5, 10, 173–175, 190, 190–193, 201, 220, 224, 225, 227
  as basic 240
hate 12, 181, 188
horror 239
humiliation 5, 8
imagery in 10, 14, 254
indignition 239
inner feelings 179, 192
joy 173, 190
  as basic 239
labels 241
lexical map of 6, 15, 66
love 5, 11, 14, 173, 176, 188, 190, 201, 216, 217, 220, 223
  as basic 239, 240
  concepts 132
  conceptual metaphor for 240
  container metaphor 9, 136, 140
  ideal 131, 133, 134, 147
    American 9, 133, 140
    Japanese 9, 138, 142
  irreplaceable 140
  lip behaviors 145
  models of 251
  physiological effects 140–142
  prototype scenario 252
  romantic 131
  stability 138
  true 133, 139, 142, 143
  visual behavior 143, 146
lust 173, 182
miedo (Span.) 225
nervous 225
nunuwan (Ifaluk) 252
Ortony, Clore and Collins' types 246
pain 225
passion 217
pena (Span.) 226
physiological reactions 177, 178, 180
postmodern approach to 4
pride 173, 182, 188, 191
prototypes 245
rage 239
reticence in 68
rules of display 146
sadness 5, 173–175, 181, 188, 190–192, 226, 245
  as basic 240, 239
  in Tahitian 254

scenario 15, 246
shame 173, 179, 188, 190–193, 237
hiya 179, 192
shock 176–178
soledad (Span.) 225–226
Solomon's dimensions of 243
song (Ifaluk) 253, 254
sorrow 190
sufferance 226
surprise 173
tranquilidad (Span.) 224
tristeza (Span.) 226
universals 248
word association 217
wrath 239
emotional 26
adjectives 152, 158–160, 162, 167, 168
intensity 108, 110, 114, 118
salience 12–13, 185
emotionalism 46, 50, 58
emotions
basic 12, 173, 238
innateness 238
intense 171
universal 238
emotive 27
emotive language 27
English 172, 173, 177, 179, 180–182, 201, 215, 218, 245
entropization 55
essentialism 248
essentialize 47, 58, 238; see also objectification
ethnicity 25
ethnopsychology 67, 76
evaluation 99
external 100
in emotion 68
in narrative 69
internal 80
experientialism 9, 11, 237, 252
experimental design 216
expert theories 251
extension 215
factory, in Indonesia 78–80
features, criterial 207
feeling states 253, 254
figurative expressions 241
figure and ground 183
first-order elements 25
focal colors 249
folk models 251
formal language 112, 119, 124
formal situation 111
formalism 207
formalized crying: See lament
French 29
fundamental elements 25
fundamentalism
quasi-religious 30
religious 31
funerary rituals 52, 57; see deathgender 44, 46, 48
genesis 237
genre 39, 47, 53–56
globalization 41
German 31
Germany, Nazi 26
givens, assumed 28
global process 7
grammar 183
grammatical constructions 191
happiness 216
harmony 65, 68
heart, word association 223
hierarchy 68, 72, 78, 92, 99
Hindi 31
hiya (Tag.) 179, 192
homonymy 214, 215
honne (Jpn.) 118, 123, 124
honorifics 74, 75, 88, 109
Hungarian 172, 177, 179, 254
hypocognized 254
Ibu Larasati 73
ideal love 131

Idealized Cognitive Models 256
identity 93, 98
ideologies 40, 54, 71
  of language 40, 53
ideology 10, 26
iklas (Jav.) 7, 65
image 151, 156, 157
imagery 156, 158, 166
  emotive 12, 27
  sentimental 27
imagination 39
improvisation 39, 42, 43, 48
India, Bihar 47
indexing strategies 8
Indonesia, Department of Labor 77
Indonesian 4, 13, 65, 244, 181, 245
in-group 107
inner speech 205, 206, 227
intensifiers 69, 99, 115, 116
interactional particles; see particles, interactional
interactivity 43, 46
Iran 54
interpsychological level 215
intimacy 107, 110, 116, 118, 124
intrapsychological level 215
Islam, reformist 45, 48
Islamist 39
Islamization 45, 51
Japanese 4, 5, 8, 9, 18, 26, 29, 107–127, 131–170, 172, 179, 181
Javanese 5, 13, 17, 18, 65, 254
  formal 71
  krâmâ 71, 73
  madyâ 72, 88
  ngoko 71, 73
jazz 42, 47
Kaluli 51
kalooban (Tag.) 192
Karunanidhi 33, 34
kasar (Jav.) 93
koi (Jpn.) 132, 133, 139, 140, 147
krâmâ (Jav.) 71, 73
L2 201, 205
lament 7
lament: Wilce chapter, 39
language acquisition 201
language community 26
language policy 31
lexical meaning 214
lexical networks 216, 227
lexical semantics 201, 227
linguistic culture 6, 26, 34
linguistic ideology 6
linguistic primordialism 34
linguistic tools 230
loan translation 31
madness 45
madyâ (Jav.) 72, 88
maternal language 25
meaning 203, 205, 215
  lexical 214
  znachenie 202
metaphor 29, 151, 152, 154, 155, 166
metaphorization 42, see also entropization
metapragmatic 44
metaphors 5, 32, 33, 172, 214, 240, 250
  conceptual 240
  conduit 229
  container 10
  container, love 136
  for consciousness 237
  ontological 191
  orientational 191
metasentiment 49
metonymy 5, 151, 154, 155, 156, 160, 162, 166, 174, 177, 240, 250
MGR (M. G. Ramachandran) 33
Micronesia 240
millennialism 31
mimesis 5
mimetics 14, see Occhi chapter
Minangkabau (Sumatra) 65, 244

missionaries 51
models
  connectionist 214
  cultural 8, 16, 238
  network 214
modernism 49, 58
modernity 50, 53, 56
modernization 45, 46, 51
modularity 207
moral order 82
mourning 60, 226
music 39, 42, 52
narrative 17–18, 98
  coherence 74
  co-construction of 84–85, 87
  evaluation in 69
  of victimization 77
  of violence 65, 97
  unified 84
national character 28
nationalism 6, 39, 40, 54, 55
nationalization 53
nation-State 39, 57, 60
ngoko (Jav.) 71, 73, 88, 91
native 31
Navajo 29
Nazi Germany 26
networks 215
  lexical 216, 227
novices 207
nunuwan (Ifaluk) 252
objectification 57, 58; see also essentialization
Old Tamil 32
Old Testament 237
omote (Jpn.) 107, 109–111, 117–119, 122–124
onomatopoeia 151, 153, 154, 155, 160, 162, 167
ontological metaphors 191
orientational metaphors 191
original elements 25
out-group 107
oversimplification 27
Pakistan 55–56
Palau, Micronesia 172, 240
participation 207
particles
  final 110
  interactional 109, 110, 112, 113, 117–119, 121, 123
  sentence 110
paternalism 78
Paxto 55–56
performance 7, 42, 47, 49, 50, 53
  performative 39, 41, 52, 53, 58, 78
Philippines 254
poise 65
polysemy 214, 215, 254
post-modern 34
postposing 111, 115, 117–119
potency 65, 69, 98
potlatch 52, 60
power 65, 69, 79, 93, 100
predicate in Tagalog 183
predication base in Tagalog 183
prejudice 27
premodern 34
primary factors 27
primary sentiments 25
prime words 216, 217
primitives, universal semantic 242
primordial bond 29
primordial devotion 30
primordialism 5, 6, 25, 32
  linguistic 34
privatization 40, 50, 57
priyayi (Jav.) values 69, 83
proclivities 28
propriety 76, 98
protest 41
prototype category 208–211
prototype scenario 252
prototypes 245; see also, categories
purism, linguistic 30
purity 31, 32

radio, Indonesian national 72
Ramachandran, M. G. 33
rape 7, 94
rapport 108, 110, 111, 113, 116, 118
rasisa (Jpn.) 152, 157, 167
rationalism 46
rationality 54
rationalization 39, 41, 45, 48, 54, 57
recontextualization 203
referentialism 7, 41
referentialist ideologies of language 41, 48, 57, 58
refinement 65, 100
reformist Islam 45, 48
relativism 244, 257
religious reformism 48, 52, 54
  reformist Islam 39
ren'ai (Jpn.) 131
ren'ai shôsetsu (Jpn.) 131
reported speech 75, 79, 81–83, 88, 99, 100
representation 229
resistance 18, 41, 44, 50, 53, 60
restraint 65
rhetoric 47, 51
ritualization 46, 48
sabar (Jav.) 7, 65
right-dislocation 111
romance fiction 131, 133
salience, emotional 183
salvific 31
Sanskrit 31, 32
scenarios 152, 157, 158, 164, 166, 167, 252, 258
schemas 160, 214
second language 204
self-consciousness 39, 54, 55, 56, 58
self-control 65, 92
selfhood, essence of 25
semantics, lexical 201, 227
sense 203, 205, 215
  smysl 202
sentiment 2–3, 12, 157, 237
sentimental 26
silence 89, 93
singer 72
slurs, class 86
smysl (Russ.) 202
snachenie (Russ.) 202
social construction 6, 9, 10, 11, 67, 237, 238, 247, 252, 258
social deictics 72, 76
sociocultural theory 201, 202–207
solidarity 113, 118, 123
Solo, Indonesia 65
song (Ifaluk) 247, 248, 253, 254
sound symbolism 151, 154, 155, 156, 160
Soviet Union 202
Spanish 11, 201, 215, 218
speech acts 239
speech community 215–216, 229
speech level 72, 75, 76, 88, 98, 99
speech styles 109, 111, 118, 122
spiritual affinity 28
Sri Lanka 32
standardization 53; see also rationalization, nationalism, globalization
state 54
  discourse of the 7, 98
  religious 31
status, high 70
stylized weeping; see lament
Sumatra (Minangkabau) 244
Sumatra, Western 65
symbolic capital 45
synaesthesia 156
syncretic heaps 203
synthesis 210, 211
Tagalog 4, 5, 10, 12, 13, 14, 171–200, 254
Tahitian 12, 13, 254
Tamil 4, 29, 31
Tamil Eelam 32
Tamilnadu 33

tatemae (Jpn.) 118, 123
Tlingit 52, 53, 59
trimå (Jav.) 7, 65, 89
trajector and landmark 183
trope 54, 55
Turkish 172, 240
unconscious 202
universal semantic primitives 242
universals 8, 10, 27, 172, 248, 249, 250
ura (Jpn.) 107, 109, 118, 122–124
urbanization 45, 46, 49, 51, 56
validity 249
utang na loob (Tag.) 179, 192
Utka Eskimo 13
Uzbekistan 211
victimization 89, 100
  narratives of 77
violence 96
  narratives of 97
vocabulary, adult 230
women, Javanese 68
Women's Crisis Center (Yogyakarta) 94
word association 202–207, 216, 227
Yogyakarta 65, 66, 71
Zulu 179–181, 254, 255

In the series ADVANCES IN CONSCIOUSNESS RESEARCH (AiCR) the following titles have been published thus far or are scheduled for publication:

1. GLOBUS, Gordon G.: *The Postmodern Brain*. 1995.
2. ELLIS, Ralph D.: *Questioning Consciousness. The interplay of imagery, cognition, and emotion in the human brain*. 1995.
3. JIBU, Mari and Kunio YASUE: *Quantum Brain Dynamics and Consciousness. An introduction*. 1995.
4. HARDCASTLE, Valerie Gray: *Locating Consciousness*. 1995.
5. STUBENBERG, Leopold: *Consciousness and Qualia*. 1998.
6. GENNARO, Rocco J.: *Consciousness and Self-Consciousness. A defense of the higher-order thought theory of consciousness*. 1996.
7. MAC CORMAC, Earl and Maxim I. STAMENOV (eds): *Fractals of Brain, Fractals of Mind. In search of a symmetry bond*. 1996.
8. GROSSENBACHER, Peter G. (ed.): *Finding Consciousness in the Brain. A neuro-cognitive approach*. n.y.p.
9. Ó NUALLÁIN, Seán, Paul MC KEVITT and Eoghan MAC AOGÁIN (eds): *Two Sciences of Mind. Readings in cognitive science and consciousness*. 1997.
10. NEWTON, Natika: *Foundations of Understanding*. 1996.
11. PYLKKÖ, Pauli: *The Aconceptual Mind. Heideggerian themes in holistic naturalism*. 1998.
12. STAMENOV, Maxim I. (ed.): *Language Structure, Discourse and the Access to Consciousness*. 1997.
13. VELMANS, Max (ed.): *Investigating Phenomenal Consciousness. Methodologies and Maps*. n.y.p.
14. SHEETS-JOHNSTONE, Maxine: *The Primacy of Movement*. 1999.
15. CHALLIS, Bradford H. and Boris M. VELICHKOVSKY (eds.): *Stratification in Cognition and Consciousness*. 1999.
16. ELLIS, Ralph D. and Natika NEWTON (eds.): *The Caldron of Consciousness. Motivation, affect and self-organization - An anthology*. n.y.p.
17. HUTTO, Daniel D.: *The Presence of Mind*. 1999.
18. PALMER, Gary B. and Debra J. OCCHI (eds.): *Languages of Sentiment. Cultural constructions of emotional substrates*. 1999.
19. DAUTENHAHN, Kerstin (ed.): *Human Cognition and Social Agent Technology*. n.y.p.
20. KUNZENDORF, Robert G. and Benjamin WALLACE (eds.): *Individual Differences in Conscious Experience*. n.y.p.